It's a kind of life, one of wind, rain, heat, sun and opposite-lock. It doesn't live in the same motoring world of "I've got a more flash, expensive car than you". It's only about the driver and his relationship with the car and each kind of day he experiences with it (never, ever the same in 10 years). In a Caterham Seven you are aware of passing trees, types of roads, the 'feel' of everything. You remember certain corners, different shades of the day; you're there, in it, doing it.

I honestly believe that had Graham Nearn only made 50 HPC Sevens like my specification, occasionally they would be auctioned for six-figure sums alongside rare Ferraris and Bugattis. Because of my Italian upbringing, I have always been a hopeless Ferrari fanatic and have been fortunate enough to drive most of the rare competition and road cars, and while there is magic, romance and mystique in bucket-loads, there is one, and *only* one, car that shares the same piece of ground; and that is my blue Caterham Seven.

It's been on the cover of a multi-million selling album; it has raced on all the circuits of England; it's been through Europe more times than I can remember; in my mind it's won GPs, Mille Miglias and Targa Florios on the way back from concerts, studios and buying a bag of frozen peas. I live for the day that I kill off the dream of dreams…a Ferrari engine in a Seven.

See me in the winter rain
Struggling to keep straight
See me when the cockpit's hot
With a wind-burnt smiling face
Don't see me with any other reason
To be blasting through the lanes
Only see me in my Seven
Being happy with the day

CATERHAM SEVENS

CHRIS REES

CATERHAM SEVENS

The Official Story of a
Unique British Sportscar

MRP

Preface by Graham Nearn,
Chairman of Caterham Cars

Foreword by Dr Jonathan Palmer

MOTOR RACING PUBLICATIONS LTD
Unit 6, The Pilton Estate, 46 Pitlake, Croydon CR0 3RY, England

First published 1996

British Library Cataloguing in Publication Data

Rees, Chris
   Caterham Sevens : the official story of a unique British sportscar
   1. Lotus automobile 2. Sports cars 3. Lotus automobile – History
   I. Title
   629.2'222

ISBN 0947981977

Typeset by Richard Clark, Penzance
Printed in Great Britain by The Amadeus Press Ltd,
Huddersfield, West Yorkshire

Contents

Preface by Graham Nearn,
Chairman of Caterham Cars

I am delighted that Chris Rees has undertaken to write the definitive and authentic Caterham story as a companion volume to Jeremy Coulter's *Lotus Seven*.

Graham Nearn, Chairman of Caterham Cars.

The year 1996 marks a milestone celebrating the fortieth year of continuous production of the original Seven, introduced by Lotus Cars Ltd in 1957. During those five decades, the Seven has survived some of the most turbulent periods in our industrial and economic history and has prevailed through safety and emission regulations unforeseen in the Fifties.

The Lotus Seven was the inspiration of Colin Chapman and, without his genius, there would be no story. Like so much of Chapman's work, the Seven was greatly underrated at the time. Yet today, it seems to have a magnetic attraction and it generates a tremendous amount of goodwill and support. It is one of a tiny handful of genuine enduring motoring legends.

When Caterham took over the Seven from Lotus, we battled against a terrible economic background and we were always at odds with public opinion – many motoring publications never really took the Seven seriously. We had a fight over getting it accepted as a racing car to contest, and had to prove ourselves over and over again. Response to change and a variety of different requirements by our foreign buyers developed in Caterham a flexible workforce who grew to evolve change with enthusiasm.

The situation today is in complete contrast. The qualities of the Seven are appreciated universally and we are widely accepted in motorsports. With the Caterham race series, we have returned to the days of low-cost motorsport, when you could race on a circuit and then drive your car home. Economic circumstances have changed, too, and in the Nineties the public is again being offered a wide variety of sportscars. The Seven is still recognized as a benchmark, and remains the inspiration for many sportscar designers, which is a real compliment. We have total support from our suppliers and sub-contractors, including the very large car manufacturers, and with their loyalty, the quality of the Caterham Seven is sustained, and this is reflected in our enhanced reputation and sales.

I am constantly gratified by the number of old friends and Seven owners who still visit us at shows and at Caterham. It is quite extraordinary the number of people who have at some time owned a Seven. The appeal is truly global: there seems to be a common language, and the enthusiasm for the Seven is as strong whether you are in Japan or America, Europe or the South Pacific.

Caterham Cars forms part of the tradition and history of British car engineering and motorsport and we are proud of the fact that we always aim for as near to perfection as we can. The company is the right size to employ the quality of staff that we do, and to enjoy a dedicated research and development department.

We have now embarked on a new course with the 21, which opens up new opportunities for Caterham and provides additional interest and stimulation for all our engineers, workforce and suppliers.

I can see the Seven providing the same level of enjoyment for future generations as it has in the past. We never neglect the young and impecunious enthusiast, although the Seven has evolved so comprehensively over the years. I am always seeing links between the generations, the father's enthusiasm being followed by his son's, with the two of them often building a car together.

There have been many people who have contributed to the continuation of the Seven, and they should be publicly acknowledged. I should particularly like to recognize the following, without whose loyalty and support the story might have taken a different course: individual friends, colleagues and staff, suppliers and sub-contractors, overseas and UK agents, motorsport clubs, owners' clubs worldwide, journalists, broadcasters and politicians for their sustaining support.

Enthusiasm is the single quality that catapulted me out of a safe prospering job into the car industry 37 years ago and it has remained the constant factor in nurturing a business and the Seven Legend. Other cars never inspired the same affection. Modern cars are too comfortable and cushioned to have moral dimension. Sevens were bare and boney, transport reduced to its basic elements, and they had a song to sing. That song is now a classic.

The book tells the story of all those who sing the same song. Those that updated the music and revised the lyrics – but essentially the refrain is the same.

I believe the ensuing years will produce just as much success and interest and I look forward to the next book to celebrate the first 50 years of the Seven and 10 years of the Caterham 21.

I have always enjoyed the loyalty and support of my family and I would like to dedicate this book to my wife, Jane, and life-long colleague David for the good times together.

Dr Jonathan Palmer

Foreword by
Dr Jonathan Palmer

It gives me great pleasure to write this foreword, for I feel so well-qualified to enthuse about the Caterham Seven in its various guises, partly because I have personal experience of the delight of driving the Seven on the road, but there is a far stronger reason. For the last four years I have run Caterham Seven Vauxhalls as part of my corporate event, The Motorsport Experience. During that time I have witnessed the pure joy of reaction from around 10,000 guests who have explored the performance of our Caterhams. In all my time I have never known any better recipe for provoking beaming looks of schoolboy exhilaration, with so many guests stepping out of the car with cries of: "I've got to get one!" And the beauty of it is, they can – it's just so affordable.

Caterham to me means real raw driving fun – the nearest thing to driving a single-seater on the road. The feeling is of a machine as an extension of your body: with a Caterham all your senses are not just involved in, but excited by, the process of control input and reaction sensation. And one of the best things about the car is that you don't have to be exceeding the speed limit to get thrills, either. Sixty miles per hour down a twisty undulating B-road on a summer's evening is driving bliss!

But, of course, Caterhams can go a lot quicker – none more so than the JPE that I had so much fun developing and testing with the Caterham lads. It was totally outrageous – 250bhp from the virtually BTCC-specification Vauxhall 2-litre unit powering an even lighter Caterham which would accelerate nearly twice as fast as John Clelland's racing Cavalier! It could stop, too, holding the *Autocar* 0–100mph–0 record in a Ferrari F40-beating 12.6 sec.

Naturally it's all down to the people involved. Credit must go to Colin Chapman for designing the original Lotus Seven, embodying the concept of sophisticated minimalist engineering. However, after Lotus lost interest, it was the confidence and foresight of Graham Nearn that provided the opportunity for the potential to be realized, with the Caterham Seven and its progressive evolution. And now, backed up by a dedicated team, who are both tremendous enthusiasts and commercial realists, the future is assured.

If this book can provide just one per cent of the pleasure produced by driving a Caterham, it will be a brilliant success!

Introduction

This book is the companion volume to Jeremy Coulter's *Lotus Seven: A Collector's Guide*. It was initially intended as an update of Jeremy's original 1986 book on both Lotus and Caterham varieties, but it quickly became obvious that the subject merited separate books for each of the Lotus and Caterham stories.

Under Caterham, the Seven has reached a far wider audience and the model is certainly more highly regarded now than at any other time. The vast majority of Sevens on the road today are Caterhams, and the company has developed a rich and interesting history of its own.

During the course of writing this book, one question has been playing at the back of my mind. What is the heart of Caterham? What is the secret of its success? Obviously, a Seven offers maximum driver involvement: the best-handling, potentially quickest car you can buy without spending super-car sums of money.

It is also British. It also has that nebulous but vital ingredient of heritage: almost 40 years of pure gold, from Colin Chapman and the very origins of Lotus to the legend it is today. As Graham Nearn puts it, Caterham Cars are the custodians of the legend.

And the Seven *is* a living legend, constantly improving, constantly keeping ahead of technological change.

Above all, the Caterham Seven is about driving – the pure pleasure of driving. I hope that some of the flavour of this superlative sportscar will emanate from the pages of this book.

May 1996   Chris Rees

Acknowledgements

With grateful thanks to everyone at Caterham who invested huge amounts of time and energy in this project: Graham Nearn, Jez Coates, Andy Noble, David Wakefield, Reg Price, Jan Russell, Mike Fleet, Mark Brewster and Jean Mallery. In addition, I would like to extend thanks to fellow author Jeremy Coulter and to publisher John Blunsden, whose constant support and extensive photo archive proved invaluable. Many thanks also to Clive Roberts, Simon Wheeler, Peter Cooper, Mike Dixon, Jonathan Palmer, Chris Rea, John Brigden, BRSCC archivist Martin Hadwen, Belinda and Jim McDougall of Entreprix, John Watson, Lol Pilfold of the Lotus Seven Club of Great Britain, Magnus Laird of Hyperion, Lotus 7X racer Tim Goss and all the overseas agents who had photography specially arranged for the book.

C R

CHAPTER 1

The Lotus Seven story

The car that helped to pay the rent

Before Caterham the Seven was a Lotus. Before the Seven, the Lotus was a Six. And before the Six was a string of specials designed by Anthony Colin Bruce Chapman. That takes us back to the humble origins from which grew the legend which became Lotus, Grand Prix championship constructor, leading sportscar manufacturer and widely employed engineering consultants.

To say that this great legend grew on the back of such a simple design as the Seven is no exaggeration. Without the Seven as a bread-and-butter earner in the late Fifties and Sixties, Lotus might well have perished as just another name among many hopefuls of the period.

But Colin Chapman and Lotus were different. Chapman's genius is undisputed and the appreciation of future generations of his talent can only increase. In the case of the Lotus Seven this consisted of a comprehension of the value of simplicity, ultimate light weight and an essential 'rightness' of design. The Seven's attractions to a generation of enthusiasts kept Lotus in profit while its other activities – notably racing and production of the Lotus Elite – were financial black holes.

The idea of the Lotus Seven as a basic sportscar using the simplest of components was not startlingly original. But it was startlingly effective. The Seven did everything better than similar cars of the period and, arguably, has continued to do everything better since, at least as far as sporting dynamics are concerned. The validity of this contention shines through in a hundred test reports and in the Seven's durability in production. At approaching 40 years old, it is one of the motoring world's great survivors.

As an engineering student at London University, Colin Chapman supplemented his studies by running a used car business in the period following the war. This was not a good time to be selling cars, and

one particular example, a 1930 Austin 7, would not shift. Using this humble old crate as a basis, Lotus was born. In 1948 Chapman built his very first Lotus, dubbed in retrospect the Mark 1. Working from a garage behind his girlfriend's house in north London, he stripped the little Austin down and created his own boxy sports body in marine ply. This was the car in which Chapman launched his competition career, driving in trials events. The following year, after he had left university and taken a job with British Aluminium, Chapman built the Mark 2, again on an Austin 7 chassis, but fitted with a Ford side-valve engine. This was used for road and competition and was rather more sporty-looking.

But with an expanding calendar of circuit racing events through the 750 Motor Club, Chapman was

Colin Chapman's Lotus Mark 2 was built in 1949 using a Ford side-valve engine. Here Eric Beaumont climbs the hill at Newry.

The Mark 3B was built specifically for racing, as Colin Chapman (driving) proves at Silverstone in June 1953.

tempted away from trials and so built the Mark 3 in 1951. Again based on a (modified) Austin 7 chassis, all-alloy bodywork was used, epitomizing Chapman's ideal of light weight. With this he began scoring notable successes and attracted the attention of other racers who were naturally interested in replicas.

As a result of this interest Lotus Engineering was born on January 1, 1952. Taking premises behind the Railway Hotel (owned by his father) in Hornsey, north London and operating as a part-time business, he built the Mark 4 (completed in 1954) for trialling. Far more significantly, Lotus Engineering developed the Mark 6 (the Mark 5 never materialized).

The Mark 6 was easily the most important Lotus to date. For the first time Chapman sketched out his own chassis design, not one based on the Austin 7, the result of a change in 750MC regulations as well as Chapman's desire to do his own thing. Two large rails formed the basis of the chassis on to

which was fabricated a lightweight spaceframe. The nearby Progress Chassis Co built the first Mark 6 chassis, while coachbuilders Williams & Pritchard (which occupied one of the sheds at Chapman's address) clothed it in a simple aluminium body with cycle wings, enclosed rear wings and a squarish nosecone. The Mark 6 was considerably lower than any previous Chapman design.

Readily available Ford parts were used on the production-form car: a 1,172cc side-valve or linered-down 1,500cc Consul engine (or the option of MG TC power), divided Ford front axle and Ford 8/10 rear axle. Since the chassis weighed a mere 55lb, the rather asthmatic Ford engine was capable of remarkable speed in the Mark 6 (whose overall weight was just 8.5cwt, or 432kg).

The first Mark 6 prototype was built in 1952, but was destroyed in a road accident. However, by 1953 the Mark 6 was ready to roll as a production proposition. Despite the involvement of several other characters at the time – notably Michael

Enthusiasts had to wait until the separate-chassis Mark 6 to get their hands on a commercially available Lotus. This 1953 example was the raw material from which the Seven would be fashioned.

Allen and some moonlighting engineers from aircraft builders De Havilland, including Mike Costin – it was Chapman himself who built the first batch of Mark 6s virtually single-handed.

Initially these were known as 'Lotus Replicas', but quickly purchasers latched on to the Mark 6 designation. Cars were sold in kit form to escape the swingeing 25 per cent purchase tax levied on complete cars. Having to build the car up was not a great hardship since most customers were typically mechanically-minded racing enthusiasts. Lotus was one of the first-ever companies to make kit-cars, but was certainly a cut above the rest in offering bodies *and* chassis (and most other specialist parts besides) to complete a car. The builder would source his own engine, gearbox and axles, taking the latter to Lotus for modification. Often customers would try to keep costs down by doing their own thing in many detail areas, but Lotus offered all parts individually. The chassis cost £110, the complete body £75, brake controls just over £12 and so on. Lotus quoted a typical on-the-road figure of around £400 – exceptional value indeed.

Almost immediately the so-called Six made its mark on the race tracks. In the hands of Colin Chapman himself, as well as campaigners like Peter Gammon (who came second to Chapman's Mark 8 at Silverstone in 1954), the successes of the Mark 6 attracted plenty of interest. This was bolstered by Chapman's formation of Team Lotus to develop and run works racers.

That the Mark 6 was, in its day, a fast and agile

sportscar there is no doubt. *The Autocar* drove Chapman's own Six and managed almost 90mph in it. They commented: "There can be few, if any, cars which are quicker through sharp S-bends". And all this from one of the most basic and inexpensive cars available!

Chapman's mind moved quickly on to bigger things. In 1954 he created the Mark 8 racing car, having allocated the Mark 7 slot to a commission for a Formula 2 single-seat racer from the Clairmonte brothers. This was never completed by Lotus (later being finished as the Clairmonte Special) so it left open the number 7 in the Lotus chain for future use. The seminal Frank Costin-designed Mark 8 was followed by the equally successful 9 and 10 in 1955.

As such the Mark 6 took a back seat. Chapman finally quit his job at British Aluminium to concentrate on development of the Eleven racing car. Despite its continued domination of its class in racing, production of the Mark 6 ended in late 1955 with around 100 cars built (later some more were constructed to use up spare chassis).

Meanwhile, all Chapman's efforts were directed towards his goal of building Le Mans-winning racers and single-seat Formula 2 cars. Team Lotus blossomed and the premises at Hornsey became rather more developed. The Eleven became the firm's mainstay, but it was almost exclusively a racing machine. Some road-going versions were built but, at prices starting from £1,511, this was hardly a car for the average enthusiast.

Edward Lewis pilots Lotus Mark 7 No 1 up a hillclimb in 1957. This original Seven had disc brakes and a de Dion rear end taken from the Lotus Eleven.

There was still, therefore, a latent demand for a successor to the Mark 6. Despite having been out of production for almost two years, secondhand Sixes were changing hands for high prices. Sales manager Colin Bennett realized the potential of a Mark 6 replacement while there was a more pressing need for a new road car to sell. Sales of racing cars were extremely seasonal, falling away to nothing over the final months of the year. Now that Lotus was becoming a more permanent institution, with staff on a regular payroll, the question of financial stability and cashflow was becoming far more important.

Chapman's idea was that the racing car business could build a road-going sportscar during the quiet period. Realizing his company could not survive on racecars alone, he had already set his sights well and truly on the sportscar market with continuing development of the all-glassfibre Fourteen, otherwise known as the Elite. This was proving a rather problematic machine to bring to fruition, whereas the replacement for the Mark 6 would be simplicity itself. As Chapman later said: "The sort of thing you could dash off in a weekend".

That car would be called the Seven (the use of the 'Mark' prefix ended with the Eleven in 1956), using up the spare numerical designation in Lotus' sequence and proving the logical successor to the Six. Chapman designed the first Seven himself at his house in Barnet. Work began in late spring 1957

and, to Chapman's drawings, Progress Chassis built the prototype chassis while Williams & Pritchard constructed the first aluminium body.

The chassis took its inspiration partly from the Six and partly from the Eleven. The centre-section, tunnel, axle mounts and scuttle resembled the Eleven, but the front and rear sections were evidently different to accommodate much less in the way of bodywork.

Like the Six, the chassis was panelled in stressed aluminium bodywork which looked rather like the Six but was lower and sleeker. The prototype was equipped with something of a racing specification, with Eleven Le Mans de Dion rear suspension, four-wheel disc brakes and Eleven S2 front suspension. The prototype's engine was a Coventry Climax 1,100cc unit.

This first-ever Seven was delivered to a celebrated Lotus racer named Edward Lewis in September 1957. Lewis had built a hillclimb and sprint special in 1956 based on a Mark 6 chassis with a de Dion rear end from the Mark 9. Its success attracted the attention of Chapman, who duly promised him the first production version of the Seven as a straight swap for the special. Lewis would campaign the Seven in sprints and hillclimbs under the Team Lotus banner: hence the fitment of the advanced suspension.

Chapman wanted Lewis' Seven to be a winner and in that he was certainly rewarded. In Lewis'

Introduced at the same time, the Lotus Elite and Seven were very different cars with light weight at their heart. Profits from the Seven propped up the uneconomic Elite.

The Series 1 Seven looked and drove like an original. The hood was a rather basic affair lacking in sidescreens, but was an advisable fitment for most owners, for whom the Seven was their only transport.

first outing at the Brighton Speed Trials, in September 1957, he won his class. The very next day at Prescott he beat a Lotus Eleven to win the 1,100cc class. As a result, before the Seven had even been launched, Lotus was receiving inquiries about the 'mystery' new car.

However, the production version of the Seven took a while to gestate. Costs were a priority, so the de Dion rear end had to be sacrificed for a live axle, disc brakes for drums and the Climax engine for a Ford side-valve. Chapman's basic chassis drawings were properly realized by an ex-Vanwall employee, Ian Jones, who had been seconded to work as a draughtsman for Lotus and given to Progress Chassis to create the production version.

While the Six chassis used two large bottom rails, the Seven's chassis was of uniform one-inch tubing with secondary tubes of ¾in. The aluminium floor and tunnel were stressed, being riveted to the chassis. The bodywork was all-aluminium: a simple clip-on bonnet, lift-off nosecone, rigid cycle-type front mudguards, flat side panels and cutaway rear wheelarches.

Front suspension derived from the Eleven/Twelve, with twin wishbones, the front upper link of which was formed by the anti-roll bar. At each side was mounted a coil spring and Armstrong telescopic damper.

The live rear axle came from BMC's Nash Metropolitan, as used on the Eleven Club. It was located by twin trailing arms and a single link from the offside end to the rear of the transmission tunnel. Again there were coil springs and dampers and the standard final-drive of 4.8:1 could be

changed to one of a variety of options.

The all-drum brakes derived from Ford. The handbrake was mounted horizontally under the dashboard, conveniently out of the way but rather awkward to operate, while steering was by Burman box.

Motive power was provided by the trusty Ford 100E side-valve engine. This was cheap, plentiful and eligible for the 750MC's popular 1172 Formula. Chapman's intention with the Seven was always to create a road car which could double up as a successful racing machine, so this was an important consideration. Mated to a standard Ford three-speed gearbox, performance was kept up only thanks to the Seven's light weight (980lb, or 444kg). Better performance could be extracted by fitting twin SU carbs, a special exhaust manifold and a Buckler close-ratio gearbox, all available through Lotus.

Progress Chassis built the new-design chassis with great haste to get the car ready for the Earls Court Motor Show in October 1957. Again it was panelled by Williams & Pritchard and completed at Hornsey. But the new Lotus Elite was the firm's priority and the Seven just failed to make it to Earls Court, being launched to the public fractionally afterwards.

Lotus offered the Seven in complete form at £1,036 including purchase tax. But they also sold the Seven as a kit, making it exempt from the tax which applied to complete cars, enabling the price to drop to just £536. Naturally, almost all Sevens would be sold in this form, making the tax man a little irate. For years, Customs & Excise played a

cat-and-mouse game with Lotus Engineering, waiting for it to overstep what was a highly ambiguous position regarding the degree of completion. For instance, no build-up instructions were permitted. To get round this, Lotus inventively printed an article in *Sports Car & Lotus Owner* magazine which explained how to strip a Seven for a major overhaul. Read in reverse the reprinted article served as a build manual!

Your £536 bought you a bare chassis fitted with rear wings, wiring, brake pipes, master-cylinder, regulator and solenoid. The dash was ready-fitted with its instruments, but the engine/gearbox assembly was supplied loose. The rest of the car was delivered in boxes and cloth bags. At least you got everything you needed to complete a car, a unique selling point among kit-cars of the period. Lotus claimed a Seven could be on the road in 12 hours, but that was certainly rather optimistic.

Even by the standards of the day, the first Lotus Sevens were very basic machines. The non-adjustable 'seats' were simply cushions placed on the floor with a one-piece foam-filled backrest. Standard finish was red Vynide with white piping, extending to the inner side panels and dashboard. There was no floor covering, no sidescreens and even the tonneau and hood were options.

As for instrumentation, the driver had a speedo sited in front of him flanked by an oil pressure gauge and water gauge, plus an ammeter sitting in the passenger's eye-line. But there was no rev-counter nor even a fuel gauge: as the special tank held only seven gallons, frequent checks were

necessary by peering in through the fuel filler!

The windscreen was detachable and top-mounted wipers could be fitted if desired. As for the headlights, these consisted of antique Lucas units, the offside light going out completely on dipped beam, while there were no indicators whatsoever, short of the driver's arms.

The first production Seven, painted pale yellow, was registered FVV 877 and hit the road in October 1957. It was a fine machine dynamically. Sales manager Peter Warr remembers testing early Sevens on the system of roads at the back of the Cheshunt works which were commonly referred to as The Mountain. "That was where the production manager of Lotus Cars used to road test all the Elites. It was a matter of some concern that the Seven would always be quicker over The Mountain than the Elite!"

Magazines thought highly of it, too. Both *The Autocar* and *The Motor* tested the prototype and praised its stability, performance and suitability for racing. The latter recorded a top speed of over 80mph and 0–60mph in 16.2sec.

Because of the man-hours being sunk into the Elite, deliveries of the Seven did not begin until early 1958. The first production Seven was delivered to Brian Luff (later to join Lotus himself as a draughtsman). While the Elite was still being readied for production, the Seven assumed a crucial role as a money-spinner for Lotus.

The earliest change to the Seven's specification was to ditch the Burman steering box in favour of a modified Morris Minor rack mounted upside-

This is what the Seven S1 builder was faced with after paying his £536 back in 1957. The main body tub came ready wired-up and plumbed in, but everything else needed to be fitted.

down. This improved feel and precision in the straight-ahead position.

For those drivers who wanted to race in other classes than the 1172 Formula, an alternative engine was offered from February 1958 in the form of the light-alloy 1,098cc Coventry Climax unit which delivered a very healthy 75bhp at 6,250rpm with twin SUs and four-branch manifold. However, the first production version of the new so-called Super Seven was not finished until December 1958, when Graham Hill raced it at Brands Hatch on Boxing Day, beating all other competitors.

The Super Seven was fitted with an Austin A30 four-speed gearbox with close-ratio gears and a slightly longer final drive of 4.55:1. Other minor changes were a three-spoke leather-trimmed steering wheel in place of the standard two-spoke plastic affair, a tachometer in front of the driver and 15in wire wheels. The price was £700 in kit form, while the standard kit (renamed Seven F) was some £120 cheaper. Top speed rose to over 100mph and 60mph came up in just 9.2sec. It was the ideal road/race machine.

Around 100 Sevens were built in 1958, stretching the factory at Hornsey to its limit. New premises had to be found and, in early 1959, were duly located in nearby Cheshunt. Shortly afterwards Colin Chapman reorganized the company into divisions: Lotus Cars (to build the Elite), Team Lotus (to run the works racing team), Lotus Developments (R&D work) and Lotus Components (to build Sevens and customer racing cars). By the time the move had been completed, the Seven was subject to a substantial waiting list, so the mezzanine first

One of the earliest adverts for 'Colin Chapman's Lotus Seven' extols the ease of build of the kit version.

floor at Cheshunt was converted as a dedicated Seven assembly area to increase production capacity. One side-effect, however, was that completed kits and cars had to be hoisted down to ground level!

In 1959 an important new move for Lotus was to cease selling cars directly from the factory. The growing company needed a proper sales network and so Chapman conceived the idea of 'Lotus Centres' to act as dealers around the country. One of the first – if not indeed the very first – was Caterham Car Services.

Export markets were also to be targeted and America looked probably the most promising. But a higher degree of specification was required for this more sophisticated market so a special Seven America was developed during 1959. This had long flared glassfibre wings instead of aluminium cycle mudguards, the BMC A-series engine and four-speed gearbox from the Austin-Healey Sprite, proper windscreen wipers, better lighting and indicators. It even had carpets, both tacho and speedo gauges, and a special tonneau to which clip-on canvas half-doors could be attached.

The twin-carb A-series engine developed even less power than the old Ford side-valve unit (only 37bhp at 5,000rpm or 43bhp in export form) but it was much more free-revving. Top speed was more like 85mph and the 0–60mph time dropped to

Part of the very first Seven brochure featuring Brian Luff's Ford-powered car, the first example to be supplied to a customer. Under 12 hours was a completely unfeasible time for a customer to build a Seven.

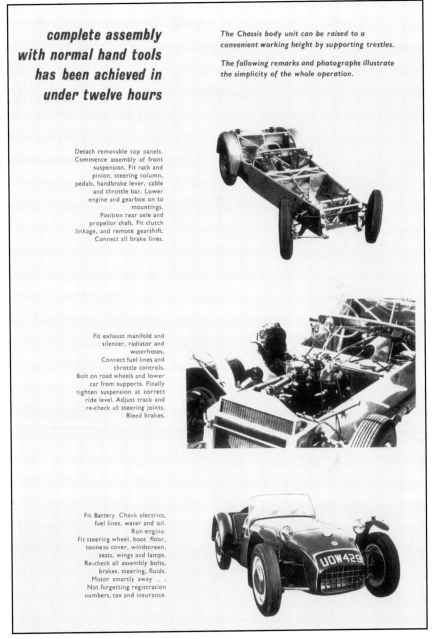

complete assembly with normal hand tools has been achieved in under twelve hours

The Chassis body unit can be raised to a convenient working height by supporting trestles.

The following remarks and photographs illustrate the simplicity of the whole operation.

Detach removable top panels. Commence assembly of front suspension. Fit rack and pinion, steering column, pedals, handbrake lever, cable and throttle bar. Lower engine and gearbox on to mountings. Position rear axle and propellor shaft. Fit clutch linkage, and remote gearshift. Connect all brake lines.

Fit exhaust manifold and silencer, radiator and waterhoses. Connect fuel lines and throttle controls. Bolt on road wheels and lower car from supports. Finally tighten suspension at correct ride level. Adjust track and re-check all steering joints. Bleed brakes.

Fit Battery. Check electrics, fuel lines, water and oil. Run engine. Fit steering wheel, boot floor, tonneau cover, windscreen, seats, wings and lamps. Re-check all assembly bolts, brakes, steering, fluids. Motor smartly away . . Not forgetting registration numbers, tax and insurance.

around 14 seconds. With tuning mods, the engine could be made to perform significantly better. As fitted with the Austin engine, the car was referred to as the Seven A.

Although the Seven was probably Lotus Components' biggest money-spinner during 1958 and 1959 (some 242 Series 1s were built in total), it was time-consuming to produce and, as a result, there were waiting lists for it. Colin Chapman identified a need to speed up the Seven's build time. Part of

the problem was an inconsistency in the dimensions of the chassis, causing Lotus fitters endless headaches during the construction of kits. The chassis were also expensive to buy in from Progress Chassis.

Therefore, in late 1959 Chapman set about creating the Seven Series 2. He proceeded to remove as many chassis tubes as he could without compromising stiffness too much. The stressed aluminium panels would take more of the strain while the

An early customer takes his Seven for a spin in central London.

the wheel line). Also the rear axle was swapped for one from the Standard Companion (even though that model had just left production) and the chassis tubing modified to suit. Instead of the large 15in wheels of the Series 1, the Series 2 adopted 13in steel wheels and wires were dropped as an option.

The fuel tank was redesigned with a greater capacity and was made in steel, not aluminium, while the battery was relocated to the front bulkhead. Inside the cockpit, the inner side trim and dashboard panels came with Vynide ready bonded on.

Externally the S2 Seven was usually easy to identify thanks to its Seven America-type glassfibre flared wings. Cycle wings were still offered initially for the S2 but they also now came in glassfibre, not aluminium as before. The rear wings were restyled to become flatter and wider and were now made in glassfibre. The nosecone was reprofiled by Elite stylist John Frayling and had less of a droopy look to it and was also now made in GRP. To enliven the look of the Seven, all GRP panels could be ordered in a choice of self-pigmented colours (red, green or yellow).

The use of GRP, along with the simplified chassis, significantly reduced the cost of production for Lotus Components. Although many chassis were still made by Progress, some were now built by Universal Radiators of Northampton. Arch Motors of Tottenham – already builders of chassis for Lotus racing cars – was approached at this time but did not yet have the required capacity.

Initially the standard engines for the Seven S2 were the Ford side-valve or, more commonly, the

inner panels and dashboard would henceforth be riveted in place. The metal undertray, however, was shortened at both ends. The main tubes removed were the engine bay diagonals, the two cockpit side diagonals, some seat back tubes and the hoop at the back of the transmission tunnel.

An A-frame was now used to locate the rear axle with radius arms, the centre of the A-frame being located by a rubber-bushed bracket to the bottom of the axle. At the front, Chapman adopted the suspension uprights from the new Triumph Herald along with its steering rack (now mounted ahead of

Potent Coventry Climax was the engine of the Super Seven which arrived at the end of 1958. With 75bhp it pushed the little Seven to above 100mph.

SPECIFICATION

	SEVEN 'F'	SEVEN 'A'

MODEL

FRAME — Multi-tubular space frame comprising 1 in. and ¾ in. square and round tubing of 18 gauge steel. The propeller shaft tunnel and floor are stressed members forming an integral part of the frame. The tunnel carries the rear engine mounting. The engine is carried on two rubber mountings at the front and a single rubber mounting at the rear around the gearbox.

FRONT SUSPENSION — Independent by transverse wishbones incorporating anti-roll bar. Springing by combined coil spring damper units reacting through a single attachment point at each end.

REAR SUSPENSION — Proprietary live rear axle located by twin parallel trailing arms and a diagonal member to provide lateral location. Springing by combined coil spring damper units.

BRAKES — Hydraulically operated two leading shoe drum brakes. Cast iron drums 8 in. x 1¼ in. diameter at front and rear. Combined master cylinder and hydraulic fluid reservoir serving front and rear brakes. Horizontally mounted hand brake operating rear brakes through mechanical linkage.

STEERING — Lotus modified proprietary rack and pinion, universally jointed steering column and 16 in. 2-spoked wheel.

POWER UNIT — Ford 100E 1,172 c.c. side-valve four-cylinder engine. / Minor 1000 or A35 948 c.c. overhead valve 4-cylinder engine.

TRANSMISSION — Single dry-plate clutch. Ford 3-speed gearbox with the following standard ratios: first 3.664:1 second 2.007:1, top 1:1; reverse, 4.79:1. Close ratios at extra cost. / B.M.C. 4-speed gearbox synchromesh on 2nd 3rd and 4th with the following ratios: first, 4.08:1; second, 2.58:1; third, 1.66:1; top 1:1; reverse, 5.17:1. Close ratios at extra cost. Single dry-plate clutch.

FINAL DRIVE — Hypoid final drive unit. Standard ratio 4.22:1. Following axle ratios available at option: 5.375, 5.125, 4.875, 4.55, 4.22, 3.89 and 3.73:1

COOLING SYSTEM — Ultra lightweight fin and tube radiator with integral header tank.

FUEL SYSTEM — Single light alloy rear tank 7-gallon capacity. A.C. engine mounted fuel pump.

BODYWORK — Two-seater bodywork with exposed wheels and separate wings. Dash and cowl readily removable for access to back of instrument panel and front suspension respectively. Dash panel covered to match upholstery. Full-width glass screen is standard, but small sporting perspex screen available as optional extra.

ELECTRICAL SYSTEM — Special lightweight 12 volt 31 amp hr. battery, weighing 24lb. located at rear. Coil and distributor, centrifugal advance and retard, belt-driven dynamo, automatic voltage control. Fuse box mounted behind dash panel. Lucas 6 in. headlamps and separate side lamps, twin stop tail lights and number plate lamp. High frequency horn. Instrument lighting.

INSTRUMENTS — 3 in. speedometer 0-120 m.p.h. with combined revolution readings in the gears. Oil pressure gauge, water temperature gauge and ammeter.

WHEELS AND TYRES — Bolt-on 15 in. lightweight wheels front and rear, all fitted with 5.20 x 15 tyres. Provision for spare wheel on rear panelling.

DIMENSIONS — Wheelbase 7ft. 4 in. Front track 3ft. 11 in., rear track 3ft. 10½ in. Overall length 11ft. Overall width 4ft. 5 in. Height to top of scuttle 27½ in. Minimum ground clearance 5 in.

WEIGHT — 918lbs. / 896lbs.

Provision is made for initial installation of the following power units and by means of interchangeable mounting brackets. Either alternative may be substituted at a later date in the life of the car.

Seven 'A' Austin A35 or Morris Minor 1000 overhead valve engine with four speed gearbox.

Seven 'F' Ford 100E side valve engine with three speed gearbox.
(N.B. The Coventry Climax 1100cc engine with Lotus close ratio gearbox may also be installed if desired—**Seven 'C'** Model).

To those who have never before driven a Lotus, the first impression on taking the wheel is one of superb driver control—instant reaction to every command.
The inherent safety of the Seven, maintained at all speeds and under extreme road conditions, enables the exhilarating performance to be confidently used to the full—high average speeds in comfort; relaxed driver.
Although successfully used in all forms of motoring competition, and race-bred in the Lotus tradition, the Seven is first and foremost a high-speed touring sports car. Full weather equipment is available and hand luggage may be stowed behind the seats. Light weight and overall mechanical efficiency result in exceptional fuel economy and negligible maintenance costs.

Manufactured by :
LOTUS COMPONENTS, DELAMARE ROAD, CHESHUNT, HERTS.
Telephone : Waltham Cross 26181

Publicity including the 1959 BMC A-series engine option. When fitted with wire wheels, the Seven was undeniably an attractive looking machine.

Austin A35 single-carb engine may have developed an anaemic 37bhp but it had great tuning potential. It was initially fitted to entice American buyers.

Warren King's Seven Series 1 was originally FVV 877, the first Lotus demonstrator.

King modified his S1 to become an S1 1/2, with flared wings and revised dash but the original droop snoot.

BMC A-series. Very quickly, however, the new Ford Anglia 105E overhead-valve engine (997cc and 50bhp with twin SU carbs) became the standard power unit, replacing the two previous engines. Another engine casualty in the S2 was the Coventry Climax, which would not fit in the new chassis.

The Seven S2 was introduced in June 1960 and was produced continuously, not on a seasonal basis as before. Therefore chassis started to pile up at the Panshangar airfield near the Cheshunt works. Lotus had to do something, and at the Racing Car Show of January 1961 it slashed the kit price by nearly £100 to £499. Lotus would also start selling cars direct again, scrapping the idea of the Lotus Centres. That seemed to do the trick and sales of Sevens soared, helped by a general improvement in the quality of construction.

In 1961 a new Ford engine appeared in the form of the 109E Classic 1,340cc power unit. Lotus employee Warren King was the first to fit such an engine to a Seven and asked fellow Lotus development man Mike Costin (who had by that time formed his famous partnership with Keith Duckworth to create Cosworth Engineering) to modify it using a Cosworth cam and SU carburettor.

This received such a positive reaction within Lotus that it became a production model, resuscitating the lapsed Super Seven name. In production form it came with a Cosworth cam, modified head, twin Weber carburettors and a four-branch manifold. It developed a stress-free and sweet 85bhp and so the new Super Seven could reach over 100mph and 0–60mph in around eight seconds: in the words of *The Motor*, "phenomenal performance". And all for just £599 in kit form.

At the same time Warren King also made special full sidescreens for his Seven, which were adopted as production items, first as an option, then as standard equipment, along with the hood. The sidescreens consisted of a steel frame covered with vinyl, hinged at the windscreen and removable by lifting them upwards. Suddenly the Seven was half-civilized!

At the London Motor Show in 1962 came another option for the S2: the 1,498cc Ford Cortina engine. This latest Super Seven could be ordered in standard 66bhp tune or in uprated Cosworth form with higher compression ratio, fully-worked head, Cosworth camshaft, four-branch manifold and twin Webers, making it good for 95bhp. This was the torquiest and quickest Seven yet with a 0–60mph time of just under seven seconds. The Cortina gearbox was also transferred with the optional fitment of close-ratio gearing. The 66bhp car cost £585, while the 95bhp Cosworth version was £645.

Coincident with the arrival of this Super Seven 1500 came improvements in the form of a hood with rear three-quarter windows and, for the first time, the option of a heater! Triumph Spitfire front disc brakes were now fitted, the exhaust was rerouted and proper dipping headlamps became standard.

Colin Chapman liked to run Lotus as an organization on the cutting edge of sportscar design. Yesterday's products were of no importance to him and he no longer had much interest in the Seven. Indeed, the only reason the Seven continued in production was that Lotus was always penniless and the bottom line was that the Seven was a consistent money-spinner. With minimal develop-

Flared wings were adopted almost immediately on the S2. This is a 1961 1,340cc Cosworth Super Seven, one of the most desirable of all Lotus Sevens.

ment – and hence minimal investment – it continued to sell in satisfactory numbers. The changes which were made during the Sixties generally had the effect of making it cheaper for Lotus to make.

However, the mid-Sixties saw Lotus become catapulted into a different class. The Lotus Elan was well-received, selling well and making money (unlike the old Elite), Team Lotus had brought home a World Champion in Jim Clark and the

Detail of the A-frame used to locate the rear axle on the S2.

Lotus Cortina finally brought volume production to the organization. The Seven took even more of a back seat.

Nevertheless, a boost was provided in 1965 when actor Patrick McGoohan asked to borrow an Elan for his forthcoming TV series, *The Prisoner*. But he saw the Seven while he was at Cheshunt and immediately fell for its rebellious charm. The TV series proved to be as popular as it was controversial and the celebrated green-and-yellow Seven S2 (registered KAR 120C) featured in the opening sequence of every episode.

However, the Seven was not really making money by this time since costs of production had overtaken it. Already there had been a mooted replacement Seven in the form of a styling proposal by Lotus chief designer Ron Hickman in 1961: a doorless targa-topped enveloping two-seater. Chapman himself favoured a low-cost mid-engined design and, initially as a proposed Seven successor, started work on the Type 46. But the Lotus Components-built Type 46 prototype got the thumbs-down as a production model and the concept was taken up by Lotus Cars and matured into a much more sophisticated car (the Europa).

By 1966 Lotus had already outgrown Cheshunt and another move was made in October of that year to a site next to an airfield in Hethel in Norfolk.

The luxury of full sidescreens was offered as an option for the first time in 1961. Rear three-quarter visibility was extremely poor and getting in with the hood on required agility and practice, but at least Seven drivers could be watertight.

The S2's interior had the speedometer on the passenger's side and the rev-counter mounted in front of the driver. The side-mounted exhaust would be changed to a rear-exit system in 1963.

A complete S2 kit laid out for its new owner. Although very complete by the standards of the day, there was still a lot of work to be done to finish it.

A rare picture of Colin Chapman driving a Seven – he lost interest in his creation almost immediately. The year is 1961, the occasion is the Guild of Motoring Writers test day and the passenger is Lotus' sales manager, who later declared he was scared out of his wits by the drive.

Just after this momentous move sales director Graham Arnold told Graham Nearn that production of the Seven was unlikely to restart, more as a matter of corporate convenience and, frankly, indifference than a firm decision against the model. Nearn can be credited with keeping the Seven in production at this crucial time by ordering a batch of 20. Lotus could hardly refuse the cash and production of the Seven looked safe again – at least for the time being. Nearn was rewarded by becoming the sole concessionaire for the Seven in 1967.

Some time before the move to Hethel the contract for chassis manufacture had passed to Arch Motors, while the aluminium panelling was now completed by Eve & Son of Norwich.

Despite the volume of racing car business which Lotus Components enjoyed – it was building the vast majority of Formula Fords in 1967 – it was not making much money and the Seven was part of the problem since over £100 was being lost on each car made (though the volume of sales made it valuable in terms of cashflow). The new head of Components, Mike Warner, decided to develop the Seven as part of a concerted revitalization programme. His original intention was to launch a radical new Seven, but the board at Lotus favoured an evolution of the existing S2, of which around 1,350 had been made.

A Seven S2 in course of construction at the Cheshunt works.

The Cosworth-tuned version of the Ford 109E Classic engine used twin Weber carbs to extract 85bhp. A 0–60mph time of 8sec in 1961 was something to write home about!

Responding to suggestions laid out in a document presented to the Board in 1968 by Graham Nearn, Lotus set about creating the Seven Series 3. The main new feature was the fitment of the new Ford 225E 'Kent' crossflow engine, a 1.6-litre single-carb unit developing 84bhp. In fact this unit was also fitted to some late S2s, which have been retrospectively called Series '2½'. As installed in the S3, it was again capable of over 100mph.

Other changes to the S3 included the replacement of the long-defunct Standard rear axle with one from the new Ford Escort Mexico, complete with its 3.77:1 final-drive (4.12:1 optional). To make it fit the Seven, the rear wings had to be widened and the propshaft modified. Ford hubs were now fitted all round, meaning a new front hub assembly and the fitment of 5½in wide Lotus Cortina wheels.

Also new were standard front disc brakes, bigger Escort rear drums and a little glassfibre bulge in the bonnet to clear the 225E engine's downdraught Weber carburettor. The exhaust was also larger in diameter and shorter, and an electric fan became standard. Inside the S3 benefited from a standard tachometer sited ahead of the driver and, for the first time, a fuel gauge and indicators! You even got

The very first Lotus Seven S3 of August 1968. The main change was a switch to Ford Kent engines and the most noticeable exterior changes were wider Lotus Cortina wheels, wider rear wings and an external fuel filler.

Note the optional Dunlop alloy wheels on this early left-hand-drive S3.

The bonnet bulge on the S3 was to clear the pancake air filter on the Ford engine's downdraught carburettor.

carpets and the option of seat belts and a roll-over bar.

The S3 duly arrived in August 1968 and was sold by sole agents Caterham Cars in two stages of kit completion for the UK market. The first was a basic kit akin to the original S1 Seven; the second was rather more ready-assembled.

The Ford Kent engine was highly tunable. Components' deal with Holbay to produce Formula Ford engines inevitably led them to create a Lotus-Holbay version of the engine with a balanced and gas-flowed head, high-lift camshaft, special pistons, 10:1 compression ratio, four-branch manifold and twin Weber carbs. Developing 120bhp at 6,200rpm, the Holbay-tuned engine was easily the most powerful yet fitted to the Seven, although the extra weight of the S3 over the S2 made it hardly any better in terms of raw speed than a Cosworth-powered S2.

A new car, christened the 'ultimate' Seven S3, was displayed at the 1969 Racing Car Show. The so-called Seven S was fitted with the 120bhp Holbay engine, but also came with uprated trim, chromed suspension, aluminium dash, full wool carpeting, Brand Lotus alloy wheels, seat belts, air horns, heater, contoured seats, matching padded side panels and colour co-ordinated gear lever and hood. The whole thing carried a price tag of no less than £1,600 fully-built (or £1,285 in kit form).

Only the single Seven S show car was ever built, being supplanted in October 1969 by the true 'ultimate' Seven S3, the Twin Cam SS. Lotus had always maintained that its Twin Cam engine would not fit into a Seven, but inevitably a private owner

Ultimate Lotus Seven: the 1969 Twin Cam SS with its 125bhp Holbay-assembled Lotus Twin Cam engine and strengthened chassis. Only 13 would be built officially by the factory.

Note the special wheels of this prototype Twin Cam SS, now owned by Graham Nearn, and the faired-in rear light units.

tried it and found that it *did* work. Graham Nearn drove the car to Hethel and Lotus Components was sufficiently impressed to take up the challenge of creating a production version.

This involved adding triangulation into the engine bay and chassis sides. As a result, the chassis was significantly stronger but also heavier. This did not matter too much since the Twin Cam engine was rated at 125bhp, enough to propel the SS to 60mph from rest in around seven seconds.

The Motor Show car had nosecone-mounted indicators and recessed Britax rearlight clusters and, at a launch price of £1,225 in kit form, the SS proved attractive to 13 customers at the Show, making it one of the rarest and most sought-after

Sevens of all. Inevitably this specification was later duplicated by individuals and even by Lotus Components itself. Production of the S3 ended officially in November 1969 with around 350 sold.

Meanwhile, Colin Chapman had given Mike Warner a £5,000 budget and a free hand to redesign the Seven for the Seventies. Warner's plans were more grandiose than just another refettling of the existing Seven. This would be virtually an all-new car, to be sold through an all-new dealer network to a much wider public. Part of the plan was also to make the loss-making Seven cheaper to produce.

Warner set Peter Lucas and Alan Barrett to work on the new Lotus Type 60 in March 1969 and the prototype was completed only seven months later. It was a completely fresh approach from chassis to hood.

Lucas designed a simple new spaceframe chassis with spot-welded flat steel cockpit and engine bay sides plus a folded steel front crossmember. Much of its strength relied on the fitment of the body. It was built by Arch Motors (with some additional chassis made by Griston Engineering).

The bodywork was drastically new. Stylist Alan Barrett created a longer and wider shape which eschewed aluminium for self-coloured glassfibre construction. The rear wings, scuttle and dashboard were integral mouldings, while the new-profile GRP wings and large tilt-forward bonnet were separate panels. The GRP bodywork was built in-house by Lotus Cars, which kept costs down. Free-standing headlamps were supplemented by nose-mounted indicators (later moved to the wings). Rear lights were bolted to the flush rear panel either side of the rear-mounted spare wheel.

Mechanically the S4 also took many new direc-

Shock! The Seven S4 broke with tradition by having an all-glassfibre body around a steel-panelled chassis. Many Seven enthusiasts felt aggrieved at the new 'soft' approach.

A hinged bonnet on a Seven! Two main engine options were offered: the standard 84bhp Ford 1600GT (as seen here) or the Lotus Twin Cam.

tions. The rear axle remained Ford Escort, but was now located by Watts linkages and a single triangulated arm for lateral location. As before there were coil spring/damper units front and rear, but at the front the suspension changed to the double-wishbone set-up of the Lotus Europa. Early S4s had no anti-roll bar (though later ones did). Brakes were carried over, but the steering reverted to Burman rack-and-pinion.

The engines offered in the S4 were the Ford 1600 (or more rarely 1300) units and the Lotus Twin Cam and Holbay Big Valve Twin Cam. The Ford 1300 unit was an awkward fit and indeed one of the chassis tubes had to be cut away to get it in! A Ford Corsair gearbox replaced the previous Cortina unit. Despite being heavier than its predecessor, the S4 returned an admirable top speed of between 108mph and 116mph, depending on which engine was fitted, while acceleration times for the 1600GT version hovered around the mid-eight second range from zero to 60mph.

Perhaps the most attractive feature of the S4 was its interior. Notably more spacious, it featured better seats (adjustable on export models), improved side-screens with Perspex sliding panels and a moulded dash with no less than six gauges fitted.

The whole project had been kept something of a secret and there is some controversy over whether Colin Chapman ever saw the design before its presentation in October 1969. However, it seems unlikely that he would not have had some contact at least with a scale model during development.

The factory presentation of the so-called Seven S4 to the Board of Directors took place in one of the hangars at Hethel. It may be stated with some certainty that those present got something of a

shock! This was not just an uprated S3 but a completely new design. Graham Nearn was also present and was asked by Fred Bushell if he thought it would sell: "With the right marketing, yes," he replied. The public got its first taste of the S4 at the Geneva Motor Show of March 1970, while there was a press launch the month before at the Grosvenor Hotel in London.

Controversy followed the S4's styling. Many thought it had lost the purity of line of the earlier Seven in favour of a beach buggy pastiche while its extra equipment and comfort were derided as unnecessary and contrary to the spirit of 'less is more' which the Chapman-designed Seven epitomized. At £895 for the GT version and £995 for the Twin Cam (both in kit form), they were not as cheap as the outgoing S3, either. However, they were good value compared with the MG Midget and Triumph Spitfire with which the new Seven was set to compete. The idea was to get young drivers interested in Lotus motoring and let them progress through more upmarket models in years to come.

Cars were built by Lotus Racing (as Components was now called) from March 1970 and, in line with Warner's desire to sell more cars, were marketed through a special dealer network after an initial awkward period through normal Lotus dealers. Up to 15 cars were built each week, promoted with glamorous advertising. This was far in excess of the level of any previous Seven model, scuttling the theory that the S4 was a sales flop. However, sales never reached the 2,000-per-year mark at which Warner had been aiming. Export markets never responded with the expected enthusiasm and the USA was never exploited due to Federal laws.

A significant problem centred around warranty claims. Customers used to top-quality servicing and cars which did not break down, rattle or leak were inevitably disappointed by the low-volume Lotus Seven. There were also problems with rear axle tramp in the powerful versions.

Mike Warner left Lotus Racing in April 1971 to be replaced by John Standen, whose task was to wind down Lotus Racing after a decision had been taken to cease selling racing cars to the public. As a result, in late 1971 production of the Seven was transferred to Lotus Cars, where it sat uncomfortably with the Elan. Chapman's plans to push Lotus upmarket were already in place (Lotus would soon cease selling cars in kit form altogether and concentrate on the new-generation Elite and Esprit) and the Seven was rather too stark a reminder of the firm's origins. Chapman had already decided to axe the model, but it stayed on in production until the large stock of chassis and parts had been run down. The last Lotus S4 left the factory in October 1972 after around 600 had been built.

But an agreement in principle already existed between Chapman and Graham Nearn of Caterham Car Sales whereby the latter would have first refusal on the tooling and rights to produce the Seven once it had ceased at Lotus. Negotiations took place and Caterham took over the Seven in May 1973, witnessing the rebirth of the model after a slow decline lasting several years.

Another difference was the moulded-in rear wings and facia. All main gauges were now sited in front of the driver and a centre console of sorts housed most of the switchgear.

In an attempt to sway Midget and Spitfire owners over to Lotus, the S4 had much more cossetting weather gear. Why, there were even Perspex sliding windows!

The later S4 had its indicators moved from the nose to an integral position on the front wings. Note the individual seats, another novelty for the Seven, and the roll-over bar.

This Seven shows the hard-top designed by Alan Barrett for the S4. Only a handful of such tops were made.

Postscript: Interview with Colin Chapman

In 1978, many years after the Seven had left Colin Chapman's mind, Graham Nearn conducted an interview with him about the origins of the Seven. It makes fascinating reading. Here are some excerpts of Chapman's words.

"Having built the Eleven we then went back and said let's build a Mark 6-type car using glassfibre wings instead of sheet metal. It was sort of a spartan-bodied Clubman Eleven, that was how the Seven came about.

"I was responsible for it and it was done at home in the evenings in Friern Barnet during 1957…. It was all very well known stuff. The chassis was virtually a Six. Instead of having two big tubes along the bottom, it had small tubes and all the running gear was virtually Eleven. There was nothing that was new on it… It was simple and just kept going. The sort of thing you could dash off in a weekend. Well, a week maybe: you could do the basic calculations, lay out a chassis, lay out the suspension, knock it out, sort of thing, and there it was!

"It was just about the simplest, most basic, lightest, highest performance little car that we could come up with for two people at minimum cost. When I first started motoring myself it was the car I dreamed about. I always only built cars for myself. If we really get down to it, the reason that Lotus has changed is that my taste in cars has changed as I get older.

"I thought that where we would get into the market was by being the first people to offer a complete kit: we literally supplied every nut, bolt and washer that was necessary to build a car.

"It was a very important car in the history of Lotus. The whole idea was that it was our first attempt at a bread-and-butter car that we could build all through the season. It was a very marginal project, but it was a good gap-filler. It was the Seven plus the sportscar [Elite] that started Lotus. The profit [the Seven] was making we squandered on trying to build a road car…. We didn't make a profit until 1963.

"I did have an affection for the Seven, but remember that all the years we were making it, it was a bread-and-butter line to enable us to go GP racing or sportscar racing and I was always involved in the senior category as it were. There was some other guy at the other end of the shop screwing together Sevens and squirting them out and making the money…. The image wasn't quite right. The only way we could really stop it was by closing down Lotus Components."

And, of course, the Seven never did die. Even the closure of Components (or Lotus Racing as it had become) didn't stop the Seven, which continued in production under Lotus Cars until the plug was finally pulled on the S4. One person at least was determined that the Seven as a model should never die. Graham Nearn, the Seven's most ardent supporter, ensured not only that it lived, but that it bred and evolved. Life was by no means any easier under Caterham, but its persistence and enthusiasm saw the Seven emerge as one of the seminal sportscars of all time.

CHAPTER 2

Caterham Cars and Lotus (1959–73)

"Custodians of the legend"

Colin Chapman conceived the Lotus Seven in 1957. Two years later, he had appointed Caterham Car Services to sell it. Apart from those first two years, Caterham has been involved with the Seven ever since.

That association began as a sales and service centre, but it blossomed as Caterham became the acknowledged experts on the Seven. Lotus were pleased to listen to the opinions of the people at Caterham who actually dealt with the car day in, day out, and would then modify the car when recommendations were made. Finally, of course, the rapport was strong enough for Colin Chapman to devolve production of the Seven to Caterham in 1973.

Caterham Cars is synonymous with Graham Nearn, who became a director on its formation and has run the company ever since. Formerly employed in the timber trade, Nearn had always held a passion for cars. He had owned a 1937 SS100, for which he paid £250 in those austere postwar years when such extravagant cars were viewed as a liability.

But cars as a full-time occupation just happened. Nearn knew some fellow enthusiasts at the Purley Rugby Club and one of them (David Holmes) wanted to buy a small garage premises which had come up for sale in nearby Caterham. This was none other than Anthony Crook Motors, a garage services business run by the racing driver Anthony Crook (who went on to take a controlling interest in Bristol Cars, which he still runs today).

Behind Crook's main Esso petrol forecourt and service bay in Town End, Caterham Hill, he used one of a set of ramshackle buildings set in an old orchard to prepare his Cooper-Bristol racing cars in which he made quite a name for himself as a driver. But in 1959 he moved on and put the premises up for sale.

So Nearn was invited to become one of the five partners in a new venture called Caterham Car Services, a forecourt business to trade and service cars and to sell petrol. One of these partners was Ian Smith, motoring journalist, Mark 6 racer, leading light of Club Lotus and author of *Lotus: The First Ten Years*, the first ever book on Lotus (also published, incidentally, by Motor Racing Publications). The other three were David Holmes, Nick Carter and Alec Bromley.

Through Smith's friendship with Colin Chapman, it was natural that the little garage at Caterham should eventually develop an association with Lotus. Smith knew that Chapman was establishing a chain of Lotus Centres to sell Elites and Sevens, so he arranged for Chapman to visit the site. Since the garage was already selling sportscars, Chapman was very keen that it should become the first of the so-called Lotus Centres. Graham Nearn clearly recalls the fateful visit one evening: "This Ford Zodiac turned up and out stepped Colin Chapman. It was a very short encounter, but enough to confirm the appointment of Caterham as a Lotus Centre."

Soon after, Caterham took delivery of a Seven kit and an Elite kit, since it was their obligation to have these available as an appointed Lotus Centre. Spares back-up did not even enter the equation at that time. Graham Nearn: "It was simply a question of here's a couple of cars, get on with it. It was never a proper marketing operation. We were never asked how many cars we could sell or asked for any kind of sales forecast or anything like that."

In fact there seemed to be little relationship between the number of cars that were being sold and the number that were being made. For the first few years it just happened to be about right. Then the market took a downturn and Lotus was left with unsold Sevens in the yard at Cheshunt and chassis littering Panshangar. Hence the £100 price cut announced at the 1961 Racing Car Show to bring the cost of a basic Seven down to a mere

Caterham Car Services' early demonstrator fitted with the Ford 105E engine, an installation which Caterham pioneered. Note the natty wheel hub-spinners.

An advert from *Sports Car and Lotus Owner* magazine of July 1960 includes Caterham as one of the first Lotus Centres.

£499. Graham Nearn learned of the price cut when he walked past the Lotus show stand. "Oh yes, we've been trying to get you on the 'phone all day," said a sheepish Peter Warr.

That price cut slashed dealer margins to just £20. On top of this, Lotus began selling direct again, which left the Lotus Centres somewhat in the wilderness. One by one they gave up their Lotus franchises and moved into other businesses. However, Graham Nearn was determined that Caterham Car Services should stay with the Seven and set about establishing the company as Britain's leading Seven specialist.

Right from his first encounter with the Seven, Nearn had recognized the car as a classic design. "It seemed to me right from the start to be the ultimate small sportscar; it didn't seem worth bothering with anything else."

But business demanded that other products flowed through the Caterham garage. With the acquisition of an Austin-Healey franchise to sell Sprites and big Healeys (a unique arrangement, since all other Healey dealers were also Austin main agents), Caterham's business moved away from selling new Lotus cars. The odd new Seven did sell through Caterham, but increasingly the business depended on dealing in used Sevens in which Caterham was the acknowledged leader. For the first time, a proper spares department was set up for the Seven: as Graham Nearn remembers, "The Lotus attitude was always *manana*". Mindful of the difficulties in obtaining insurance and finance that people commonly encountered when buying a

Seven, Nearn negotiated deals with an insurance company and a finance house to make purchasing much easier.

Then in 1962, the Government removed Retail Price Maintenance from petrol, allowing forecourts to set their own prices. The partners in Caterham Car Services saw a price war looming and, faced with the prospect of falling profits from petrol sales, they sold the filling station to Esso. The

doors at the front) and the old building where Anthony Crook had tuned his racing engines. The sales side of the operation became known as Caterham Car Sales, while the coachwork business was called Caterham Coachworks. The latter proved to be highly important in 1962 when Lotus axed its Lotus Centres and started selling cars direct. Caterham Car Sales might not have survived alone, but it was underwritten by the coachworks side which built up slowly to become the mainstay of the business.

In 1964 Nearn placed an advertisement locally for a manager for the expanding bodyshop. A disenchanted Ford main dealer bodyshop employee called David Wakefield applied for the job. As a Seven enthusiast and racer, Wakefield was accepted to become the workshop manager, while Nearn concentrated on car sales. As Nearn later said: "David Wakefield became the other half of me: we complement each other perfectly." They both raced Sevens during the Sixties. Using cars from stock they competed in the 1965 Clubmans Championship and also won a six-hour relay and sprints at Brands Hatch.

The tiny Caterham Car Services stand at the 1960 Racing Car Show, featuring all sorts of Lotus paraphernalia. The upper picture on the wall shows how the old Caterham site used to look.

The unprepossessing facade of Caterham Car Services in 1960: a basic Esso forecourt with a workshop behind. The Esso station remains today, but the rest of the scene is virtually unrecognizable.

partners split up, leaving Graham Nearn in sole control of the premises behind the forecourt to carry on the car sales and service business.

Nearn bought the freehold on all the buildings, consisting of a house which became a sales office (and later stores), the horseshoe of lock-up garages (between which a roof had been installed with

One of Wakefield's early tasks was to prepare a 109E-powered Seven to duplicate the car used in Patrick McGoohan's cult TV series *The Prisoner*. Having found that the original car, KAR 120C, was no longer at Lotus, McGoohan needed one at the last minute to film a sequence in the last episode and Wakefield laboured overnight to have the car

Nearn also helped out Patrick McGoohan, instigator of the TV classic *The Prisoner*, by creating a replica of KAR 120C to be used in the final episode. McGoohan responded by posing for some publicity shots with Nearn.

Inside the workshop area can be seen the Elite which Caterham was obliged to keep as part of the agreement as a Lotus Centre, plus the Speedwell Sprite record-breaker, which just happened to be around when the picture was shot.

ready. It was painted, unusually, in green with a yellow nosecone; according to popular myth the yellow nose was on there because the previous nose had been damaged and the yellow one was all that Lotus had available!

Graham Nearn drove the car to the filming location in London and quickly found himself seconded as an extra. In the episode *Fall Out* he could be seen cleaning the car and delivering the

keys through the letterbox. McGoohan repaid Caterham's fast work by posing with Nearn and a Seven for some photographs which appeared in Caterham adverts for some time afterwards.

As the business grew it went limited and became known as Caterham Car Sales & Coachworks Ltd, with Nearn and Wakefield as co-directors. Caterham would eventually become sales agents for other British specialist sportscar firms TVR, Gilbern

In the yard at the back of the workshop in the early Sixties, Sevens mingle with other more mundane machinery which provided the mainstay bodyshop with its business. Caterham was also a dealer for Austin-Healey, hence the Sprite.

Graham Nearn became the official Seven man on Lotus show stands. This is the 1969 Racing Car Show, and Colin Chapman brushes up on the Seven with Nearn at the Caterham Cars stand with, second from right, former Caterham director and show organizer Ian Smith.

and Marcos, but these never took off in the same way as the Seven.

When Lotus moved from Cheshunt to Hethel in October 1966, it became clear that, while no decision had been made to drop the Seven, Lotus Components hadn't started building it again. Sales manager Graham Arnold told Nearn that production was unlikely to restart as there was talk of the model being axed. Nearn was understandably concerned and at the Racing Car Show in January 1967 he approached Colin Chapman directly.

Chapman seemed surprised that a demand still existed for the car and told Nearn to contact David Lazenby, ex-mechanic for Jim Clark, who was at that time running Lotus Components, to see what could be done.

Having received the go-ahead from the highest authority at Lotus, Graham Nearn confidently attempted to make contact with Lazenby, but he proved rather elusive. For two months he was passed on to someone else. Then, on March 27, Nearn's first son Robert was born. Feeling he could do anything, he decided to ring Lotus just one more time. He got through to Graham Arnold, who said: "It's David Lazenby you want and he's sitting right in front of me; I'll pass you over."

Nearn travelled up to Wymondham in his trusty Aston Martin DB2/4 to meet Lazenby for a historic appointment. Lazenby explained that Components were heavily committed to building Formula Fords, but that there were sufficient parts in stock to build 20 S2 1500 Sevens. Nearn agreed to purchase them there and then. Faced with continuing demand for the Seven, Lotus had little option but to resume proper production and the numbers built up again. As Lotus Managing Director Fred Bushell put it: "We just couldn't bring ourselves to turn down ready money."

At the same time, Nearn suggested that Caterham Car Sales should become the sole distributor of Sevens in the UK. This was a timely suggestion which suited Lotus admirably: Graham Arnold was freed from having to market the car. An agreement was reached whereby, from 1967 until the advent of the S4 in 1970, all Sevens except those sold overseas passed through Caterham's hands. There was no binding agreement as to how many cars Caterham would guarantee to sell. Arnold realized that Components could only make four cars a week and that was just about the level at which sales averaged out.

Graham Nearn became a regular visitor to Hethel. He bought a Land-Rover and trailer in which he would pick up each batch of new kits on a weekly basis, personally checking that everything was in order before loading the kits up. The Land-Rover had a reversible sign on its flanks that read 'Caterham Cars – Lotus 7 Specialists' while transporting kits and 'Caterham Coachworks – Body Repair Specialists' when running around the town!

Nearn quickly got to know more faces at Lotus and became increasingly involved with the marketing of the Seven. When he offered to act as resident Seven specialist on Lotus show stands, Graham Arnold could hardly believe it. He'd been looking for someone to answer the endless questions about the Seven on show days and here was someone who was prepared to do it for nothing!

Caterham's experience with the Seven was also heeded at Lotus. For example, the Standard Com-

panion rear axle was never really up to the task of transmitting high power outputs to the rear wheels. Ron Davies at Caterham pioneered the technique of welding on a reinforcing plate to the rear of the casing, something which Lotus subsequently adopted. And when supplies of Companion axles started to dry up, Caterham would locate more and supply them to the factory.

At the Lotus Open Day in summer 1968, Graham Nearn discovered that David Lazenby was no longer head of Lotus Components, having been replaced in April 1968 by Mike Warner. Nearn met up with Warner, who wanted to firm up the production arrangements for the Seven. He asked Nearn for the first time to come up with a monthly schedule of the number of cars he would need. Under Warner's regime, Components always produced the required number of cars on time.

Warner also hinted at some of the radical ideas that he had for the future of the Seven, but these were not to bear fruit and instead 1968 saw the introduction of the Seven S3. The changes incorporated on the S3 were largely the responsibility of Graham Nearn. As a regular visitor to Hethel he had got wind of a plan to reorganize the distribution of the Seven and he feared for his position. He acted decisively by presenting a document outlining his proposals for the future of the car.

This was Caterham Cars' first S3 demonstrator of 1968. Unusually, the main body was left unpainted.

Colin Chapman saw the document, was impressed by it and that effectively made secure Caterham's sole concession – for the time being.

The material proposals in the document were that the latest Ford 225E crossflow engines should be fitted and that the equipment level be increased. When Mike Warner took over as head of Components he was keen to see changes instituted and Nearn's plans were entirely logical. Hence the new S3 came with the 1600 Ford Cortina engine.

Graham Nearn arranged the S3 launch party. His brother owned a very fine old inn called the Ringlestone Arms, in Kent, and Nearn had a metallic blue Seven S3 delivered from Lotus by transporter to the pub. He placed an advert in *Motor Sport* to announce the launch, expecting a handful of enthusiasts to show up. In the event, the pub was swamped by a sea of eager people all desperate for a glimpse of the new car.

The car had arrived swathed in polythene and with its rotor arm missing – a deliberate Lotus ploy so that it could not be driven! Nearn was having none of that and transferred a rotor arm from a Cortina in the car park so that, at the appointed hour, it drove out of a nearby barn to be greeted by the throng. Three orders were taken that night and there was a flood of interest in the following weeks based on that evening's work.

Undoubtedly the ultimate Lotus Seven was the S3 Twin Cam SS. Once again Graham Nearn had a hand in this model. Lotus' official line on the Twin Cam engine was that it would not fit in the Seven's engine bay. Nearn knew that it would, however, because he had met a man who had done just that at an earlier record-breaking attempt to build a Seven in the shortest time possible. With the 1969 Motor Show not far off, Nearn arrived at Hethel on one of his regular visits driving this chap's car, which was fitted with a Twin Cam engine from an Elan. Faced with clear proof that a Twin Cam *did* fit in a Seven, Lotus Components was persuaded to enter production with the Twin Cam SS. Graham Nearn acquired the very first car, chassis 2564/TC1, which he owns to this day.

Then in 1970 came the S4. Nearn was obviously aware that a revised Seven was in preparation. Just as he had done with the S3, he supplied a proposal on how the new car should be, including more interior space, better weather protection and more standard fittings.

"I thought they were simply going to make a bigger S3," says Nearn. "When I actually saw the car I got quite a surprise." Like many other people,

he found the S4 something of a shock. Although he had been a regular visitor to Hethel, he had not seen the new Seven before its factory unveiling in October 1969 (indeed, some reports state that Colin Chapman himself had not seen the car until that moment). The advent of the S4 also marked the end of Caterham's sole concession. In the event it was recognized by both Nearn and Warner that Caterham could not sell the number of cars which Lotus wanted to sell. As a competitor in the MG Midget market, the S4 had a much higher sales forecast than the old S3, so several new dealers were appointed around the country in addition to Caterham Cars. Each had to undertake to sell a certain number of cars per year.

Nearn had serious doubts that Lotus' sales targets could be reached at all. For this reason he was quite happy that other dealers should take on the job of selling new Sevens: "Frankly I didn't want the responsibility of having to achieve sales targets which I considered to be unrealistic."

To begin with, this was not the case. Despite all the controversy about its styling and the problems surrounding its production and warranty claims, the Seven S4 was a healthy seller in its first year. It was even good for Caterham Cars because the service department, run by Peter Cooper, was always fully booked since the type of owner who bought an S4 was happier to pay someone else to do

At the launch of the Seven S4 in 1970, Graham Hill asks Graham Nearn for his thoughts on the new model. Nearn was not as sure of the sales potential of this model as the outgoing S3.

LOTUS

GROUP LOTUS
CAR COMPANIES LIMITED

NORWICH NOR 92W   Wymondham 3411
Telegrams Lotus, Norwich   Telex 97401

19th July, 1971.

Graham Nearn, Esq.,
Caterham Car Sales,
36/38, Town End,
CATERHAM-ON-THE-HILL,
Surrey.

Dear Graham,

    Whilst it is still at least eighteen months away, this letter is to confirm that when we discontinue the manufacture and sale of the Lotus 7 from the factory here, we will give you first option to purchase these operations. This would, of course, include handing over all necessary drawings, specifications, body tools, chassis manufacture jigs, etc., etc., and coming to an arrangement on spare parts, etc.

    In view of your past and present association with the Lotus 7 I am sure you will be in a far better position to take over this operation when the time comes than any other organisation that might be interested, and we will be pleased to give you every assistance to see that this becomes a reality.

Yours sincerely,

Colin Chapman

the servicing. Caterham continued to be the country's leading specialist in older Sevens.

Then in early 1971 Mike Warner left Lotus. The S4 had been his baby and he had defended it through thick and thin. With Warner gone, the future of the Seven began to look shaky, especially as the economy was beginning to enter another uncertain period. Plans were already afoot for Lotus' move upmarket and it was only a matter of time before Lotus could no longer swallow its pride over the Seven.

Therefore, Graham Nearn approached Colin Chapman to sound out the possibility of Caterham Cars taking over the manufacture of the car. Chapman was receptive to the suggestion and in a letter dated July 19, 1971 he said: "Whilst it is still at least 18 months away, this letter is to confirm that when we discontinue the manufacture and sale of the Lotus 7 from the factory here, we will give you first option to purchase these operations."

The Seven S4 continued to be made at Lotus Cars without any real enthusiasm, and Nearn was undoubtedly far more interested than anybody at Lotus in the Seven. Despite the fact that it was looking increasingly like a doomed animal at Lotus, he had a singular lack of success persuading anyone to finalize a deal regarding the transfer of production.

However, with the introduction of VAT, the imminent launch of the Elite and Esprit and a general desire to get rid of old wood, the time was ripe. By 1973 Graham Arnold had moved on to Moonraker (a boat company owned by Colin Chapman) and his place in sales had been taken over by John Berry. One of his tasks was to clear out the debris left after the closure of Lotus Racing. A priority on Berry's list was to get rid of 54 Formula Fords which had been left standing in Lotus Racing's hangar at Hethel for a couple of years. Many of these were in a dilapidated state, covered in bird droppings and brake fluid corrosion where the master-cylinders had leaked. Berry asked Nearn if he had any interest in the Formula Fords. Nearn certainly was interested, but only if this deal could be linked with another – namely the takeover of Seven production.

This time Nearn's offer looked too tempting to resist but, even so, problems over the terms of the deal dragged discussions on until John Kelly took over as Lotus service manager. Anxious to steam ahead with fitting out for the new range of Lotus cars, he pushed for the Caterham deal to go through.

Finally, a draft agreement was worked out and Nearn found himself commuting between Caterham and Hethel almost non-stop. Fred Bushell yielded up more information about the Seven's production costings, which did not make encouraging reading for the people at Caterham. Much of the car was sub-contracted out and prices had been kept low against bulk orders. The whole parts supply position was obfuscated by the discovery that some helpful soul had put all the computer records relating to suppliers – addresses, prices, parts numbers, ordering schedules etc – into a shredder, on the basis that the Seven was now out of production and so the paperwork wouldn't be needed any more....

By May 1973, Nearn was convinced that the project was viable as a whole (taking into account the spares and servicing sides) and, for their part, Lotus were happy with the terms of the deal and were probably happy to be rid of the 'bobble hat brigade', knowing that they would be in better hands at Caterham. Caterham Cars paid an undisclosed sum to take on the whole Seven operation plus the Formula Fords and more than 50 Lotus Twin Cam engines. As well as the main payment, Lotus would receive a royalty on each Seven sold up to a mutually agreed cut-off point.

Another clause in the deal stated that Colin Chapman would attend an official handover ceremony and also that Lotus would design a new badge for the car. This was necessary because, under the terms of the agreement, Caterham was forbidden from using the Lotus name, mainly due to fears over the product liability position of a car bearing the Lotus name but not produced by Lotus. Caterham could call the car Seven, but not Lotus Seven. An artist at Lotus duly came up with a badge design reminiscent of the traditional Lotus badge but bearing the numeral '7'. As such the subliminal association was with Lotus without actually calling it a Lotus. This badge was fitted to the last of the Lotus S4s as well as the Caterham-built cars to emphasize the continuity of the model.

The formal handover took place in June 1973 at Pub Lotus in Primrose Hill, north London. This remarkable establishment was the brainchild of Graham Arnold. He had negotiated with Char-

The June 1973 handover of the Seven to Graham Nearn took place at *Pub Lotus* in London. Colin Chapman shakes Nearn's hand to confirm the deal.

ringtons to fill its pub with Lotus artefacts ranging from tables made from Brand Lotus wheels to specially mounted Europa seats at the bar. There was even a Seven Bar, and it was here that the handover ceremony took place. Colin Chapman duly turned up to give Graham Nearn the official handshake for the benefit of the assembled photographers, before spending a pleasant afternoon chatting about cars and motor racing.

"This was an early experience of dealing with the press for me," recalls Nearn. "I handed out a press release before coffee and lunch, with the ceremony last. Everyone went back to Fleet Street at the earliest possible moment and missed an opportunity to talk with a relaxed Colin Chapman for a whole afternoon. These days I save the press release till last."

This sort of deal is almost unique in motoring history. Manufacturers rarely hand over to a third party the rights to a model once it has gone out of production. One could cite the Lotus Elan, sold to Kia in 1994, but otherwise it is hard to think of such an event ever happening.

The story of what happened to Caterham after all the excitement of becoming a manufacturer had died down is related in the following chapter. In the years that have unfolded since 1973, the perception of all Sevens has drifted away from Lotus and towards Caterham. Even in the Lotus years, Caterham Cars had consistently shown more enthusiasm for the car than the people who were actually making it and the passion for the Seven redoubled when the company became a manufacturer.

All Caterham's efforts were directed at promoting the Seven worldwide, and constantly improving the beast until virtually nothing of the original Lotus Seven remained. As such the Seven, which started life under Caterham as an almost hallowed object – to be preserved as Lotus had conceived it – evolved into something which was Caterham's own, though no-one ever lost sight of the Seven's heritage. As Nearn would say later, Caterham became "custodians of the legend". In practice, that meant preserving the external dimensions and shape of the Seven, and religiously applying the Chapman doctrine of engineering out unnecessary weight.

Caterham boldly relaunched the S3 Seven in 1974 but with important modifications. The Britax rear lights were mounted proud of the rear wing, which in turn was reprofiled.

CHAPTER 3

The Caterham years

A cottage industry on the hill

It would be easy to look back at the history of Caterham Cars since 1973 and conclude that it was all plain sailing. After all, there has been consistent growth and development from start to finish and the popularity of the Seven has never once faltered.

However, it was far from certain that, had the Seven been taken on by Caterham as an isolated project, it would have succeeded. It was quite simply not self-supporting, a fact well recognized by Graham Nearn before he embarked on his career as a manufacturer. Until then, the business had needed only minimal overheads to operate successfully. But even as the leading sales and service centre for the Seven, Caterham Car Sales was not in a position to make a seamless transition into profitable manufacture.

In the beginning, manufacture of the Seven would be supported by the busy and profitable body repair business, Caterham Coachworks, which was run by David Wakefield. The Seven would be given some breathing space in which to establish itself while, at the same time, secondhand car sales and servicing would continue to provide bread-and-butter income. Graham Nearn continued to operate his sportscar showroom in Hampstead, retailing new and used Lotus, Marcos, TVR and Gilbern cars.

The agreement with Lotus stated that initially Lotus would supply complete kits of parts for the Seven until Caterham were in a position to source them themselves. However, the shredding of the computer records at Hethel threw Lotus into disarray and complete kits were never forthcoming, although all the stock at Hethel was transferred to Caterham.

As such, Caterham were thrown in at the deep end with the challenge to transform from retailer to manufacturer; it was evident that there was a lot of work to do before the first Seven could be built at Caterham. Dave Merritt was taken on as foreman in charge of building Sevens and he found that the chassis posed no problems. Arch Motors had never stopped building them and it was simply a matter of delivering them to Caterham, instead of Hethel. Alan Barrett supplied the glassfibre body panels, but the other parts were the problem.

Those items not held in the stockpile from Lotus had to be sourced from existing suppliers. Many of these, who had been happy to deal in multiples of 100, were less than happy when Caterham rang up to ask about just 10.

Despite the difficulties, the first Seven was built in about two months in the workshop at the bottom of the Caterham yard where Anthony Crook had once prepared his racing cars. The first car was fitted with one of a batch of Twin Cam engines that Lotus had agreed to supply. Other than the badging, the Caterham-built Seven was indistinguishable from the Lotus Seven S4.

The press release announcing the takeover of Seven production said: "A special manufacturing company (to be called the Seven Car Co Ltd) has been set up by Caterham Car Sales to produce the Seven as a fully built car. The name of the car will be changed to Super Seven Series IV".

As it transpired, that never really happened. The idea of selling cars fully built (at £1,487 for a Twin Cam and £1,195 for a GT) came about because of the imposition of VAT on kits: previously purchase tax had not been payable on kits, giving them a huge price advantage, but that was eliminated by the arrival of VAT. In fact, said Caterham, British customers preferred to build a car themselves. The reality was that the law had been changed by Norman Fowler, the Minister of Transport, at virtually the same time as VAT arrived, in 1973, so that 'amateur built' cars could be exempted from the tough Type Approval regulations which were then coming into force. Caterham could never afford to go through full Type Approval so, in

This is the first Caterham demo/press car of 1975, the 42nd S3 made. Both the bonnet and nose were slightly higher than the old Lotus S3.

The first Twin Cam cars that Caterham built did without air filters over the carburettors, but the noise they generated was unacceptable.

Therefore the mouths of the carbs were protected and quietened by two small rectangular filters. The bonnet had to be modified to fit round them.

Britain at least, its cars *had* to be supplied with some degree of incompletion to accommodate an element of 'amateur build'. Caterham simply chose to sell the Seven in complete component form with all-new parts and not as a bare-bones basic kit.

There had been some trepidation over the title for the Seven and how the car would establish itself without Lotus badging. Although launched simply as the Super Seven, enthusiasts themselves solved the problem since they continually referred to the car as the Caterham Super Seven. "That name just happened," says Graham Nearn, "it's not the one I'd have chosen." At least it gave it an identity of its own.

One element of continuity from the Lotus days was a six-month warranty which would be honoured throughout the Lotus dealerships.

Despite the intention to retain the Lotus design intact, Caterham announced it would be improving the car in certain areas, notably legroom, better hood and carpets, improved exhaust, a low-cost hardtop and the availability of a towing bracket. In practice, Caterham never had the chance to implement any of these changes. The choice of colours encompassed red, yellow, blue, white or – that icon of Seventies paint schemes – lime green.

With one car per week being built at Caterham, Graham Nearn set about divesting himself of the Formula Fords which were still in store at Hethel. Nearn was obliged by his agreement to take them away within six months of the May takeover. The sale of these cars was achieved with considerable marketing finesse. Realizing that many people would like to buy a racing car but were prevented by lack of finance, Nearn arranged a readily available finance deal with a rugby-playing friend, Bob Holland, that made even uncompetitive Lotus chassis seem appealing! Most were sold in this manner; some chassis which had deteriorated too far were refurbished by Group Racing Developments (GRD), a company run by none other than Mike Warner, late of Lotus Cars; and the final batch went in a special deal with Motor Racing Stables, the driver-training school at Brands Hatch.

Problems for the Seven were quickly gathering like storm clouds on the horizon. Firstly, the early Seventies was not the best time to be building a sportscar. The price of oil, rampant inflation and interest rates and Prime Minister Edward Heath's looming confrontation with the miners and the three-day week left the UK economy in recession.

Then there was the problem of parts supply. The stock items from Lotus were quickly being exhausted and it was becoming more and more difficult to find alternative sources. The final blow came when there was no more weather gear. Weathershields of Birmingham had a patent on the mouldings for the windscreen and weather equipment for the S4. The final quota of the original run had gone to Steele Brothers in New Zealand and Weathershields were uninterested in restarting production – unless Caterham placed a big enough order. That meant a minimum of £50,000, a figure which was clearly out of the question. The fact had to be faced that the S4 had come to the end of the road, despite the strong demand for it.

David Wakefield suggested going back to the Seven S3. The idea was always at the back of Graham Nearn's mind and seemed to make sense: it was estimated that the S3 could be built in half the time it took to make the S4, and it was preferred by enthusiasts. Some of these enthusiasts had even been buying replacement S3 chassis from Caterham and attempting to build their own S3 replica! As a matter of courtesy, Graham Nearn went to Hethel to tell Fred Bushell, Colin Chapman's right-hand man, about the plan and Bushell agreed that it was the right thing to do, especially as Lotus was still getting royalties on each car sold.

Caterham put an advert in *Motor Sport* stating that "a limited run of 25 S3 Sevens" would be built, one of the first examples of a limited-edition

The Lotus Twin Cam engine as supplied to Caterham. The 'Big Valve Twin Cam' lettering on the top of the engine at the front led to the bonnet line being raised slightly. Headaches with supply eventually brought the Twin Cam engine to its end.

47

car. As Graham Nearn recalls: "The 'phone never stopped ringing. All that remained was to produce the cars."

David Wakefield took on overall responsibility for the S3 project. Peter Lucas, formerly of Lotus, was brought in to explore ways in which the chassis could be improved. Service manager Peter Cooper, in conjunction with Ron Davies, set about putting easy-sounding theory into practice.

the standard bonnet and nosecone. There was no alternative but to raise the bonnet line and remould the nosecone accordingly. Arthur Francis, manager of Caterham Coachworks, built a buck for the new nose moulding, while Peter Cooper attended to the bonnet.

The first Caterham S3 was complete and running by April 1974, even before production of the S4 had finished (the last S4 left the works in June).

Al fresco was the only way to drive a Seven. Note the optional roll-over bar on this 1977 model.

The interior was very similar to the old Lotus S3. This press demonstrator is fitted with Dymo tape labels by all the switches, but identifying them for owners was second nature.

This was the time of the three-day week and electricity rationing. Working quite literally by gaslamp during the frequent power cuts, Cooper and Davies depanelled a standard Lotus S3 chassis which had been produced by Arch Motors and held in the spares department and set about uprating it to Twin Cam SS specification by adding triangulation to the engine bay and cockpit sides. In fact, the chassis was given even more stiffness by the addition of diagonal tubes in the rear and sides of the cockpit, reinforcing plates for the gearbox mount, improved steering rack mounts and a strengthening hoop in the transmission tunnel. The stressed aluminium cladding was then refitted.

The prototype was to be fitted with a Big Valve Lotus Twin Cam engine, but this presented a problem. Even on the original Seven SS model, the Twin Cam had been a tight fit: it rubbed against the underside of the bonnet and parts of the nose-cone had to be cut away to clear the carburettors. But now it was discovered that the extra height of the 'Big Valve' lettering cast into the cam covers meant that the engine simply would not fit under

Standard finish for Caterham Sevens was an unpainted aluminium body with painted wings and nosecone. A full paint scheme could be ordered as an optional extra.

Peter Cooper tested the first Series 3 with its Big Valve Twin Cam engine running on twin Dellortos with no air filters. There was a terrific rattle, which sounded as though the engine had shot its bearings. In fact, it was just the induction thump from the carbs, which was simply rectified by fitting air filters.

The beauty of the S3 was that most of the components were simple in design and could be sourced relatively easily, unlike the S4. Caterham Cars already manufactured glassfibre wings for the spares department so it was an easy matter to make more for the new car. Likewise, the propshaft, instruments, wiring and most other fittings were either held in stock or obtainable without too much difficulty.

The Twin Cam engine was mated to the normal Elan-type Ford 2000E gearbox and the rear axle came from the Ford Escort. One of the few problems was finding a suitable radiator but judicious reference to a parts book revealed that the Hillman

Avenger would yield a radiator of exactly the right size and capacity. The first S3 was fitted with Brand Lotus wheels and Goodyear tyres and at the rear it was distinguishable from the Lotus Seven Twin Cam SS by the fitment of top-mounted three-in-one Britax lights rather than units recessed into the wings.

Arch Motors still held the Lotus S3 jigs that had devolved to Caterham with the takeover and indeed had been supplying S3 chassis for Caterham's spares department. So there was no problem increasing production to cover the new car's requirement. By that time, Don Gadd (who had run Lotus' development workshop back in the Cheshunt days) was manager of Arch Motors and was delighted to see the S3 revived. He built the new chassis to S3 Twin Cam specification, but with judicious alteration to some of the tubes to increase strength still further.

The Caterham S3 Twin Cam was officially introduced in September 1974 at a basic price of £1,540 and the first car, like many to follow, was sold to an

The Ford 1600GT Kent engine was offered from 1975 but did not prove at all popular until the Eighties. With a single carb, the engine turned out 84bhp, much less than the Twin Cam, but then this model also cost considerably less.

Building a kit from Caterham took 20 hours, or a good weekend's work. During the Seventies and early Eighties, complete component form was the usual way to buy a Seven in the UK.

overseas enthusiast. The first batch of around nine S3s was built pretty much from stock items and thereafter the initial announcement of a limited run of 25 cars was quietly forgotten about and production steamed ahead.

Yet the mid-Seventies was still a difficult time to be selling sportscars. Caterham faced constant supply problems – strikes and the three-day working week were always cited by suppliers as the reasons, which may have been true, or simply an excuse for late deliveries. In addition to the economic chaos, the change in the British tax laws in 1973 meant that kit-cars, which had previously been exempt from purchase tax, were now not only charged VAT at the standard rate, but were also burdened by the special Car Tax, which had to be paid before they could be registered in the UK. Inevitably, the price of the Seven leapt up, but even so, the Seven would continue to be sold in kit form in Britain, while Caterham concentrated on fully-built cars for foreign markets.

Despite these difficulties, a six-month waiting list opened up for the Seven almost immediately, while other specialist firms were going to the wall. Why? Partly because the Seven really had no competition and was excellent value. But mostly, it was because export markets were crying out for the Seven, where it was widely regarded as the epitome of the British sportscar. Strong exports would remain a vital part of Caterham's business for the company's future.

Many export markets required left-hand drive, and the first left-hand drive chassis was created as

an exact mirror image of the right-hand drive version. This may have seemed logical to the fabricator at the time, but areas like the pedal box went in mirror-image too. No-one had thought to remind him that, despite their strange ways, foreign drivers did *not* use their left foot to accelerate and brake!

There were other minor problems with the left-hand drive chassis. Different exhaust manifolds had to be fitted on the Twin Cam engine to allow space for the steering column, and the alternator mounting bracket and belt had to be modified.

With the 126bhp Big Valve Twin Cam engine in place, the Caterham was the fastest Seven yet. In *Autocar*'s test of 1975, a car fitted with Goodyear 5½in alloy wheels and G800 tyres running on a standard Ford axle and 3.89:1 diff achieved a top speed of 114mph and reached 60mph in a scorching 6.2 seconds. The car weighed only 1,162lb (527kg), so the power-to-weight ratio was a remarkable 242bhp/ton. As one noted Lotus enthusiast commented, that was "reminiscent of the downfield runners in the 1961 Grand Prix season!"

All of the early S3 cars were fitted with Big Valve Twin Cam engines but, with the demise of the Lotus Europa in 1975, supplies of these engines started to run out. Part of the contract that Graham Nearn had negotiated with Lotus said that Lotus was under an obligation to assist Caterham in the production of the Seven. Mindful of this clause when Twin Cams finally ran out completely in 1976, Lotus announced that it proposed to supply kits of Twin Cam parts to Vegantune, a well-established engine building and tuning company

The site at Caterham Hill was modest to say the least. This was the small showroom with the workshop to the left. Out of sight to the right was the house.

run by George Robinson. Vegantune would build these up into complete engines and supply them to Caterham, a process which began in 1977.

In the meantime, the Ford 'Kent' engine had been introduced as a cheaper alternative to the Twin Cam. Both 1600GT and even 1300GT units were offered, but neither proved particularly popular, the latter hardly selling at all. It was only when the Twin Cam finally died in the early Eighties that the Ford 1600 would become one of the mainstay engines.

In 1978, Lotus finally ran out of engine blocks for the Twin Cam. David Wakefield was forced to obtain supplies of Ford 1600 blocks and Vegantune pressed ahead, building these up with Twin Cam heads to create the 'tall-block' Twin Cam with its modified front casing. The Lotus Twin Cam had been designed around the Ford 1500 block, bored out to 1,558cc, whereas the tall-block displaced 1,598cc. Both units produced a quoted 126bhp but the tall-block did this at lower revs and with a slightly lower compression ratio, which meant that the engine no longer needed five-star fuel. The first of the new Twin Cams supplied to Caterham was not a success as the compression ratio was too low and the cams too mild. With some adjustment and the fitment of livelier cams, the new engine revealed itself as a sparkling performer and subsequent units were built to that specification.

Then production stumbled into a new and chronic obstacle when Lotus ran out of cylinder heads. The situation was getting desperate: at one point in 1978 there were 20 Japanese-specification rolling chassis sitting in the yard at Caterham waiting for Twin Cam engines (the Japanese would not consider any other engine). Japanese market cars had

such luxuries as dual-circuit brakes and a steering column lock, items not offered on UK-spec cars at that time.

David Wakefield approached Lotus direct and obtained permission to have use of the cylinder head pattern equipment at the foundry that had originally supplied Lotus. Caterham managed to conjure up another 53 heads in this way before the foundry was involved in a takeover. Caterham was asked to remove the pattern equipment, but before it could do so, Lotus itself carted it back to Hethel, a misunderstanding which was quickly straightened out. Caterham regained the moulds and struck a deal with a new foundry, but its castings were of such poor quality that the project ground to a halt.

The final straw came when Lotus changed its policy with regard to reproduction of the engine. Anxious to safeguard the copyright position of their engine design, Lotus was also concerned about the product liability position of engines bearing the Lotus name, particularly in the United States. Technically, Twin Cam engines should not have been getting into the States, but people have always found a way! This time it looked as if the Twin Cam had finally reached the end of the road.

Production of Sevens was rolling along at a steady rate and in 1976, the production line was moved to the main 5,000sq ft Caterham workshop. The general accident repair business, Caterham Coachworks, was wound down and the Seven finally became the sole business at Caterham.

Between 1975 and 1980, the specification of the Seven had changed in many detailed respects, generally because a particular part had become obsolete or because of a change of supplier. One significant early improvement was a widening of the axle

John Miles of *Autocar* demonstrates the difficulty of getting in and out of the Seven with its roof in place. This is a Ford Kent-powered car, identifiable by its bonnet air intake to clear the top-mounted single carb.

brace to take the ends beyond the radius-arm mounting brackets. Caterham had found that with grippy tyres and a powerful engine, even reinforced axles could crack unless the brace was extended. In 1975, supplies of the Mk1 Ford Escort rear axle dried up and the Mk2 axle was as yet unavailable, being too new. Caterham was forced to scour the country to find a batch of Mk1 RS axles, nine of which were fitted to Sevens. This in turn was quickly superseded by a standard Mk2 axle and then, from 1978, a Mk2 RS unit, which gave the benefits of a longer final-drive as standard and bigger brakes.

In 1977, Clive Roberts became the first graduate recruited by Caterham, joining as production buyer, having previously worked as an engineer for Triumph. The addition of his practical and theoretical engineering skills did much to speed up the pace of development of the Seven. Gradually the philosophy shifted from change in response to parts difficulties, to improving the car for its own sake.

Roberts: "It's easy with a 'traditional' car like the Seven to sit on yesterday's laurels, especially when it was so difficult just to source and build existing parts into a car, without adding new changes. I think David Wakefield has never received due credit for the toil of putting that side together – not the most glamorous task, but I doubt Caterham would have survived as a manufacturer without his diligence.

"We were very conscious that in the Seventies most customers wanted to regard the Seven as a *Lotus,* and there was a persistent demand for the traditional instruments, wheels, badges and so on. This meant changes had to be made with due regard for the traditionalists – 'improve the car without changing it'! I'm sure that Caterham is now well enough established in its own right to relax that position and dare to make the changes we would have loved to make long ago."

Another influential new character at around this time was Reg Price. Although he worked in a nearby school in Merstham – and continued to do so – his face was well-known at Caterham. A gifted and intuitive engineer, he had built and prepared the famous Modsports racer of David Bettinson. Price joined Caterham by asking Graham Nearn if he needed some help. As a teacher, he had plenty

Inside the workshop at Caterham, space was at a premium and each department merged with the next. Up to 12 cars could be in build at any one time.

of holiday time and worked at Caterham during school breaks.

At first, he believed that the Seven was an immutable object which could not be altered from the 'sacred' Lotus design. Clive Roberts once saw him correcting what Price knew to be a common bump steer problem by jacking the suspension up, a process which Price had discovered would cure it. When Roberts understood the problem, he said: "Why haven't you changed the design? It's there to be improved." Within a week, the bump steer had been dramatically cut by suspension modifications, and soon Price was contributing to much of the development work on the Seven.

His attitude could be summed up as: "I can make one and bolt it on faster than we can finish the discussion about whether it will work." Examples of his hands-on approach were the models he made in pre-computer days; often these would be full-size working creations in strip steel.

Price and Roberts always worked extremely well together. Their partnership evolved over the years so that the pair became the hub of research and development at Caterham.

Clive Roberts said of Reg Price: "Generally Reg came up with the bright idea, I might sort out the details and translate it into a financially and socially acceptable form and we would then develop it together. I know of *no-one* better at making an idea come alive."

One of the major problems faced in 1980 was Ford's adoption of front-wheel drive for the new Escort. Reliable supplies of the Escort rear axle dried up almost instantaneously and Caterham was forced to cast about for an alternative axle. "This consisted of Clive Roberts and Reg Price crawling around car parks looking at what sort of axles they had," remembers Graham Nearn. "There were surprisingly few small cars around which still had a front engine and rear-wheel drive." They looked at Rootes and Vauxhall, but the trouble with both these axles was that the differential fitted from the rear, not from the front, which would have introduced problems with bracing the axle.

Eventually the decision came down in favour of the unromantic Morris Marina/Ital. Although it was theoretically weaker than the Ford unit and had smaller brakes, the Ital back axle was more compact and 30lb lighter than the old Escort axle. It was also slightly wider, so it filled out the wheel-arches better. A final plus point was that the Ital axle had the same wheel fixings as standard Triumph Spitfire front hubs, which meant that the front uprights no longer needed to be modified and fitted with Ford centres.

In reality, there were never any problems with the strength of the Ital axle. As its weight was unsprung, it could handle up to 150bhp reliably. The brakes, if anything, were better than those on the Ford axle, which had been hindered by a cumbersome self-adjusting mechanism that gave a dead-feeling two-stage action. Initially, Reg Price attempted locating the Ital axle on four links and a sliding A-frame, but the sums looked better with the existing Seven A-frame as long as it sat lower, below the chassis.

By 1980, the Twin Cam engine story was looking critical. Production of the Lotus engine had definitively ended and, although many Twin Cams continued to be built by scouring the country for immaculate used cylinder heads, a new high-powered engine was obviously needed.

David Wakefield decided that the best route would be to produce an uprated version of the Ford Kent pushrod engine. It may not have the same magic as the Lotus unit, he reasoned, but it could certainly be easily tuned to roughly the same power output as the Twin Cam, added to which it

When the Lotus Twin Cam became unavailable, Caterham offered the Vegantune-built VTA twin-cam engine in its place. Power was comparable with the Lotus engine and the VTA filled a need for a Twin Cam replacement for a short while.

In 1982 the Seven celebrated 25 years in production. So Caterham launched this Silver Jubilee edition, which featured colour-matched trim, silver paintwork and all the options you could wish for, all for an extra £1,400.

would be much cheaper and simpler to manufacture and maintain.

Wakefield, Roberts and Price came up with a simple but effective specification using a Cosworth A2 camshaft, gasflowed head and twin Weber carburettors on a Holbay manifold (although Caterham quickly developed its own manifold). Webers were chosen instead of the Dellortos used on the Twin Cam because Dellortos simply wouldn't fit without modifying a chassis tube in the engine bay. The Webers, on the other hand, fitted neatly, although an aperture was needed in the bonnet to clear the air filters.

The new engine, christened the Sprint, bumped up the output of the standard Kent engine from 84bhp to a smooth and untemperamental 110bhp. The first car to this specification was on the road in May 1980 and the engine was immediately popular. By 1983, when the last Lotus Twin Cam-powered Seven left the factory, the Sprint was the most popular model.

Apart from seeing the introduction of the Sprint, 1980 was also the year when supplies of Corsair 2000E gearboxes ran out. Fortunately the Escort Sport 'box was suitable for the Seven and this was duly fitted. To suit the new gearbox, a clever remote-control mechanism was devised by Reg Price which gave an improved feel to the change, at the same time moving the lever back from the base of the dashboard where Lotus Seven drivers had traditionally skinned their knuckles! A pre-engaged starter was fitted in association with the Escort gearbox and a lighter clutch unit made standard. For the first time this was cable-operated and it was altogether more pleasant to operate than the unnecessarily heavy hydraulic system.

Meanwhile, George Robinson of Vegantune had been working on another project that held out hope for Caterham for a genuine alternative to the Lotus Twin Cam. This was the Vegantune VTA Twin Cam engine. Through David Wakefield, Caterham actually funded the development and pattern equipment of the VTA, which drew its inspiration from Lotus, Fiat and Cosworth BDA twin-cam units. Based on the Ford Kent block, the 1,598cc unit developed 130bhp and made a highly agreeable noise.

But two out of three proved to be sub-standard, with oil leaks, camshaft breakages and mismatched and rubbing pulley belts. Supplies from Vegantune were also erratic, with only 41 engines being delivered over a four-year period from 1981. This was regrettable because Caterham had a market for probably 150 Twin Cams and there would usually be cars lying around the factory waiting for engines. Staff were called on to drive up to Vegantune in Spalding in an overloaded old Ford Granada estate to pick up as many as three engines at a time.

In 1981 Clive Roberts and Reg Price started experimenting with a turbocharged Ford engine in a Seven. They installed a Garrett AiResearch turbo unit, sucking through a 2in SU carburettor. A smooth 150bhp was produced at 6,000rpm by the turbo but, although there was plenty of power at the top end, it became very flat indeed at lower speeds and this characteristic proved impossible to overcome without an extended development programme. Moreover, the amount of power and torque produced by the turbo engine was not significantly greater than a modified normally aspirated engine; also the addition of the turbo made the engine note very un-Seven-like. Consequently, this interesting project was dropped, but not before David Wakefield had enjoyed the experience of the turbo wastegate sticking closed. This shot the boost gauge right off the scale and gave Wakefield the most exhilarating run he'd ever had in a Seven!

"I have mixed memories of that car," remembers Clive Roberts. "It was fiendishly fast and its 150bhp seemed to be *everywhere*. On the other hand, having it catch fire at 5am on the M1 was less endearing. Reg, in his inimitable way, decided to tackle my complaint of footwell heat by taking a hammer and chisel and carving three large GTO-style vents in the side panels. He seemed fairly

In 1982, Avon Coachwork of Warwick reached an agreement with Caterham to offer a Super Seven 'A'. This sported two-tone paintwork, alloy wheels, extensive soundproofing, wind deflectors, trimmed interior and extra instruments, all for an extra £1,250 – but the world was not yet ready for a luxury Seven. Incidentally this was the first production car fitted with the Vegantune VTA engine.

The Pace turbo installation on a 1600 Ford Kent engine was a disappointment and, despite several factory attempts to turbocharge a Seven, such an engine has never been offered. A turbocharger somehow detracted from what a Seven was all about.

pleased with the result, although I felt a can-opener would have been a more useful tool."

There was one further attempt at installing a turbocharger on a Ford engine. David Wakefield still knew David Lazenby from the Lotus days (Lazenby had been responsible as manager of Lotus Components for working with Nearn to resurrect the Lotus Seven S2 in 1967). By 1981, Lazenby was running a tuning company called Pace, in Essex. At the height of Wakefield's problems finding Twin Cam engines, he and a team from Caterham visited Lazenby to discuss its 'bolt on' turbo conversion. A Pace Fiesta Turbo was borrowed for a while and Wakefield thought it worthwhile going ahead with a Caterham version. A base 1600GT Seven registered GPL 39V was delivered to Pace and duly converted.

Reg Price recalls that it was not a great success: "It was horrendous. There was a big alloy block on top of the carburettor and the whole thing looked awful. Neither did it produce any appreciable power increase so it was something of a non-starter." In any case, a new and more powerful version of the Ford Kent engine was soon to arrive in the Supersprint engine.

At 6ft 3in tall, Clive Roberts was a man who had plenty of experience of another Seven problem.

Legroom in the Seven made driving for over six-footers rather uncomfortable as it had remained basically the same as when Colin Chapman designed it in 1957.

Roberts realized that, because the recently-introduced Ital back axle and differential were so compact, it was possible to reposition some tubes in the rear of the chassis. Ostensibly this was to make the rear end stiffer, but when Roberts and Price locked themselves away in the workshops to take a torch to the chassis, they found that the rear bulkhead could be moved backwards. An extra 2¼in of cockpit space was liberated as well as stiffening the chassis significantly.

The so-called Long Cockpit chassis was introduced in 1982, initially as an option, before eventually supplanting the old short-cockpit set-up completely some 10 years later. As far as Arch Motors was concerned, it was no problem to introduce this variant into the chassis programme, even though a new chassis jig needed to be built at Arch.

Graham Nearn, understandably, was delighted with the arrival of the Long Cockpit Seven as it opened up new marketing opportunities and removed the gripe that so many people had about the Seven – not being able to fit into it! Now anyone up to 6ft 2in tall could fit comfortably. The opportunity was taken to develop adjustable seats for the first time (this was a requirement of the German market). However, most cars continued to be supplied with the traditional covered foam bases and backrest for the time being.

In 1982 Caterham celebrated 25 years of the Seven. This anniversary was commemorated by a special-edition Jubilee version. This was a £1,400 option consisting of silver paintwork done by Jim Whiting with contrasting stripes, luxury grey trim, stainless exhaust, nickel-plated front suspension, tinted windscreen, satin black underbonnet, grey-painted chassis and lockable fuel cap. The first example was shown at the 1981 London Motorfair, at a premium price of £7,250 in CKD form. Only a handful of Jubilee Sevens were built over a two-year period, but the fact that upmarket Sevens were selling at all was, for Graham Nearn, the first sign that the market was lifting. Not all Jubilees were painted silver: at least one was finished in Jaguar green with matching trim.

Another new engine option, introduced in 1982, was a Holbay R120 modified 1700 engine. Only five Sevens were ever fitted with this power unit because it was later superseded by Caterham's own modified Kent engine, the Supersprint.

Triumph had dropped the Spitfire in 1980 and it was only a matter of time before the steering racks and front uprights that this model provided became unavailable. Clive Roberts modified the rack mountings on the chassis and fitted a re-geared Mini rack in 1983, optimizing the steering geometry as far as possible in the process. Bump steer was dramatically reduced and the feel of the new system was much improved. The front upright problem was solved by negotiating directly with the company that had forged them for Leyland. This particular deal was set up in association with Jem Marsh of Marcos, whose cars used similar uprights. Marcos and Caterham continued to enjoy a close working relationship throughout the Eighties.

In early 1983 David Wakefield received a 'phone call out of the blue from Len Newton, of Cosworth

An experiment from 1983: a Ford CVH engine installation which proved to be unacceptably harsh. Note the tunnel-mounted handbrake lever, another idea which was rejected.

A Seven in an early stage of build. Cars were hand-finished up to a point, with the buyer expected to turn a few spanners to complete the car, for official exemption from National Type Approval laws.

Engineering. The gist of the call was that Cosworth was putting a BDA-type 16-valve engine back into production and would Caterham be interested in fitting this engine in a Seven? The engines were being built up by Langford & Peck, who had considerable expertise with Cosworth as the builders of its Formula 1 engines.

Cosworth was offering to supply complete cylinder head, camshaft and valve kits to be built on to a basic Ford Kent block. The resultant unit, they said, would easily produce around 150bhp, and much more with tuning. Graham Nearn was immediately enthusiastic. The Seven had strong historic associations with Cosworth, so the BDR, as this revised BDA was called, appeared to be the long-awaited Twin Cam replacement.

A Super Seven BDR was up and running by early 1984. It managed a top speed of nearly 120mph and reached 60mph in a shade over five seconds. Here indeed was a worthy successor to the Twin Cam – indeed, it was the quickest factory Seven yet built. The new 150bhp model was listed at £9,000, making it not only the fastest but the most expensive Seven to date. Mike Costin himself told Graham Nearn that he was delighted the Cosworth name had returned to the Seven after the memorial parade for Colin Chapman at the 1983 British Grand Prix, in which an example of every Lotus ever made was driven around the track, Graham Nearn piloting his Lotus Seven Twin Cam SS.

A logical experiment was carried out, beginning in 1983, with the fitment of a new-generation Ford Escort CVH engine in a Seven. At this stage, Clive Roberts simply wanted to see if the engine had potential for use in the Seven, given that it was thought the Ford Kent engine might have a limited life. Running on twin Dellorto carburettors, the CVH engine, complete with a Ford Sierra five-speed gearbox, was run in a development chassis for around one year with very disappointing results.

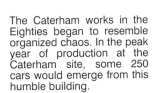

The Caterham works in the Eighties began to resemble organized chaos. In the peak year of production at the Caterham site, some 250 cars would emerge from this humble building.

1984 was another anniversary year: 25 years of Caterham Cars' association with the Seven. To mark the occasion, a special all-aluminium-bodied car was built, playing on memories of the all-metal Lotus Seven Series 1.

At the beginning of 1983, a highly significant newcomer arrived at Caterham. Leyland Trucks employee Jez Coates made the move as something of a known quantity. He had first been contacted by Caterham in 1981 when, after modifying his Lotus Elan, he advertised a couple of Lotus Twin Cam engines in *Motoring News* and David Wakefield of Caterham Cars rang to buy a cylinder head: "I offered to bring it down – all the way from Lancashire – because I wanted to have a look round. David Wakefield was very keen because the Japanese market was crying out for Twin Cams and he was reduced to scouring the magazines for mint secondhand cylinder heads to refurbish. I provided several to Caterham, building up a relationship with David Wakefield. Off-hand one day I said I was bored at Leyland and if you ever need an extra hand a Caterham, give me a shout. The next time I was down, he said come and work for us!

"My mother thought I was mad to leave the security of Leyland to work in a selection of tin shacks in Surrey. Of course, Leyland Trucks has since gone bust under Daf, while Caterham has gone on to ever greater heights."

Jez Coates began as an understudy to Clive

Roberts, soon evolving a buying capacity and doubling up with Roberts and Wakefield in sales. As he lived in Essex and commuted each day, he was entrusted with the CVH development car to accumulate mileage.

"I was amazed they gave the new boy the valuable development car. I thought, this is great, I'm the only one driving a five-speed Seven and the only one with the new Ford engine. However, one Saturday I was acting as salesman and drove the 1700 Supersprint four-speed demonstrator. The sad fact was that that car was so much sweeter to drive than the CVH – more refined, better gearchange, nicer to drive.

"Ford invented the term NVH (noise, vibration and harshness) but do not seem to be able to engineer it out of their own products. Despite Reg Price's development of a sophisticated engine-mounting system, the CVH engine was dreadfully harsh – if you took it above 5,000rpm, it felt like it was going to explode – and in a Seven the noise was just appalling."

So Roberts and Price opted to abandon the CVH project. The pushrod engine was still available – and in fact remains available today – so the CVH engine and five-speed gearbox were simply sold off and the chassis re-engined. The CVH engine would return, however, in a later version for the Swiss market.

In late 1983, the Caterham management team – Graham Nearn, David Wakefield, Clive Roberts, Jez Coates, Reg Price, Mick Lincoln and Peter Cooper – went down to the *King & Queen* pub in Caterham to discuss what would happen after the imminent demise of the (Morris Ital) live axle. Roberts had drawn up a list of potential donor axles and it didn't make promising reading – it included things like the Hillman Hunter (which was still being made in Coventry for assembly in Iran) – so, short of buying the rights to the Morris Ital axle, there was little alternative but to abandon the live-axle set-up.

Roberts thought they should aim for a fully independent rear, but Reg Price's suggestion of a de Dion rear struck a chord as Sevens in the early Lotus days had been fitted with this system, so there was a historical link and some racing Sevens had also been adapted to a de Dion rear system. The idea also sounded good from a technical point of view: combining a live axle-type wheel location with a chassis-mounted diff meant less unsprung weight without the complexity of fully independent suspension. The thought of having to develop

The German-spec car was finalized and put through 'TUV' testing in 1984. Differences included cycle wings, a windscreen-mounted mirror, lowered rear lights, special rear foglights, different number-plate plinth and rear-exit exhaust.

a fully independent rear end within Caterham was not relished since it would obviously have represented a major engineering challenge. With the de Dion rear end, at least there was a beam axle involved, so the geometry was easier to fathom. A third reason for favouring the de Dion route was that it could be mounted on the chassis in much the same way as the live axle for less cost – and there would be no necessity to build chassis stiffeners from the seat back (with an independent rear, a supporting structure would have been necessary – more expense, more headaches).

Roberts roughly costed the de Dion rear end and found it would be £100 cheaper than going fully independent, so the de Dion idea was rubber-stamped over a pint.

The de Dion suspension was developed by Roberts and Price, the latter working almost exclusively using equipment at his school. In those pre-computer days, Price used real life models made from strip steel. Within weeks a system based around a Ford Sierra differential was conceived

and it took just one month to transfer the idea on to a chassis. From the Sierra came the diff, CV joints, hubs and brakes, while Caterham devised its own de Dion tube, locating links, hub-carriers and driveshafts. The de Dion tube was located by trailing arms and an A-frame, while the tubework at the rear of the transmission tunnel was completely revised to carry the differential. The de Dion tube itself became probably the only straight tube in production, for the simple reason that there was no machinery available at the school to bend the tube. Instead, ears were used at either end.

Numerous problems were encountered but, by April 1984, the first prototype was running successfully. Roberts and Price tested the de Dion rear end during 1984, taking it over *pave* at Chobham testing ground to try to break the suspension. Price drove some 10,000 road miles in the development car. One welcome side-effect of the chassis modifications was a significant increase in stiffness, partly a result of the addition of tubes along the transmission tunnel for the first time.

The Cosworth BDR engine was available from 1984, producing easily the fastest Seven to date. In 150bhp 1,600cc form it was capable of 0–60mph in 5.6 seconds, while the 170bhp 1,700cc version could do it in 5 seconds flat.

The de Dion Seven demonstrated much-improved ride quality because of the dramatically improved ratio of sprung to unsprung weight. The torque was taken directly into the chassis, rather than trying to twist the axle with a live set-up, so traction was also much improved, particularly in the wet. It was also just as easy to set up as the old live axle system because both wheels always pointed in the same direction and had the same camber angle.

The first productionized de Dion car was launched at the 1984 Birmingham Motor Show. It had the novelty of a tunnel-mounted handbrake lever, but when Clive Roberts left to work for Lotus in 1985, Coates repositioned it in its more familiar but unconventional site under the dash so the tunnel could be used to rest the driver's forearm. The new rear suspension also allowed the boot floor to be lowered, in turn releasing an extra 30% of luggage space.

Another significant event in 1984 was the submission of the Seven for official testing by the German authorities. Development for this important test was supported by a grant from the UK Government as it was an example of 'Technical Innovation for Export'. This was the only occasion on which Caterham received any government funding.

Clive Roberts and Graham Nearn towed a Seven behind a Ford Capri in diabolical rain all the way to Volkswagen's Wolfsburg testing ground. "We were very impressed with the German engineers," recalls Nearn. "They adopted a positive attitude, saying that the car was essentially very well engineered. They spent three solid days driving the car."

After extended development work to ensure that all aspects of the car could pass the stringent requirements on noise, brakes, safety and emissions, the Seven was duly granted its 'TUV' certificate, allowing it to continue to be sold in the German market. A number of unique features had to be incorporated, such as cycle wings and rake-adjustable seats. Similarly, the Seven was accepted in other European markets to be sold complete.

Meanwhile, more developments were occurring on the engine front. There was a strong latent demand for more powerful Kent engines and there were continuing problems over supplies of the Vegantune VTA engine. Initially Caterham had turned to Holbay, but soon decided that doing the work itself would be easier and more profitable.

Peter Cooper had built a special Kent engine for a customer who ran a Seven in sprints and hill-climbs. So impressed was Cooper when he tested the engine on the road that it was soon agreed to offer it as a regular option. And so the Supersprint

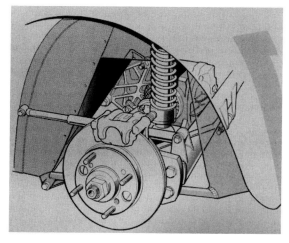

Cutaway of the de Dion rear end. The tube was entirely straight with 'ears' to connect it with the suspension.

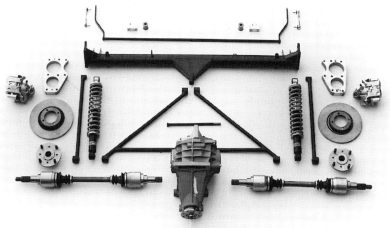

Exploded rear end showing the de Dion rear suspension available on Sevens from 1984. This system offered a vastly improved ride and superior traction qualities, as well as an ability to handle almost limitless amounts of power reliably.

was born in 1984. This pushrod engine was bored out to nearly 1,700cc, and received lighter, larger valves designed by Reg Price and special springs by Clive Roberts (both were made especially for Caterham), a balanced and lightened flywheel, fully gasflowed head, high-lift camshaft, twin Weber 40DCOE carburettors and a high-pressure oil pump. The first 250 heads were worked by Reg Price, who kept a record of the numbers and dates of completion on the wall of his dining room, where he did the modifications!

The Supersprint produced a lusty 135bhp, which slotted well in the engine range. Although only 15bhp short of the 1600 BDR version, it cost some £2,000 less and was also much cheaper than the Twin Cam. This was a powerful sales tool and the Supersprint engine took off. Almost immediately, it became the most popular engine choice.

At the same time, Caterham asked Cosworth to supply a kit of parts to build a powerful 1,700cc Cosworth BDR unit. This version was rated at 170bhp on the dynamometer, which equated to 100bhp per litre. This made the Seven a quite astonishingly quick machine, inspiring Caterham to apply a kind of insurance policy against the wrong kind of person getting behind the steering wheel. Caterham Cars made it a condition of purchase that owners should attend the High

This well-known car is the 1985 Motorfair show model which went on to become Caterham's press car the following year. It was one of the first examples to be fitted with the all-new de Dion rear suspension.

The local MP for Caterham was Sir Geoffrey Howe, seen here visiting the works along-side Graham Nearn in 1985. Sir Geoffrey had a proper interest in supporting local businesses.

Performance Course, a performance driving course run by John Lyon.

Caterham's line was: "It takes skill and responsibility to drive safely and well and a fast car needs a special kind of skill that can only be fully developed with training. Caterham Cars does not wish to release the car to anyone who has not got the skill or experience to drive safely."

Graham Nearn added: "I had always wanted to run this type of exercise. Legend has it that Bugatti used to do the same with the Type 57: if he didn't like your style of driving, he wouldn't sell you a car. The market wants cars which can do 0–60mph in such-and-such a time; personally, I think this is only one part of the specification: handling and braking are just as important. The point is that you can end up with a car which is potentially lethal in the wrong hands. We were just being responsible about it." Newspapers seized on this piece of information and Caterham got more valuable exposure for its products.

When fitted out with an optional package, the 1700 BDR-engined car was dubbed the HPC and given a special 'HP' chassis number. This package consisted of a rear anti-roll bar, limited-slip diff and individually adjustable seats. The first example to be so fitted was built in 1986 for racer John McLean. This provided the blueprint for the HPC specification, although the chassis plate recorded this car as a BDR, not an HPC.

When Clive Roberts left to join Lotus in 1985, Coates took on the mantle of chief engineer (as well as continuing his buying role for a while). He almost immediately recruited Andy Noble, another Leyland Trucks refugee, as his understudy, taking over the purchasing function.

Coates and Noble occupied an old Portakabin in the yard at Caterham, which leaked in the wet and became an oven in sunshine. It became affectionately known as the Chip Shop because some droll members of staff would knock on the window and ask for two cod and chips, please…

"My first job", recalls Jez, "was to productionize the de Dion rear end. The driveshafts were the single most difficult thing, as they were based on Sierra items. We were buying standard Ford shafts, taking them apart and changing the central piece for a specially-made item – a very expensive operation. In the end, GKN were prepared to make bespoke driveshafts for us."

During a two-year period from 1984 to 1986 (when Austin Rover finally ditched the Ital back axle and Caterham rejigged the chassis), the factory built a run of about 40 of the first de Dion cars with the old-style chassis and a Ford Escort Mk2 four-speed gearbox.

But supplies of the old Ford four-speed gearbox were drying up and it was decided, after investigation of the alternatives, to replace it by the close-ratio five-speed 'box from the Sierra in 1986. This version was not the standard Ford five-speed unit (which had quite different ratios that were unsuitable for the Seven) but the one seen in V6 versions of the Sierra. Compared with the four-speed 'box, its first and fourth ratios corresponded almost exactly, but second and third were slightly more highly geared, while fifth became a cruising gear with a ratio of 0.82:1. For a short time until the last four-speed 'box was used up, the new five-speed was offered as an optional extra.

In turn, fitting this new 'box meant modifying the chassis. Over the years, the chassis had previ-

A typical Saturday morning at Caterham Hill: chaos! David Wakefield's dog looks on implacably.

Cosworth power returned to the Seven in the Eighties in 1600 and 1700 forms. The latter was dubbed the HPC after the High Performance Course which all new purchasers were obliged to attend – just in case they couldn't handle the 170bhp they were in charge of!

Various five-speed gearboxes were trial-fitted to replace the old Escort four-speed during 1985. This was a Toyota 'box from a Lotus Excel but the final choice was the Sierra XR4 close-ratio unit, offered from 1986.

ously evolved in a somewhat piecemeal manner as and when changes were needed. As a fresh face, Coates, working together with Price, took the opportunity for the 1986 model year to redesign the chassis in a fairly major way. He set about creating the so-called universal chassis. The basic chassis would now be symmetrical: the same for left or right-hand drive and would be capable of taking either four or five-speed 'boxes. Arch Motors was very glad to change to the new universal chassis as it made their job very much more straightforward!

Sales manager Simon Wheeler suggested one significant part of the chassis modifications. This was that the upper engine bay diagonal on the exhaust side should mirror the one on the right. No Lotus had ever had it, and initially the idea was viewed with scepticism due to the difficulty of persuading the exhaust manifolds to miss it. The problem was passed to the exhaust system suppliers, who suggested modifications which allowed the diagonal to be fitted. The symmetry this brought to the engine bay was carried right through the redesign.

Previously there had been a lot of dead space between the passenger foot box and the gearbox. By revising the positioning of the tubes on the universal chassis, the foot boxes were made larger (on the passenger side, no less than 7 inches of extra length was created). The chassis was now also torsionally stiffer.

Despite the arrival of the de Dion rear end, in practice live axles never left the Caterham range because in 1984, basic kit-form Sevens were relaunched and builders were now expected to locate their own reconditioned live axles.

The story of the basic kit-form Caterham began

as a result of the Seven's own success. As demand boomed for Sevens during the mid-Eighties, there was a sudden emergence of 'copies' of the Seven in the kit-car industry. There were two main reasons why this happened: firstly, the extended delivery period and secondly, the price, which was relatively high for a kit-form car, due to the high standards applied during manufacture and the comprehensive nature of the kit which required no donor vehicle parts. Since 1973, the Seven had always been sold essentially as a complete car in knock-down form (although rolling body/chassis units were available to those who knew).

That all changed in 1984. In response to several Caterham Seven-style kits selling at lower prices, Caterham introduced a far more basic kit-form version of the Seven.

The Seven car could now be bought as a basic kit minus engine, gearbox and rear axle (at £1,850 plus VAT) and completed with various mechanical and trim packages which would bring the total kit price up to just over £3,250, or £4,500 with literally everything supplied (except the engine, 'box, axle, wheels and tyres). As a base model, it was still impressively complete for a kit-car, with all the important safety items supplied and fitted – brakes, fuel tank, instruments, switches, wiring loom, windscreen, plus wipers and washers and all glassfibre parts. On top of this basic chassis/body unit there would be a choice of front suspension packages, front uprights, packages for the rear suspension, for the engine, gearbox, axle, steering, cooling, trim, weather equipment and lighting. These could be mixed and matched according to the customer's taste. Starting from the absolute minimum, the build time was quoted at around 150 hours.

Three types of chassis were offered: the original Lotus-style short-cockpit Ford live-axle chassis,

the long-cockpit Ital live-axle chassis and the long-cockpit de Dion chassis. The short-cockpit chassis actually lasted right through until 1992, when demand died. Since 1957, when the Seven was designed, people have basically become taller and the short cockpit was simply too small. (Another brief chassis option was to have a five-speed gearbox allied to a live rear axle, but the uptake was so poor that this was soon withdrawn).

The main problem was the bewildering choice of specifications which could be selected by the basic kit buyer. So Caterham chose not to list all the packages in detail in their price lists, generally preferring to inform buyers on an individual basis. One last significant advantage of the kit-form Seven was that, because the major mechanical components were secondhand, the payment of Car Tax could be avoided.

Something which really helped that situation was comprehensive computerization at Caterham so that the works were able both to order up component packages from stocks and to record the detailed individual specification of every single car sold.

The more basic kit-form Seven quickly took off. About 50 were supplied in the first full year; by 1987 the basic version was consistently out-selling the traditional component Seven in the UK by a ratio of about four to one, and considerably more in some years.

There is no doubt that the kit-form Seven did much to boost fortunes at Caterham. Certainly the economy was in full boom, but the availability of cheaper Caterham kits unlocked a latent demand for what people saw as a quality product. "We spoke to a lot of people who had bought kits from other manufacturers which had taken hundreds of hours to build and which actually came out costing *more than a complete Caterham* to finish," recalls Jez

Just before the move from Caterham, some idea of the strain on space can be gleaned from this picture. In time-honoured fashion, chassis units were stored outdoors prior to being fitted out in the works.

Coates. "People realized they were on to a better bet with the proven quality and resale value of a Caterham."

The whole business of kits which sought to duplicate the appeal of the Seven was very drawn-out. "Basically, people were trying to sell in our shadow," says Graham Nearn. "We are the Rolex of the business and it's just part of life that people try to sell cheap replicas."

Caterham acted quickly to defend its product copyright through the courts, particularly defending the shape of the Seven as a copyrighted item, something which was quite new in legal terms. Several companies were put out of business and others were required to destroy tooling. "We got the legal side of things down to a fine art," says Nearn. "We knew exactly what we could and could not sue for. We always come down hard on anybody using the trademark of Caterham, or indeed Seven. We are very sensitive if the intention is to deceive

that the product is linked with Caterham.

"However, we have to recognize there is such a thing as fair competition, and at first it did help to keep us on our toes, but now there are so many copies that the question is rather boring, and customers are aware of the differences. We believe we offer good value because of the quality and specification of our product and because it has an exceptionally good resale value. And our cars have an excellent safety record. We are the original and the best and I suppose it is a compliment that people copy us.

"Most customers are undoubtedly price-conscious. We attracted a lot more people into the showroom with a sticker price of £2,500 and so the kit-form Seven has been very valuable for us."

In 1986 the Seven was rewired and also deprived of the much-loved traditional Smiths gauges purely because supplies were so unreliable. German VDO instruments were substituted instead and have been

Caterham's Supersprint demonstrator for 1987 was the first to be fitted with a five-speed gearbox. It also came with colour-matched hood, leather seats and leather steering wheel: heresy for purists, perhaps, but popular with the late Eighties yuppie set. Note the softer rear wing profile which was introduced at this time.

run ever since – until the 1996 model year, that is.

With Coates in the engineering hot-seat, the Seven began evolving in a more structured way. There was usually an annual package of specification revisions and so a 'model year'. People also began getting the luxury of proper job titles and did less sharing of the general running of the company.

In about 1987, Coates was contacted by the German shock absorber manufacturer Bilstein, who wanted to develop a damper tailored to the Caterham. Flattered by the offer, Coates agreed that a team should come over from Germany and do a damping exercise – as long as the quality was better than Caterham's current supplier (which more or less went without saying) *and* as long as there was an immediate improvement in ride quality.

The team duly came over and spent two days there. But the end result was a poorer ride. So Bilstein requested that they borrow a car, which they did for 10 weeks. Reg Price and Jez Coates went to Germany and were extremely impressed by the feel, ride and suppleness. They drove back to Britain in the car, feeling happy. Only when they reached home did Jez Coates comment that the car felt fidgety somehow, and Reg Price agreed.

"We always trust our instincts," affirms Jez Coates, "and it turned out that the frequency of the surface irregularities of British roads were different from German roads and the dampers were too stiff! Bilstein remained amazingly patient when we rejected them again.

"Eventually – and it was 1990 by this time – we opened up the parameters so that the damper settings, spring rates and anti-roll bar rates were all free. Together with Bilstein's highly talented UK consultant Roddy Harvey-Bailey, we spent a whole week in Derbyshire in three cars testing the whole suspension. This was major league development work – it reminded me of my Leyland testing days. The week resulted in us fitting different anti-roll bars for K-series, Ford and Vauxhall cars. It eliminated minor traces of understeer and has been very successful: we've kept the same suspension ever since – at least until the 1996 model year."

In 1987, improvements included a powder-coated chassis and the introduction of a Triplex heated and tinted windscreen (demisting the Seven's screen with the hood up was always problematic). With the economy now in full boom, demand for Sevens was very strong and production was running at a very healthy level. Despite increases in production, the waiting list for delivery remained the same at about 18 months. As a survivor of the bad old days of the three-day week and oil crisis, Nearn had always resisted expanding in response to increased orders: they had a tendency to fall away as soon as you expanded; or, as Nearn put it, "God has always got a custard pie up His sleeve for those who are too greedy".

However, it was becoming clear, and had been for the last two years, that the 6,000sq ft factory at Caterham was close to bursting. The antiquated production line resembled a chaotic merry-go-round and the best one could say of it was that it was probably very like how Lotus ran its operation in the 'good old days' at Hornsey. Patently, the limits of Seven House had been reached.

Graham Nearn was already on the look-out for a new base for Caterham. In 1987, he found one. This single discovery was set to become probably the most momentous event in the history of Caterham Cars, as it upped stumps and transferred lock, stock and barrel to a brave new world, not in Caterham but in Dartford, Kent...

When the Caterham site was vacated, there was a farewell party to celebrate the 30 years the Seven had been there.

CHAPTER 4

Dartford to date

"Hey, boys, I've just bought a factory…"

By 1987, with demand for the Seven soaring, the limit of the Caterham factory's capacity had been reached. It had developed piecemeal from an old blacksmith's forge with an orchard and lock-up garages in the Fifties and was plainly unsatisfactory for an expanding company with a steadily rising output (in the last year at Caterham, around 280 Sevens left the factory).

From 1985, Graham Nearn had started to look around for somewhere new. It was firm company policy to own premises rather than rent them, so the new site would have to be purchased outright, with all the long-term commitments that this involved. There was an investigation of local sites, including the old Garrod & Lofthouse printing works, but the Eighties property boom was then well underway and real estate in Surrey was looking impossibly expensive. In addition, commercial property was being redeveloped for housing and offices. Nearn tracked down a suitable site in Edenbridge, Kent, but he was outbid by John Surtees. He also had a contract for another site from a receiver, but the receiver got sued for underselling, so the deal fell through.

Finally, David Midcalf, a friend in the Rotary Club, told Nearn of a site in Crayford, near Dartford, Kent. The whole site had previously been occupied by Cray Engineering, a large electrical firm which had been badly affected by lost government contracts. A development company had taken over the site and wanted to sell one of the units for cash.

"At that time," remembers Nearn, "the property market was in chaos. Things were moving ridiculously quickly and I needed the ability to close a deal straight away. The bank finally agreed to let me do this, so I came to Dartford and had a good look around the site. I shook hands instantly over the bonnet of the agent's BMW, with the proviso that I would come up with the cash within 10 days – which is what happened.

"I went straight back to Caterham after the handshake and said: 'Hey, boys, I've just bought a factory'. Once they'd got over the shock, everyone was very supportive."

The industrial site in Dartford may not have been in a particularly salubrious area, but the factory itself was ideal: light, airy and spacious. Indeed, with 20,000sq ft of factory space to play with, plus about 5,000sq ft set aside for offices, everyone felt optimistic about how the new factory could function. With the deal firmed up so quickly, preparations began immediately for the big move.

Amazingly, the move coincided with the infamous Hurricane Gilbert in October 1987 – a storm which all but destroyed the tin shack encampment at Caterham. The roof was blown off, the walls of the showroom fell down and there was a lot of internal damage. If production had not been ready to transfer to a new building straight away, this would have represented an absolute disaster.

"It seemed like the Gods were willing us on," said Graham Nearn. The move was brought forward by a week since nothing could now happen at the decimated Caterham works. A graduate production engineer called Mike Dixon had joined Caterham from Rover as production manager for the new factory. Along with Jez Coates and Andy Noble, Dixon went to Dartford and walked round the factory with pieces of chalk, marking out where the walls should go. "This was a tremendous opportunity," said Andy Noble. "We were designing our own factory from scratch. How many people get a chance to do that?"

As well as putting up walls and shelves, an area was dedicated for research and development: for the first time there would be a dedicated and secure zone for the R&D team to work in. A showroom area was also created in the front of Unit 2 (which remained in use until 1990).

This is how the Dartford factory looked before Caterham Cars moved in – little more than a shell.

Needless to say, the move was a major operation. Endless lorry loads of tooling, parts, equipment and records were ferried from Caterham to Dartford during a full three-week period, during which time the company was officially closed for business. To cap it all, it rained solidly for the entire three weeks!

There were other problems: someone had fly-dumped several tons of concrete on the site, but luckily the council agreed to remove it. And the builders kicked three large drums around from the back of the factory – but these the council would *not* remove as it transpired they were filled with

cyanide! The previous owners agreed to dispose of them.

The staff at Caterham were given the opportunity to decide whether or not they wanted to continue working at a site which was now 30 miles distant from Caterham. Almost all transferred happily, but a handful took the offer of redundancy. A works bus was laid on to transport employees who continued to live in Caterham to the Dartford works.

Graham Nearn: "Commercial removals are a black art. I had studied the fate of other companies that had done so and concluded that this was the

The purchase of the new factory in Dartford in 1987 was the biggest metamorphosis in Caterham's history. Graham Nearn certainly appreciated the vast increase in available space which allowed Caterham to keep pace with expanding demand.

The frontage of the Dartford factory was a lot more noticeable than the old Caterham site. Rows of Sevens awaiting delivery habitually occupied the parking area.

Part of the Caterham site after the October 1987 hurricane which all but destroyed the buildings. The whole site was razed to the ground and rebuilt.

An early visitor to the new factory was singer Chris Rea. He owned several Caterhams over the years and raced in the Caterham series. Note the revised sidescreens and the popular option of German-style cycle wings.

most vulnerable time for a firm. I was nervous about moving the entire operation to Dartford, so we kept the old Caterham site. People knew where it was and it made sense to continue it as our sales base. In fact what has happened is that the place at Caterham resembles a sales agent for us, rather like we were in the old days with Lotus."

The old Caterham site, now in tatters, had to be thoroughly redeveloped. But there was something of a Catch 22 situation. Local laws in Surrey stated that the Caterham site needed a change in planning and so housing had to be developed on it. However, the council also said that the amount of commercial activity should not be decreased!

A compromise was reached whereby the Caterham showroom would be rebuilt as part of a mews complex with flats above. The planners were in favour but the Highways Officer was against it. The reason? He couldn't authorize the access because he didn't recognize the site as a commercial site (it had never been registered as such). But if they got planning permission for it to become a commercial site he would still object because the access road was too narrow for commercial activity. Objections that there would actually be less traffic than before went unheeded. So Graham Nearn was forced to acquire a house adjacent to the site so that it could be chopped in half to provide wider access to the area. The main buildings were flattened and the site redeveloped into flats with garages below, Caterham's showroom occupying one wing of this new building.

"During the work, the showroom actually operated out of the adjacent house. The demonstration cars were in the garden and the office was in the kitchen! If you wanted a demonstration drive, you had to help manhandle the cars over some planks to get over the builders' ditch...

"One rainy morning we looked out of the window to see Rowan Atkinson hunched under a holly tree trying to keep dry. I would recount this story to people who had been saying that Caterham was moving too upmarket!"

In the light of the tremendous upheavals caused by the move to Dartford, Graham Nearn took the opportunity to restructure the company for the coming era and in 1988 he installed Jez Coates, Andy Noble and Mike Dixon as co-directors alongside himself, his wife and David Wakefield.

Considering the upset of the move, it was amazing that product development continued at all during 1987 and 1988, but in fact there was considerable activity. The drum brakes on the de Dion

rear end were replaced by 9in discs with Sierra Cosworth calipers and asbestos-free pads. The French-made drums were becoming difficult to source reliably and the disc brake package looked logical from both supply and sales points of view. Like most of the improvements made by the factory, the disc brake package was designed so that it could be retro-fitted to earlier Caterhams.

At that time, Lotus was in the process of developing the new Elan, a project being run by ex-Caterham man Clive Roberts. Lotus actually borrowed a Seven from Caterham as a benchmark in handling and, after spending some time with it, returned it with some recommendations about the front suspension. As a result, Caterham changed the caster, camber, toe-in, spring rates and bump steer in 1988. Ironically, after years of striving to eliminate bump steer, Lotus actually recommended *more* toe-out in bump as a measure to improve stability on rough roads.

Also in 1988, the weather equipment was improved, with increased-visibility sidescreens, requiring a modified hood. These sidescreens incorporated a glassfibre lower section with a bulge in it for the occupants' elbows; in addition, the screens could now be folded in half and put in the boot. The pedal bracket was also replaced by a pedal box, which at last stopped the ingress of water on to the driver's feet (it used to come through the bonnet louvres). The traditionally

New improved-visibility sidescreens from 1988 also incorporated rigid lower halves with bulges for extra elbow room and the ability to be folded in half for storage in the boot.

70

Caterham Cars

In 1989, new 15in alloy wheels were designed especially for the Seven, providing increased levels of grip, ride and stability. They were initially commissioned for the Prisoner limited edition.

stove-enamelled chassis was also epoxy powder-coated from this time on, and there was a larger radiator with a cowl for the electric fan.

As the Eighties progressed through the boom years of economic expansion and easy credit, the market for Sevens extended further and further upward. Customers wanted ever more equipment, fancier paint finishes, more luxury. Colin Chapman might have sighed, but in these matters the customer is always right. In response to the trends of the time, Oxted Trimming, the interior upholsterers who supplied almost all the Seven trim, developed an S-type interior package with special seats, leather trim and Wilton carpets.

In 1989 came an unmistakable limited-edition Seven called the Prisoner. Who cannot have heard of the timeless TV series created in 1966 called *The Prisoner* in which Patrick McGoohan proclaimed: "I am not a number. I am a free man!" In the opening sequence to each episode, he was seen

driving a green-and-yellow Lotus Seven – the very symbol of individuality and freedom.

Graham Nearn had been involved with the original TV series when he was called upon to build a replica for the final episode, *Fall Out*. Actually two cars were used in the series because, when McGoohan needed to be filmed driving the Seven in the last episode, it was discovered that Lotus had long since disposed of the car originally loaned to him – to South America, it is thought. David Wakefield stepped in and mocked up a doppelganger virtually overnight. Graham Nearn was actually seen in the TV episode playing the mechanic who delivered the car to McGoohan's London house.

Three main considerations led Nearn to launch a Prisoner 'replica': first, the TV series was part of the Lotus heritage and folklore (he commented that "*The Prisoner* is very much part of the charisma surrounding the Super Seven"); second, the origi-

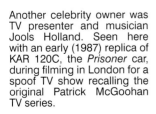

Another celebrity owner was TV presenter and musician Jools Holland. Seen here with an early (1987) replica of KAR 120C, the *Prisoner* car, during filming in London for a spoof TV show recalling the original Patrick McGoohan TV series.

Spurred on by continued interest in *The Prisoner*, Nearn created the official Prisoner edition Seven in 1989. Fitted with the yellow nosecone of the original and Prisoner alloy wheels which were reminiscent of the Elan wheels used on the original KAR 120C, the effect was evocative.

nal series was being screened again on ITV; and third, he had always been strongly in favour of special editions from a marketing point of view.

So Nearn set about tracking down Patrick McGoohan to seek his endorsement for this special Seven. McGoohan was eventually traced to his new home in Hollywood. Graham Nearn remembers: "I asked: 'Is this Patrick McGoohan?' and this very clipped voice on the other end of the 'phone just said: 'Yup'. I was so surprised actually to reach him, I was lost for words.

"He agreed to me going over to California to see him and he was very charming. He remembered the car and was basically amenable to the idea of having his signature appear on a dashboard-mounted plaque and a special certificate. He would endorse the specification of the car.

"We arranged that he would come over to Britain

for an official presentation of the car at the 1990 Motor Show. That was actually the first time he'd been back to Britain since the TV series.

"I picked him up from Birmingham airport and the airline had lost his luggage, but he handled the stress of such a visit as a true professional actor does. I had the Wogan show on to me asking about an interview with McGoohan, but he wasn't happy about it. He said: 'I can't *ad lib*. Give me a script and I'll be whoever you want me to be, but just don't ask me to improvise'.

"At the Motor Show, he was anxious about being mobbed, so we brought him in through the back door. He couldn't wait for the presentation to begin – he was a bundle of nerves. In fact, he became quite relaxed when he got into the swing of it. As a conclusion, I handed him the keys of chassis No 6 in the Prisoner series (he was always referred to in

Apart from the wide rear wings, fat wheels and tyres and colour-keyed roll-over bar, this could be 1965 and you could be Number 6...

Each example of the Prisoner limited edition had a dash-mounted numbered plaque. Numbers were allocated more or less upon customers' preference rather than in sequential order.

the TV series as 'Number Six'). Patrick now owns this Seven in the USA."

The whole event had been another excellent publicity opportunity for Caterham, attracting widespread coverage in the press and on TV.

True to the original Prisoner car, the modern replica had a special British Racing Green paint scheme with a yellow nose, Lotus Series 2-style red interior (including red leather seats and red Wilton carpet) with chrome bezels for the instruments, chrome rear number-plate light and white edging to the side screens, hood and boot cover. To mimic the wheels on the original KAR 120C, special 15in alloy wheels with a design which mirrored the Series 2 Elan-style hubcap were commissioned specifically for the Seven.

As well as a Prisoner penny-farthing motif on the steering wheel boss and a numbered dashboard-mounted plaque, Prisoner owners received a special certificate of authenticity with some words from Patrick McGoohan:

"Back in 1966 when we were preparing *The Prisoner* series we needed a car for our hero. Something out of the ordinary. A vehicle to fit his personality. The first time I saw the now-familiar Lotus Seven KAR 120C, I had that certain feeling. It sort of looked me straight in the eye. I test drove it. This was it. A symbol of all The Prisoner was to represent: standing out from the crowd, quickness and agility, independence, individuality and a touch of the rebel...

"Many people now know there were two versions of the car in the series, the second being a replica of the original Lotus demonstrator, produced by Caterham Cars and used in *Fall Out*, the final episode.

"The Seven has been associated with the *The Prisoner* ever since and I am delighted that it remains in production today as the Caterham Seven. There have been many unofficial replicas over the years so now it's fitting that Caterham Cars should be producing an official, limited edition, Prisoner replica. This they do with my full blessing.

"I am sure you will enjoy your new acquisition. Be seeing you,

Patrick McGoohan

'Rover', the weather balloon-turned-surreal policeman in the TV series, stands guard over Prisoner chassis number one, which was one of only about 50 Caterhams fitted with a 1600 BDR engine.

The uncompromisingly red interior mimicked the original S2 Lotus trim. Instrument bezels were chromed and the steering wheel boss incorporated the penny-farthing motif used to such effect in the 1965 *Prisoner* TV series.

Escape! I am not a number, I am a free man!

The Prisoner edition was also endorsed by the Six of One Society, of which free membership was granted to each purchaser. About 40 Prisoner cars were sold (priced at £16,951 for a Supersprint version, although you could specify any current engine). In theory you could still buy one at the time of writing.

As part of Caterham's continuing attempts to homologate the Seven in as many markets as possible, in 1989 the car passed its 30mph barrier test in France as a condition of full French Type Approval. The front end absorbed the impact with flying colours, the chassis emerging largely unscathed with only localized distortion. The front suspension displaced backwards by 2in, while the rear axle moved forward by 1in, still leaving the car to roll freely. The crucial measurement – the movement of the steering wheel at less than 10mm – was vastly

At the 1990 Birmingham Motor Show, Patrick McGoohan receives his own Prisoner special edition (chassis No 6, of course) in a handover ceremony conducted by Graham Nearn.

within permitted tolerances and demonstrated the inherent safety of the Seven.

Towards the end of 1989, Reg Price developed an improvement to the front suspension in the form of an extra half-link added to the top wishbone. The need arose because of instability during braking, causing the castor angle to change. Price and Coates took an unmodified Seven to Goodwood and drove it for several laps to reacquaint themselves with the 'baseline'. Then Price fitted the top link: "Almost as soon as I'd left the pit lane I knew this was a quantum leap. The feel was completely different." It was quickly adopted on production cars.

In 1990, as a result of the experience with Alex Hawkridge's stiffened racing Seven *(see Chapter 5)*, it was decided to adopt some side impact protection on road-going Sevens. Hawkridge's Adrian Reynard-designed carbonfibre inserts were impractical because they would have cost almost as much as the rest of the chassis put together. Caterham employed much cheaper aluminium honeycomb – technology specified by Ralt for their Formula 3 tubs built by Arch Motors in the early Eighties and mandatory for Indy Cars until the Nineties. Neither were the inserts bonded in: the bonding glues used by Ralt had proved to be carcinogenic, so the

One engine installation which was doomed never to work in the Caterham: the Ford Sierra 2-litre eight-valve engine stood no chance of being squeezed under the narrow confines of the Seven's bonnet, as this 1988 experiment proved.

As part of the French Type Approval process, a Caterham was 30mph crash-tested in France. It's difficult to guess, but this was taken after the impact.

impact protection panels were simply sandwiched by the cockpit side frame triangulation and the inner trim panels. All 1990 model year Sevens therefore came with ½in thick aluminium honeycomb chassis reinforcement corresponding to where the shins, thighs and hips were sited. The chassis triangulation had to be reduced to ½in tubes to provide space for the honeycomb.

The year 1990 also saw the expansion of the Dartford factory to take over Unit 3, an adjacent unit of some 6,000sq ft. This was pressed into service as a stock area and goods despatch point: Caterham no longer accepted personal collections from the factory, delivering each kit to its new home itself. A mezzanine floor was later installed in Unit 3, which houses Caterham Cars' collection of historic Lotus products.

From the late Eighties, perhaps the biggest decision in Caterham's history had been looming on the horizon: what to do about the Ford pushrod engine. Sevens had used the Ford Kent unit since 1968, but the end was now in sight. It had been superseded by the CVH unit in the Escort in 1980 and it was becoming much less familiar in Britain (only being fitted in the Eighties to Ford Transits, P100 trucks and Formula Fords).

In fact, Graham Nearn did manage to secure supplies of new pushrod engines for many more years, as he recalls. "While visiting South Africa on legal business, I contacted Samcor in Port Elizabeth, which was originally a Ford subsidiary in that country. I knew it produced trucks with the Kent engine and discovered they were the suppliers to Ford UK of the P100 truck. Samcor was concerned that there were insufficient numbers going to the UK and I agreed to buy engines by the container

At the 1989 Earls Court Motorfair, Caterham celebrated 30 years with the Seven with a special multi-car display including all versions from the basic kit-built car up to the BDR-engined HPC.

A much needed extra storage area and despatch point was created in 1990 when Caterham bought Unit 3 next door to the Dartford factory. Here an impressive collection of wheels and body/chassis units fresh from Arch Motors are stored awaiting fitting.

Beauty and integrity of the later-type (post-1991) chassis shines through.

load. Samcor has now stopped making the Kent engine but our supplies should last us until at least 1997."

Knowing that the Kent engine's days were always numbered, the search for a successor continued.

The then-current Ford CVH engine had already been rejected as the replacement mainstream choice for the Seven's engine bay (although it was later used in Swiss-market Sevens to satisfy local emissions laws where it was also locally turbo-charged). Some 93 CVH cars were built between 1986 and 1991, of which 75% were turbocharged by the Swiss importer, Fredy Kumschick.

Another Ford engine, the Dagenham-built I4 2-litre eight-valve twin-cam unit (as fitted to the Sierra and RS2000), was considered and rejected at a later stage because it was too tall to fit, and because Jez Coates became convinced that Caterham should only be using 16-valve engines.

It was not just the supply of the Ford pushrod engine which was causing some concern in the late Eighties: the Cosworth BDR twin-cam unit which had been so successful in the Seven was also in doubt. The cost was horrific and there was no certainty that Cosworth would continue producing the unit.

"In the end we dropped it in the UK market because it was something of a liability," admits Jez Coates. "It was an old engine (first launched in 1968) and the type of customer who bought the (rather expensive) Cossie – doctors, professionals – weren't used to Cosworth's weeping cylinder head gaskets, comparatively temperamental running and carburettor flat-spots. They wanted fuel-injection driveability. But the odd Cosworth engine is even today still built for Japan – several were made in 1995, for example. A total of 480 BDR engines have been built to date, and only two remained unfitted to cars at the time of writing; 331 were 1700s, the remaining 149 being 1600s. Some 400

As ever, most Sevens were supplied in CKD form with a body/chassis unit ready fitted with wiring, piping and instruments, but requiring major mechanical items to be installed.

After an extended development period, Bilstein dampers became standard fitment on Caterhams from July 1991 as part of a package of suspension changes which also included an adjustable rear anti-roll bar.

Cosworths went to Japan – they're crazy for twin-cams and go absolutely ballistic for the Cosworth."

Of the genuine HPC models, only 62 examples were ever made. "In my opinion, these are likely to become the most collectable Caterhams in years to come," says Coates. "They have the legendary name, the historical link with the much-loved S2 1500 Cosworth Lotus Seven and all the Cosworth magic: the first serious 16-valve engine, the engine which powered Roger Clark to win the RAC Rally and the engine which went into the Ford RS200."

The search began for not one but two new engine ranges, before phasing out the BDR. The attitudes behind choosing which engines to use were changing. Jez Coates: "Our engineering confidence was growing. Rather than bolt in the next Ford engine we were better positioned to consider all the alternatives. For years, the development of the Seven had progressed along the lines of 'firefighting': when a problem arose (such as the demise of the Escort rear axle), an alternative was quickly found. But at Caterham, the emphasis was moving towards engineering on the basis of what was best for the car."

The leading service agent for the Seven from day one, Caterham Cars built up a strong picture of what modifications and improvements were required with the Seven. Engineering confidence grew alongside ever-widening customer feedback and respect for the product. Typically, buyers would pay to have extra sophistication. For example, they would opt for the de Dion rear end which, although it was more expensive than the live axle, was

regarded as the set-up to have – because Caterham had engineered it.

In this way, Caterham kept ahead of the market. Although Caterham sometimes appeared from the outside to be following an absolute and unchanging formula, the reality was very different. For sure, there was (and still is) an unwritten but golden rule that the shape of the Seven should remain untouched – after all, Caterham had paid Lotus for that specific shape. But under the skin, Caterham increasingly responded to the expectations of a generation brought up on the Golf GTI. Handling,

Perhaps the most significant development in Caterham's recent history was the adoption of Rover K-series power. The 103bhp engine came from the Metro GTi, but of course was mounted longitudinally, not transversely as in the Rover.

power, grip, braking and suspension sophistication were all in a completely different class to the original Sevens made by Lotus.

Jez Coates recalls: "When it came to replacing the Ford engines, the R&D team adopted first principles: rather than saying Sevens have always had Ford engines, so we'll use Ford, we asked what was *best* for the car. This would mark a major departure for the Seven: it had not had a change of engine block since 1961!

"I had an old friend, Geoff Calvert, from the Leyland days with whom I used to rally a Saab 96, and by the late Eighties he was working for Rover. He told me about the new all-alloy, incredibly lightweight K-series engine they were developing. That sounded exactly the right concept as a replacement for the Ford pushrod engine in the Seven, a car which always derived its dynamic ability from its light weight. Historically it was also appropriate because the Lotus Seven had used the BMC A-series engine as early as 1959. I reckon that Lotus dropped the A-series when it got a bit

antiquated and Ford engines were used as a fill-in for over 20 years until the A-series replacement arrived!

"I immediately became enthusiastic and I met Roger Stone, chief engineer of the K-series project, in 1988 – well before the K-series came out – and quickly established a very good relationship. Rover were extremely supportive and our liaison officer at Rover, Dave Fender, had boundless enthusiasm and an ability to persuade people to give up their time for the project. The K-series was the right product for us and Rover recognized the benefit they could gain from an association with us. They agreed to loan us engines as early as May 1989."

Caterham actually fitted a K-series engine into a Seven for the first time in July 1990, virtually at the same time as the K-series Metro made its debut.

The K-series engine was a 16-valve 1.4-litre twin-cam unit with excellent power-to-weight potential. However, it provided some unique engineering challenges which Caterham had not had to face before. One of these concerned the gearbox.

The Rover K-series was a neat fit in the Seven chassis, which was revised with splayed upper engine bay diagonals and a narrower pedal box. The whole K-series power plant installation weighed significantly less than the Ford pushrod.

Rear of the K-series chassis showing the aluminium honeycomb panel above the fuel tank and twin-tailpipe rear-exit exhaust, plumbed to cope with a catalyst. Later K-series cars reverted to side-mounted exhausts.

The K-series engine was only used in front-wheel drive format, and therefore no longitudinal gearboxes were available for it. It was felt that the Ford five-speed gearbox was still the best 'box to use (the Rover SD1 five-speed was considered, but rejected on grounds of weight, bulk and poor change quality). The trouble was, it would need a special bellhousing.

In the best Colin Chapman tradition, Jez Coates added lightness by casting a special alloy bellhousing (and a special alloy sump for the engine). In the end, the K-series power plant installation came out some 30kg lighter than the old Ford pushrod. A further 5kg was lost from the radiator, as the K-series cooled more efficiently.

Sooner or later, European markets would insist on fuel injection and a catalytic converter. So the original choice of Weber carburettors was abandoned in favour of fuel injection. The trouble was, Rover's original single-point fuel injection unit would not fit under the Seven's bonnet. Coates knew that a multi-point fuel injection system would soon be launched by Rover and that it *could* be squeezed in – if they changed the angle of engine installation, together with modifying the bellhousing and sump to suit. This was duly done; ironically, the angle now matched that of the Rover Metro in which the engine was installed transversely, not longitudinally as in the Caterham.

The chassis had to be modified in detail for the new engine. The upper engine bay diagonals were spread by an inch each at the rear to accommodate the width of the inclined cylinder head, while the pedal box was narrowed.

Another problem was where to put the catalyst.

Worried by the heat generated by the 'cat', Caterham decided to site it in the engine bay. Installation in this very limited space was accomplished by Caterham's exhaust suppliers, Cheesman Products, who had to create an intricate and costly manifold. The catalytic exhaust exited at the rear of the car instead of the side. Due to the cost and difficulty of assembly, this system was later dropped, and all catalyzed Sevens now have the converter within a side-mounted exhaust protected by an extended exhaust guard. During 1991 and 1992, before the EC emissions laws came in, the catalyst was an (unpopular) option. From 1993, of course, the catalyst became mandatory on all new engines.

At the launch of the K-series car at London's Docklands in July 1991, Graham Nearn managed to underscore its significance by pulling off another publicity coup in the form of an official presence

Rover's 1.4-litre K-series unit had the advantage of being emissions-tested for overseas markets. Technically, this 16-valve twin-cam unit was very advanced and its character suited the Seven extremely well, even if the Ford traditionalists had a hard time accepting it.

from Sir Graham Day, chairman of Rover Group, who enthused that he was "delighted to have been able to work with Caterham Cars", a comment which greatly enhanced the company's credibility.

K-series was launched at £13,883 in kit form. That may have seemed a lot of money, but this reflected the wide scope of the development programme and the state-of-the-art engine. Performance was every bit as a Caterham should be: 0–60mph in 6.7 seconds and a top speed of 112mph. Because of the lightweight engine, it was also probably the best-handling Seven yet made. As Jez Coates said: "It's the most Seven-like Seven we've produced."

At that launch was another interesting option: lightweight body panels with aluminium wings and nosecone. Offered as a (rather expensive) option, the so-called Lightweight was intended for those who wished to get the maximum performance out of their Seven and who were not concerned about cost. It also offered the opportunity to duplicate the all-aluminium style of the Lotus Seven S1.

Caterham has never been one to miss out on its links with the past…

Demand for the new Rover Metro was so strong that managing director George Simpson indicated that he required all K-series engines for the production line. Graham Nearn visited him at Cowley and found him very supportive when he understood that the off-take of engines would be very small in the first year, after which time K-series engine production was scheduled to increase.

By the time the K-series finally arrived in the Seven, the problem of finding a replacement for the Cosworth engine had already been solved. Caterham turned not to Ford but to a completely new name for the Seven: it was a Vauxhall engine which took over from the Cosworth as the high-performance unit in the range. Vauxhall had introduced its 2-litre DOHC 16V engine in the Astra GTE in May 1988. It had the right contextual position, too: the double-overhead-cam conversion was devised (and initially built) by Cosworth.

The lavish launch of the K-series at London's Docklands in 1991. Canary Wharf looms in the background.

Rover's chairman, Sir Graham Day, attended the launch of the K-series. His presence underlined the benefit Rover saw in being associated with a high-profile sportscar maker such as Caterham.

"Everybody loved it," remembers Jez Coates. "It got rave reviews and it seemed right for us because it was a mainstream product, cheaper than the Cosworth BDR, *and* Vauxhall were keen to sell it to us."

Installation work actually began after K-series. Again there were problems with fitting the Ford gearbox, since the power train assembly needed to sit lower and further back in the chassis to make it fit. As a result, the Vauxhall engine was an easier fit under the Seven's bonnet than the Rover, even though it was a larger engine and was installed upright. New gearbox mounts, another new bell-housing and another new sump were needed. It may appear surprising that Caterham went for carburettors instead of injection, but the main

consideration was the attitude of Japanese customers, by far the company's biggest market for twin-cam cars. Put simply, at that time in Japan, customers were not interested in injection systems on Sevens: they wanted two carburettors, full-stop.

As a prestige market, Japan had always liked the 'business' on their cars. The previous BDR engine had been dry-sumped with a separate tank especially for the Japanese market and it was decided to dry-sump the Vauxhall engine, too – but in a state-of-the-art way, with the oil in a dry-sump bell-housing, not in a separate canister (an old Lotus formula trick). This also meant that the dry-sump tank, which had reduced the passenger footwell in the BDR, need not impinge on legroom. The dry-

Launched at the same time as the K-series car was the all-aluminium-bodied Lightweight. It's seen here at the Geneva Motor Show.

A highly significant new model was launched in 1990 in the form of the Vauxhall-powered HPC. This superseded the old Cosworth HPC and was the fastest Seven yet made.

sump treatment made the bellhousing a very complicated and expensive casting but, as it was an option directed mainly at Japan, Caterham knew it would find customers.

So there were two separate bellhousings and two separate sumps for Vauxhall engines, all approved by Vauxhall themselves. Caterham also made its own cast alloy cam inserts which featured the wording 'Caterham Vauxhall' (as opposed to just 'Caterham' on the Rover engine) – one of the first times that Caterham had tried bespoke engine branding (it had previously been used on the Vegantune engine). Customers liked it and Vauxhall wanted the association.

One major advantage of the Vauxhall engine was the amount of power it had on tap as standard. Once Caterham had fitted twin 45DCOE Weber carbs (in place of the standard GM fuel injection) and a special manifold, the engine produced a storming 175bhp. That was in sharp contrast with the 1700 Supersprint Ford engine which had to be stripped down, rebored and rebuilt with specialist parts to obtain a high output. The Vauxhall engine could simply be bolted straight in.

On the performance side, the new HPC was unmatched. Caterham claimed a top speed of 126mph and 0–60mph time of just 4.8 seconds. It was simply the best Seven yet made, as reflected in its rather steep launch price of £18,492.

The Vauxhall-engined HPC was launched at the newly acquired unit at Dartford in August 1990 with factory tours and speeches from Graham Nearn and Vauxhall's parts director, Peter Lord (a Caterham Supersprint owner himself). Lord said: "We see the association with Caterham as extremely

Attending the launch of the HPC was Peter Lord, director of Vauxhall Parts. As a Caterham owner, he was an enthusiastic supporter of the HPC project from day one and was very keen for Vauxhall to become associated with Caterham.

positive, since they are the acknowledged leaders in their specialist field. Jez Coates and his team must take credit for the vehicle as it stands here today. Having driven it, I have to say the results are stunning." Later, on August 1, 1993 he put his money where his mouth was and bought the very first low-volume type-approved Vauxhall HPC injection Seven.

Just as with the old BDR-engined HPC, much play was made of the HPC title. Customers under the age of 25 were obliged to take the half-day High Performance Course – the name of John Lyons' high-speed driver training course. Costed into the product, it was optional but recommended above the age of 25. Despite the fact that the scheme was not new, the renewed publicity generated from its relaunch brought Caterham yet more media attention.

At 126kg, the Vauxhall engine was 10kg heavier than the Ford crossflow. That made it slightly less sharp on handling than the K-series Seven. But in performance terms it was an extremely quick car – the car that Seven owners aspired to own. Standard equipment included a limited-slip differential, adjustable cloth seats and specially designed lightweight 16in KN-manufactured alloy wheels (weighing only 6.7kg each) and correspondingly wider tyres.

Initially, the HPC was a very healthy seller. But by 1994 its popularity had started to wane as the

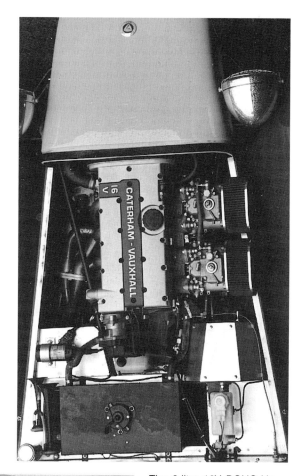

The 2-litre 16V DOHC Vauxhall engine developed a storming 175bhp when fitted with carburettors, endowing the lightweight Seven with a 0–60mph time of less than 5 seconds. A special cam cover insert was designed for the engine.

This is how the HPC kit looked when delivered to your door. The special five-spoke 16in alloy wheels were new for the HPC and provided new levels of grip for a Seven.

Fully-built Caterhams came on stream in 1993 and Peter Lord of Vauxhall Parts (standing with Graham Nearn) took delivery of the first fully-built Vauxhall HPC. Caterham's penchant for Vauxhalls can be seen from this collection: Lotus Carlton (Jez Coates), Senator (Graham Nearn), Carlton Estate (David Wakefield) and Calibra Turbo (Andy Noble).

Another fan of the Caterham was Prince Michael of Kent, seen here inspecting the K-series at the 1992 Birmingham Motor Show with Simon and Graham Nearn.

effects of the recession made the relatively expensive Vauxhall engine a less popular option. Also a small performance edge was knocked off when emissions laws required Caterham to return to fuel injection and catalysts, blunting the power down to 165bhp.

In terms of sales, 1991 proved to be Caterham's best year to date. With all the new engines now on stream and the kit versions proving to be consistently popular, the remarkable total of almost 800 Caterhams were built in 1991. This is all the more impressive when you consider that, only nine years before, Caterham had made just 80 cars a year. So by 1991, Caterham had become the fifth largest independent British manufacturer behind Rover, Rolls-Royce, TVR and Reliant.

Then the recession hit. The British specialist car industry suffered heavily during the early Nineties, but Caterham survived better than almost any of them. One reason was the long waiting lists for Sevens – typically nine months – so Caterham was still working through its back orders while others were going to the wall. The lengthy delivery times – which were a big disincentive to purchasing a Seven – began to shrink (down to about 12 weeks) and this did have a positive knock-on effect on sales, particularly among kit-car buyers. In addition, exports were a strong and growing area and helped smooth out the effects of weaker domestic demand.

But the recession certainly did have an effect on Caterham and production levels fell by 25%. Sadly, Caterham was forced to cut its 60-strong staff back by six. Probably around 300 other jobs among Caterham's suppliers depended on the strength of orders. Caterham Cars was the biggest customer of Arch Motors (chassis), Oxted Trimming (trim) and MES (wiring looms). At the time of writing Caterham even remains the third largest external customer of Rover Cars.

Caterham Cars was well placed to consolidate its position in the Nineties. It now had two brand-new engine ranges from Rover and Vauxhall. The highly successful Ford engines remained available and, despite the new powerplants, were overwhelmingly popular. Initially, this was a cause for

The 35th Anniversary model, with its special yellow-and-green paintwork, was launched in 1992. Here it is pictured with a Series 1 Lotus Seven outside the redeveloped sales site at Caterham.

some concern: there was considerable customer resistance to the Rover K-series engine. Firstly it was not a Ford engine, something that had seemed almost obligatory for Sevens. Secondly, it was smaller than the old Ford engines at only 1.4 litres *and* it had ECUs, catalysts and fuel injection, not carbs, and was therefore not a 'real man's engine'. For the same money as the 110bhp K-series you could buy a Seven with a 135bhp Supersprint engine.

What changed people's minds? One of the answers was the success of K-series-engined racers *(see Chapter 5)*. Caterham also pushed the K-series engine as *the* new engine for the Seven: press cars and demonstrators were always K-series, not Ford; and Caterham introduced a hire fleet for public use, all of which were fitted with K-series engines.

The final solution was to extract more power from the K-series. Taking the head off and changing the porting or pistons would have been so costly that it was pointless: you might just as well buy a Vauxhall engine. Likewise, turbocharging and supercharging were considered, but rejected as expensive options. So Jez Coates approached Rover's powertrain director Sivet Hiljemark, saying he wanted to up its power to 100bhp per litre. Hiljemark replied that he could not sanction any money or manpower for such a project but that, "if Rover employees wished to get involved in their own time, I wouldn't have a problem".

So the 'Saturday Morning Club' was born. With no official backing, six engineers at Rover (Steve Wood, Tim Sieple, Alan Warburton, Ronnie Gibson, John Ruddy and Dave Fender) worked in their spare time to develop an engine which almost matched Coates' request – a K-series which pumped out 128bhp. This boasted reprofiled camshafts from the Project Pride Metro record-breaker, a new larger-bore free-flow inlet manifold and plenum chamber, and a specially mapped Motorola ECU allowing the engine to rev much higher.

And so the K-series Supersport was created. Launched in 1993, this was finally a match for the old Ford-based Supersprint, boasting a 0–60mph time of well under 6 seconds and a top speed of

Prince Edward and Lord Montagu of Beaulieu sample the Anniversary Seven in the grounds of the National Motor Museum. Caterham donated this car to be raffled to raise funds for the museum.

After the exciting debuts of the HPC and K-series, in 1992 Caterham returned to its roots with the budget-priced GTS: 100bhp 1600 Sprint engine, live axle, four-speed gearbox and a price of just £8,995.

112mph. A useful fringe benefit of the ECU was redundant air conditioning software, which was rewritten so that a gearchange light on the dashboard lit up at 7,400rpm (the rev limit was 7,600rpm). "You can play at being a Touring Car championship driver for the day," commented Jez Coates.

There were also customers who wanted even more power than the standard carburetted Vauxhall's 175bhp. In early 1992 Caterham approached Swindon Racing Engines, builders of Vauxhall's own BTCC engines, and acknowledged leaders in tuning this power unit. Three SRE levels of tune were offered: 218bhp, 225bhp or 235bhp, by changing camshafts, working the head and so on. The cost of conversion ranged from £1,175 to £2,585 and these proved very popular for a short time until two factors conspired against the options: the continuing recession and the standardization of fuel injection.

Now that the K-series and Vauxhall Sevens had revitalized the top end of Caterham's range, it was felt that something had to be done at the entry level – especially as the economy was still in the grip of a full recession and the proportion of buyers with a lot of money to spend had fallen dramatically. Caterham Cars did not wish to neglect the enthusiast who had formed the backbone of Seven sales for 35 years.

So in February 1992, Caterham relaunched the live-axle model with a 100bhp Ford 1600 Kent engine, reconditioned Ital rear axle and Escort four-speed gearbox; otherwise the car was all-new

and supplied complete in kit form. This was the GTS, a model intended as a low-cost way into Seven ownership and, in Graham Nearn's words, "to maintain links with the grass-roots enthusiast".

Initially, the GTS had a different coloured chassis to indicate that it was simplified, having less triangulation. The paint scheme recalled the old Lotus Seven Series 2 chassis. The standard engine was a 100bhp version of the Ford 1600, but a 135bhp 1700 Supersprint engine was an option at £1,175. A further option at £455 was a Race Pack to enable you to enter your GTS in Class C in the Caterham race series.

As an affordable 'real' Caterham selling for £8,995, the GTS was a great success, selling around five per month. Then later in 1992 Andy Noble was flicking through a copy of Jeremy Coulter's book, *The Lotus & Caterham Sevens* and saw an old advert for the original Lotus Seven extolling its low price. "No wonder it was so cheap," he thought, "there's almost nothing to it." So he suggested taking the GTS concept one stage further: an even more stripped-down, old-style, cheaper car.

Launched at the 1992 Birmingham Motor Show and named the Classic, the model took its cues from the specification of the Lotus Seven. So the Classic came with a specification which really was classic: no carpets, no rev-counter or fuel gauge, no spare wheel, no heater, no weather gear, a bench seat, a single downdraught-carb 84bhp engine (which necessitated the fitment of a bonnet bulge) and Brooklands aero-screens. That shaved another

£1,500 off the purchase price, taking it to £7,450. However, the Classic still retained the aluminium honeycomb and safety features of all other post-1990 Caterhams.

Perhaps the most significant effect of the Classic was to bring new blood into the showroom. Attracted by the low initial price, customers would come in fully expecting to spend just £7,500. But then they were told that for an extra £1,500 they could have a Special Equipment (SE) package which included five alloy wheels instead of four steel wheels, a full set of instruments, carpets, 100bhp engine with twin Weber sidedraught carbs, and a proper windscreen and weather equipment. Every Classic customer, virtually to a man, went the extra mile and ordered a Classic SE, not a Classic. In fact, over 100 Classic SEs were sold before a single basic Classic left the factory!

Another facet of the Classic story was that it saw the introduction of Caterham's guaranteed depreciation buy-back scheme. If you returned to Caterham to part-exchange your Classic for a Supersport or HPC, you would get a generous guaranteed sum back.

In 1992, there was a new shadow looming in the form of The Law. From January 1, 1993, all cars sold with new engines in the EEC needed a catalytic converter, so the Vauxhall engine had to be switched from carbs to fuel injection for the UK and Europe. The HPC engine did not look as evocative, neither did it produce as much power

(down 10bhp to 165bhp), nor did it have the same raw sound, but fuel injection was a 'necessary evil' to satisfy the legislators. In fact, carburettor Vauxhall engines remained available as Caterham had stockpiled a batch of pre-1993 engines. However, by summer 1996 this stockpile will be – if you will pardon the pun – almost exhausted.

Despite the publicity and glowing reports of the Rover and Vauxhall-powered Sevens, it was the Ford pushrod engine which continued to be the mainstay of the Caterham range. Many customers felt a historical affinity with the old Ford lump, besides which it was a very cheap engine to buy and to tune. Its cheapness accounted for Caterham's ability to offer a Classic with a brand-new engine for under £7,500. As previously described, Caterham Cars had secured a supply of new engines from Samcor, the South African manufacturer of the Ford engine. They ordered a large batch of them just before the emissions regulations of 1993 came into force, and that is how Caterham was still able legally to fit carburettor Ford engines to Sevens post-1993.

Another event of major importance which occurred on January 1, 1993 was a change in the law which allowed Caterham Cars to sell fully-built cars in the UK for the first time. Full Type Approval had always been too expensive an option for Caterham to consider, but the introduction of less stringent Low Volume Type Approval (LVTA) laws made the process much easier – and cheaper.

Even more back-to-basics was the Classic. For £1,550 less than a GTS, you made do without a windscreen, fuel gauge, weather gear, carpets, heater or spare wheel.

In fact, Caterham Cars was closely involved in getting LVTA up and running. In 1985, a self-regulatory group called the Specialist Car Manufacturers Group (SCMG) was set up within the Society of Motor Manufacturers and Traders (SMMT). Graham Nearn became chairman of the SCMG, a role he continues to fulfil at the time of writing.

Even before the idea of LVTA was discussed, the SCMG had run a 96-point voluntary code of practice for manufacturing standards. For Caterham, this meant a minimum standard for kit-supplied cars: for example, instruments and wiring already fitted, brake pedals, cylinders and piping already installed, brand-new fuel tank and fuel line, jigged windscreen, wings and nosecone and a full assembly guide supplied. As part of the process, each of the models Caterham sold was inspected and passed by an independent body (Bob Brayfield's TUV UK). A free post-build check was also available to all purchasers as a requirement of the code.

As the SCMG grew in stature, it worked closely with the Vehicle Certification Agency to devise a set of Type Approval standards for car makers which produced only a small number of fully-built cars per year (less than 500).

Caterham Cars was keen to be allowed to sell its cars in fully-built form in Britain, in addition to the component form packages it was used to marketing. So the non-Supersport K-series and standard Vauxhall cars were put through all the necessary tests during 1991 and 1992, a process of mind-numbing tedium, but also, thought Caterham, of great long-term value.

So Jez Coates and his team endured the rigours of endless noise, emissions and radio interference suppression tests. These were tough to pass, as Jez Coates remembers: "The noise limit as the car accelerates flat-out in second gear is set at just 77dB. When you realize that the Seven rolls past the noise meters at 70dB *with the engine switched off,* you can appreciate the difficulties involved."

The K-series and Vauxhall were finally passed as LVTA-approved fully-built cars in 1993 (May and July respectively). In effect the 'turn-key' version was the same as the component car, but with all components fully fitted. The main differences were that the fully-built cars had to have a catalyst

Another view of a Classic shows just how pared-down this model was. Plain steel wheels, 84bhp engine and aero-screens gave a stark feel, but at under £7,500 the model attracted much new blood into the showroom.

Most Classic customers in fact opted for a few extras such as full windscreen and wipers, twin carburettors, full complement of instruments and alloy wheels in place of these steel type. Such an upgrade was offered by Caterham in the so-called Special Equipment (SE) package.

engine with the rear-exit exhaust system and, because of the regulations on visibility, the LVTA version could not be sold with a roll-over bar; nor could sidescreens be supplied because these were required to have glass, not plastic, windows. Customers had to go back to the factory and buy weather gear and sidescreens as aftermarket items!

With baited breath, the sales department waited to see what effect supplying £14,995 fully-built cars would have. There was some suspicion that there was perhaps a class of doctors and dentists who would prefer a complete vehicle. In the event, there were remarkably few customers who wanted to pay extra cash to turn up and drive a car away. Over 95% of UK buyers still wanted to do some of the work themselves.

At least LVTA gave Caterham an extra level of credibility in the UK, and allowed the company legally to register its demonstrators, development cars and press cars without having to prove some element of amateur input into the construction. Also it has provided a recognized platform to gain Type Approval in other countries such as Australia.

The whole LVTA procedure had taken a tremendous amount of time and energy. All the legislative work had added weight to the car and was of no direct benefit to the customer – it just needed to be done. There was a strong feeling that, after this period of dull and soul-destroying labour, the team ought to do something completely fresh. With the new emissions laws due to arrive at the beginning of 1993, Jez Coates decided to embark on one last, end-of-an-era, ultimate-spec project.

Mike Dixon, Caterham's production director, had built a special Seven for himself, essentially a Vauxhall racer with the minimum added to make it

Just before emissions laws outlawed such a machine, Caterham launched the awe-inspiring JPE, a projectile whose sole purpose was to catapult its occupants at maximum velocity towards some escapist horizon.

JPE stood for Jonathan Palmer Evolution. Ex-Formula 1 driver Palmer, pictured here, contributed to the test regime for the car and endorsed it. Buyers were entitled to attend one of his motorsport days for personal tuition. But then, they had spent £35,000 to buy the car…

road-legal: lights, horn, speedo and a cooling fan. It retained the Perspex screen, 13in wheels, total lack of trim, and racing mechanicals (188bhp engine with 48DCOSP carbs, straight-cut gears and LSD). The car was painted Kermit green and in this form Dixon persuaded Jez Coates to drive it back from Snetterton in 1992. "Subtle it wasn't," recalls Coates, "but it was a very focussed car which went like stink."

Coates felt inspired by Dixon's car and also by the Light Car Company's Rocket, designed by Gordon Murray – "another focussed product," he commented. And so the JPE was born. "Just for once, we weren't concerned about cost. We wanted to build a car that was over the top. For the engine we turned to Swindon Racing Engines, who offered us a '92-spec Touring Car version of the Vauxhall 2-litre engine, which put out 250bhp. It had Weber Alpha fuel injection, which was expensive but necessary for drivability. OK, the engine cost £13,000, but we weren't bothered about the cost, were we?

"We were going for ultimate speed and ultimate lightness, so we did without such fripperies as a windscreen and wipers in favour of a smoked Perspex wind deflector, carbonfibre wings and nose instead of GRP, individually-tailored carbon Kevlar bucket seats, no roof, no heater and no spare wheel. That brought the weight down to just 530kg (1,168lb) for a power-to-weight ratio of a gulping 472bhp per tonne (as a comparison, a Jaguar XJ220 has 369bhp per tonne and a Bugatti EB110SS 458bhp per tonne).

"Then we really upped the spec with an aluminium saddle tank repositioned above the rear axle, aluminium radiator, Quaife straight-cut close-ratio gearbox, exhaust matched to the engine, aluminium-cased steering rack, four-pot alloy brakes with vented discs, magnesium wheels, fat tyres, six-point harnesses, and personalized helmets and steering wheels."

Attracted by the brash green colour scheme of

The JPE engine was essentially a BTCC Vauxhall unit as produced by Swindon Racing Engines. Reputed to cost in the region of £13,000, it developed 250bhp at a screaming 7,750rpm. Indubitably the hairiest Caterham there has ever been.

Jonathan Palmer gives his JPE launch speech at the 1992 Birmingham Motor Show.

Mike Dixon's road-racer, Coates consulted with Caterham's paint shop, TSK, for a suggestion of an equally striking – or preferably even more striking – colour. Proprietor Tony Whiting came up with two proposals: fluorescent pink or fluorescent yellow. The ability of Luke Harnesses to supply webbing for standard six-points in fluorescent yellow sealed the decision. This pulsating colour scheme was adopted as the JPE's signature, with colour co-ordinated yellow cam cover and exhaust guard inserts, instruments and seat belts.

The JPE got its name because of the involvement of ex-Formula 1 racing driver and tester Jonathan Palmer. Already linked with Caterham through his corporate entertainment company, Jonathan Palmer Promo Sport, which used Sevens in its so-called Motorsport Experience, he was invited by Andy Noble to do some testing in the car. Within just a few laps of the test track, he was able to identify several areas of fine-tuning on handling, gearing, wheels and tyres. The car became known as the JPE for Jonathan Palmer Evolution.

Palmer explained the ethos of the JPE: "It's the nearest thing to a Formula 1 car on the road, for a price quite a few people can afford. It's a difficult car to drive on the limit, but that's the whole challenge. The engine is very peaky: the power only really comes on strongly at 6,500rpm. But the

great thing about it is that it's also very docile lower down in the rev band. It's the most intoxicating adrenalin pump on the road."

Palmer was pictured widely in the national press seated in the car. He made himself available to meet JPE buyers at Bruntingthorpe test ground and assess their driving ability. The result of all this was that the JPE got tremendous publicity when it was launched at the 1992 Motor Show. It was also hardly the sort of car you could miss, painted in fluorescent yellow with colour-matched dials (which would glow green in the dark). The instruments themselves also created a stir because initially the speedo was not calibrated above 70mph and the rev-counter had virtually no markings below 6,000rpm. After some consternation in certain officious quarters, the instruments were recalibrated: now the rev-counter was fully marked (albeit with a *green* band, not a red band between 6,500 and 8,200rpm) and the speedo was half-heartedly marked up to 150mph, presumably as a licence-saving measure!

Yet more publicity arrived when people came to road-test the JPE. As well as having the fastest top speed of any Caterham to date (thanks to the improved aerodynamics, it was a genuine 150mph car), it transpired that it was a phenomenal 0–60mph machine. Running the close-ratio gearbox, the JPE could pull 60mph in first gear, opening up the possibility of very rapid 0–60mph times. Derek Bell achieved it in 3.815 seconds, but then John Barker of *Performance Car* magazine

The massive four-pot alloy disc brakes which gave the JPE perhaps the most decisive braking power of any road car.

Jonathan Palmer, Jez Coates and *Autocar*'s James Thomas find plenty to laugh about just before the JPE's crushing attempt to sprint to 100mph from rest and back to zero again at Santa Pod raceway.

Jez Coates leaps out of the way as Jonathan Palmer prepares to tackle the 0–100mph–0 run.

Palmer confirms the test results: he achieved the sprint-stop attempt in just 12.6 seconds, fully 4 seconds faster than a Ferrari F40. A JPE also broke the record with a 0–60mph sprint of 3.46 seconds.

recorded a time of just 3.54 seconds. However, the best time was set by Mark Hales of *Fast Lane* magazine, who achieved the 0–60mph sprint in 3.46 seconds.

The Caterham was all set to make it into the Guinness Book of World Records as the fastest road car in the world. But in response to the Caterham, other groups began trying to go one better, building bespoke 0–60 machines. A matter of weeks after the record-breaking run, a faster run was recorded by Graham Hathaway in a specially boosted Ford RS200 with some 600bhp on tap (at 3.3 seconds). The difference was that you could buy a JPE off-the-peg from Caterham and use it on the road!

A JPE was also provided for *Autocar & Motor* for their competition to find the quickest car from zero to 100mph and back to rest again. Jonathan Palmer performed a perfect 0–100mph–0 run at Santa Pod

The original dials which caused so much controversy: a rev-counter with virtually no markings and a speedo which was not calibrated above 70mph!

And this was how they were made 'acceptable'. The rev-counter incorporated a green band upwards of 6,400rpm because that was where you would find the real power of the engine.

in an astonishing 12.6 seconds – over three seconds faster than a Ferrari F40. His F1 skills meant that the engine didn't bog down off the line, gear-changes were super slick and the car never exceeded 101mph! Apart from the driver, the JPE's advantage derived from its phenomenal traction and braking power.

The cost of the JPE to the customer was expensive by Seven standards, with a price tag of £34,950 – and that did not include paint! "We gave customers the moral dilemma of deciding whether or not to add an extra 2kg of weight by having it painted," comments Jez Coates wryly. Even at such an astronomical price, the JPE proved attractive to many buyers. It was, and will undoubtedly remain, the ultimate Seven. To date, the JPE has sold no less than 33 examples, beginning in September 1992. Nine went to the UK, two to Germany, one

to Australia and 21 to Japan. JPEs are still being built (Japan ordered four in May 1995, for instance). But in the UK, the supply of pre-1993 engines will eventually run out, so the JPE has a limited domestic life.

In another important way, 1992 was a landmark year for Caterham. It represented the 35th year of Seven production and a special Anniversary model was launched in May 1992 to celebrate. Featuring a classic Lotus-style yellow-and-green paint scheme, 'Prisoner' alloy wheels and a dash-mounted plaque, the Anniversary was offered in CKD or complete component form and was touted as the last new Caterham to have the Ford engine's characteristic Webers protruding from the bonnet – the reason being that the 1993 emissions laws were about to come into force. In fact, Caterham is still building them at the time of writing!

This JPE pictured in build in 1994 was, like almost all JPEs, destined for a lucky owner in Japan.

MODEL JPE-MOD'D
2000 VAUX INJ
DE DION
DESTINATION JAPAN

Also on the standard spec list were a heated front screen, rear wing protectors, side mirrors, heater, inertia-reel seat belts, roll-over bar and full weather gear. You could also choose a Sprint, Supersprint or Vauxhall HPC engine. Prices ranged from £12,999 for a CKD 1600 Sprint up to £14,897 for a component-form 1700 Super Sprint.

An Anniversary car was donated to and displayed at the National Motor Museum in Beaulieu throughout the summer as a raffle prize (which netted no less than £50,000 in ticket sales). That process was repeated the following year. Obviously, this was a useful publicity exercise, made all the more so by Prince Edward being widely pictured in the national press piloting the Seven alongside Lord Montagu.

The year 1993 proved to be a historic one for Caterham. In the face of a worldwide recession, the company had recorded its fourth successive rise in exports the previous year. Representing some 55 per cent of sales, this feat was enough to earn Caterham Cars the Queen's Award for Export Achievement. At a ceremony at Dartford, the award was presented by Field Marshal The Lord Brammall, Lord Lieutenant of Greater London. The Queen's Award flag has flown outside the Dartford works ever since. Buckingham Palace also sent an invitation to Caterham to attend a function. Graham Nearn went as MD, David Wakefield as the person responsible for exports, and Ian Cowdrey as one of the longest-serving production workers.

Another project, which began in January 1993, was no less than a turbocharged version of the Vauxhall 2-litre Seven. Vauxhall had introduced a turbo engine in the Calibra, featuring a state-of-the-art Garrett T2.5 system built into the exhaust manifold, providing the shortest possible distance between exhaust valve and turbine, minimizing turbo lag. Another reason why Caterham was interested was the extremely compact installation – small enough to fit into a Seven without modification.

The main driving force behind the project was Reg Price, who was a strong advocate of turbocharging. He had built a Clubmans racer for John McLean some 20 years earlier (McLean in fact asked Caterham to build a second Vauxhall turbo car for his own use). Jez Coates was less enthusiastic, but could not deny the potential market for such a car.

The first turbo car took one year to build and was registered L7 VXT. The boost gauge revealed that less than 0.5bar pressure was the maximum used. With so little use being made of the turbo, 'chipping' the installation was irresistible, and 250bhp

Not all JPEs were fluorescent yellow. This black car was the first UK-customer JPE and the first road-equipped JPE. It was the seventh JPE built, all previous production having been exported.

and 250lb.ft of torque were achieved, but the car was hair-raising to drive with the standard chip, at least for Coates: "That car provided me with a unique driving experience: lift-off power oversteer in the wet! It was building boost pressure and power faster than I was lifting my foot off the throttle pedal! Reg Price said that it was driver error and I just needed to get used to it."

It was decided that Caterham should work with the chip manufacturer to tailor it to suit the Seven. Coates was still not convinced and there were problems packaging adequate engine cooling within the confines of the standard bodywork. The final nail in the coffin was the news of the Vauxhall engine's impending demise. L7 VXT was subsequently converted to Rover power.

That was not the last turbocharged Seven. Caterham's Swiss importer, Fredy Kumschick, decided to take up the challenge and develop a limited-edition left-hand-drive Vauxhall turbo car for personal registration in Switzerland. This developed no less than 300bhp! Total cost? No less than £65,000! To date seven cars have been built in Switzerland, and the exciting car made its public debut at the 1996 Geneva Salon.

Meanwhile, John McLean's car, which was completed by the factory in 1994, was fitted with an external intercooler just behind the offside front wheel. The result was an astonishingly rapid, unique, factory-built car capable of 0–60mph in 4.6 seconds and a top speed of nearly 150mph. Although it boasted a power output of 240bhp, the real benefit came in the mid-range where the turbo provided a huge amount of torque – significantly

more in fact than the JPE. McLean went on to race the car regularly, with reliable finishes at the Circuit Paul Ricard 500km and at Spa.

Another abortive project in 1993 was the introduction of a live-axle chassis suitable for a five-speed gearbox, but it is thought that only two such cars were ever built. The live-axle/five-speed 'box concept would, however, be revived two years later for the Rover K-series-engined chassis (see below).

Yet another major problem area where supply difficulties would soon be faced was the gearbox. The mainstay gearbox throughout the late Eighties had been the five-speed unit from the Sierra. In the Rover-engined Seven, especially, the ratios were too tall and there was a certain amount of criticism in the press about this. Additionally, Caterham realized that the old Sierra 'box would not last forever (production in Germany was set to end in September 1995), so it began to think about a replacement. In 1989, Ford had introduced the MT75 gearbox, which was impossible to fit as it had an integral bellhousing which bolted only to Ford engines.

Most gearboxes, by that stage, were exclusively for front-wheel-drive vehicles. The seminal German-made ZF rear-drive 'box was just too expensive, the in-line Rover 'box used by TVR was too big, some alternatives were too heavy, and others had a limited shelf-life. A feeling grew that Caterham would have to develop its own gearbox. A sub-contractor contacted Caterham saying that they could do just that and so work began – not just a replacement five-speeder, but one with six forward ratios.

The K-series cried out for more power to confirm its position as the next-generation engine for the Seven. In 1993 came the 128bhp Supersport version of the K-series, which finally gave the Ford Supersprint engine a run for its money.

The six-speed gearbox represented the single largest engineering task ever undertaken by Caterham, easily the most complicated item on any car, short of the engine. Frankly, Caterham underestimated the complications involved, taking far longer than anticipated to reach production. Having said that, the project progressed with remarkably few technical glitches. The main problems centred around sub-contractors: two out of the original three teams had to be replaced, costing a full year in getting the 'box to the marketplace.

Although launched at the 1993 Motor Show, the six-speed gearbox took until April 1995 to reach true production. It was the first British-made six-speed gearbox on the market.

As a piece of design it was quite advanced, with all-alloy construction (making it 3kg lighter than the old five-speed 'box despite the additional ratio), diecast exterior cases, needle-roller bearings on the mainshaft and helical gears inside. But clever use was made of Ford parts, particularly in the difficult area of synchromesh technology, so that although all the casing, gears, shafts and selectors were Caterham-designed, over half the parts were actually derived from Ford.

The effectiveness of the 'box was readily appreciated by the motoring press. The ratios were chosen specifically for the Seven, and the impact – particularly on the K-series, which was always over-geared with a five-speed – was dramatic. Instead

By 1993 the K-series Seven was fitted with spoked alloy wheels as standard.

In 1993 Caterham Cars was presented with the Queen's Award for Export Achievement by Field Marshal Brammell at the Dartford factory. Over 50% of production had been exported the previous year.

of an over-driven top gear, the six-speed had a direct-drive top gear, the equivalent of fourth on the old five-speed 'box. Higher gearing could be achieved if required by using a higher differential ratio available from Ford.

Initially, first gear equated to 3.05:1 with top gear driven directly, but when design responsibility for the 'box was brought back in-house in 1994, the ratios were revised to stack them even closer. "It makes the six-speed unit in a Ferrari F355 look like a tractor 'box in terms of the spread of ratios," commented Jez Coates.

It was immediately a popular choice as a £1,350 option. In premium markets like Japan, a six-speeder became *de rigueur*. Ultimately, of course, the six-speed 'box will become the *only* brand-new gearbox option when the Ford five-speed 'box dies.

Since the creation of the universal chassis in 1986, chassis developments had continued apace. Both the Vauxhall and the Rover engines needed their own special chassis, so there were now six types of de Dion chassis (right-hand-drive and left-hand-drive versions of Ford, Vauxhall and Rover power). So in 1994 the chassis was redesigned to be capable of fitting any engine by incorporating several sets of mounting points and bolt-in upper engine bay diagonals to make engine installation easier for the factory and for kit customers. The 1994 chassis had the effect of reducing the number of chassis Caterham needed to keep in stock from 70 down to between 10 and 15. That saved Caterham around £150,000 in freed-up stock.

Another development for the 1994 model year

From 1993 the HPC gained standard fuel injection so there were no longer carbs sticking out of the side of the engine. Also new for the HPC was a smart grille incorporating the '7' logo.

was an enlarged foot box which gave about two inches of extra legroom.

As the world recession dragged into 1995, price-sensitive markets like Europe were always looking for more economical ways to buy Sevens. In Europe, the only engines Caterham could sell were catalyzed units (*ie* Rover and Vauxhall). So in 1995 Caterham began offering a K-series engine with a live rear axle, which was a considerably cheaper option than the de Dion system. Such cars were initially sold to Belgium and Japan, but other countries will surely follow suit.

With this possibility in mind, a new universal live-axle chassis was created for 1995. This was capable of taking Ford or Rover engines and four or five-speed gearboxes. In some ways this was an ironic situation because 10 years after the supposed demise of the live rear axle, here was Caterham still

developing the live-axle chassis, apparently more popular than it had ever been!

Graham Nearn smiles as he recalls the press presentation at the Caterham stand at the 1995 Motor Show. "A number of other manufacturers were launching cars they described as Sevens for the next century. I said: 'Here's our Seven for the next century' and pulled the covers off our £9,000 Classic model! That's my view on the whole thing – any new Seven ought to undercut the existing one, not cost twice as much."

But there was no denying the changes in attitude towards Caterham, as Jez Coates confirms: "There has been a sea-change in the way people view us. In the Eighties it was quite usual for people to say: 'I want to fit some Revolution wheels and different tyres to my Seven – what do you recommend?'. We would say, you should fit such-and-such a size of

The size of the main Dartford workshop can be appreciated from this shot. In build are well over a dozen Sevens, including one of the rare JPEs.

Jez Coates, Graham Nearn and Jonathan Palmer with the brand-new six-speed gearbox at its launch at the 1993 Earls Court Motor Show.

wheel and such-and-such a tyre. But people wouldn't listen and would go out and fit whatever they wanted to fit. But today, customers by and large follow the advice we give because they appreciate our experience and development work with the car and the reasoning behind our recommendations.

"Also there are far fewer cars fitted with non-standard engines. The standard-specification car has a lot more value in the marketplace. There may be other power units which seem attractive, but the resale value of a Seven fitted with a non-standard engine will be much lower."

Today, Caterham's customer base is wide-ranging, from the impecunious enthusiast seeking to buy into a legend, to the professional who demands one of the best-handling and quickest cars money can buy. As a result, Caterham's range of cars is correspondingly wide. In fact, in an idle moment someone calculated that the total number of permutations of Seven packages numbered '6 billion billion' – excluding paint and trim combinations!

There are three forms of build: CKD kit (complete knock-down in kit form, taking 80 hours to finish), component form (needing just 20 hours' work to finish) and fully-built. If someone knows about it, it is still possible to buy a really basic kit and source some of the mechanical parts yourself.

There are Ford engines for the traditionalist, Rover and Vauxhall engines which appeal to customers looking for a modern Seven (who do not necessarily place such high value on the Lotus and

Caterham never forgot its kit-built roots. Here a body/chassis unit is displayed at the 1995 Stoneleigh National Kit Car Show.

A new parts and service reception area at Dartford enhanced the public face of Caterham in 1995.

Ford origins of the car), and full-house engines for the serious driver or racer.

Caterham's patience and efforts with the Rover engine were at last rewarded in 1994 when it proved to be the most popular engine choice in the de Dion car, which is good news as Caterham moves towards the next century and Ford power inevitably fades away.

Caterham has continued its quest to place its customers first, and the tales of satisfied customers tells all. There is a comprehensive build manual for buyers of kit-form Sevens, detailing every last task to be performed. In addition, there is a video entitled *Building the Legend*, which demonstrates the build process in glorious technicolour, as they say. A customer helpline for queries is open every day except Sundays and reassuringly takes only 10–20 calls daily.

Whereas in the Eighties there was one development car and one press/demonstrator, it is a measure of the company's growth that today there are at least two dedicated demonstrators, at least two K-series hire cars, usually two or three press cars and a fleet of development cars.

The 1996 model year Seven, available from January 1, 1996, incorporated some significant changes. The chassis was once again stiffened (by some 30%).

To accompany the chassis changes, it was decided that the suspension should receive some attention, as it was now five years since Bilstein dampers had been standardized. Jez Coates and Reg Price travelled up to Derbyshire, just as they had done five years before, and played around with what Coates described as 'shades of grey' changes. "It was very difficult to pick holes in what we already had," said Coates, "and it got to the stage where we were taking hump-back bridges at 85mph to make tiny changes in the suspension. We realized that it would be very hard for anyone to discern the differences, so I suggested adopting a different approach: try to improve ride quality, which would mean that 100% of people would gain an immediate benefit."

The Bilstein dampers were revalved and lengthened for more consistent performance, while the anti-roll bar rates were revised and roll-on camber increased, while the suspension was improved with anti-dive geometry. The overall effect was to smooth out the ride, particularly over bumpy surfaces.

The interior of the 1996 Seven was much improved: note the Caterham-branded instruments and, significantly, the resited handbrake lever.

Also, the roll-over bar was increased in height by 1.5in (3.8cm) and sloped forward, still fitting snugly under the hood. Caterham-branded instruments replaced the VDO items and a new lightweight wiring loom was introduced (the wiring for the front lights was now carried inside the wing tubing to improve tidiness). Rover's immobilizer became a standard fitment on 1.6-litre K-series-powered cars and uprated and lightened seats (almost half the weight of before) were fitted.

Perhaps the most significant change for 1996 was the adoption of the 1.6-litre Rover K-series engine in place of the old 1.4 (except for race cars). As early as 1993, Caterham had trial-fitted the 1.8-litre K-series engine, which it was able to do by courtesy of its special relationship with Rover. Jez

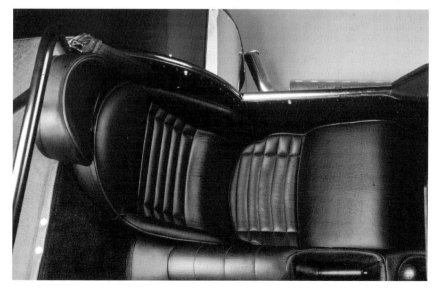

Another advance for 1996 was this new lightweight seat design.

The last factory-built 1.4-litre Sevens were a run of the limited-edition Road-Sport in January 1996. Almost £4,000 worth of extras was added, making this a bargain Seven.

The last factory-built 1.4-litre Sevens were a run of the limited-edition Road-Sport in January 1996. Almost £4,000 worth of extras was added, making this a bargain Seven.

Coates remembers: "The development engineers at Rover came back to us and persuaded us that the 1600 engine was a better choice: for instance, it produced peak power at 500rpm higher than the 1800, because the 1600 had a shorter-stroke crank, and it had better NVH (noise, vibration and harshness) characteristics. We could also produce a much more effective Supersport package on the 1600, as the valves were a limiting factor on the 1800 unit (we reckoned that a 1800 Supersport would produce only a few extra horses than the 1600 version). Finally, there was a cost implication which could not be ignored. But we have not totally discounted the 1800 unit: only time will tell whether it has a place in the Seven."

The 1.6-litre K-series developed significantly more power than the 1400 (at 115bhp), and more torque, as well as answering those critics for whom a 1400 engine never seemed big enough. For Caterham, the changes meant moving into a new era of engine management systems, since the Rover unit incorporated a computerized engine immobilizer, set up to communicate with the ECU. It also meant another round of noise, emissions, fuel consumption and radio interference suppression tests.

As an aftermarket option, there was once again a Supersport package, boosting power as high as 138bhp. This was developed by Rover especially for Caterham.

And a 38-year-old tradition was ended when the last remaining item from the original Seven – the handbrake – was resited from under the dash to a position on the stiffened tunnel (on de Dion cars only). This was developed from work completed on the 21.

As the 1.6-litre K-series took over the reins in the Seven's engine bay, a run-out limited edition of 30 1.4-litre K-series Supersport Sevens was announced in January 1996. Called the Road-Sport, it was based on the new '96 chassis and came with a six-speed gearbox as standard. The Road-Sport had several unique features: carbonfibre front wings and stoneguards, metallic paint finish (green or yellow), anthracite-finish alloy wheels, black grille and windscreen surround, lightweight leather seats, Momo steering wheel, painted roll-over bar, personalized jacket, unique decals and a free driver training day.

Each of the 30 Road-Sports carried a numbered plaque on the dashboard and retailed at £16,995 in component form, or £20,155 fully-built. It was also possible to upgrade it to race spec.

Looking ahead, the Vauxhall engine will eventually die (it ceased to be fitted to Vauxhall cars in 1995) and a replacement will have to be found. It is a distinct possibility that the larger K-series engines from Rover will be fitted: the 1.8-litre variable valve timing unit from the MGF looks a natural, if Rover have enough capacity to sell it to external customers. And of course Caterham introduced its VHP (Very High Performance) version of the 1.8-litre engine for the 21 in the course of 1996 *(see Chapter 9)*.

One final twist to the tale is occurring at the time of writing, in summer 1996: the Caterham Cars sales site is moving! Graham Nearn learned that a Layhams Vauxhall agency in the centre of Caterham town was ceasing and he asked them what they were doing with the site. When they said: "Selling it!", he realized here was a great opportunity.

"It was too good to miss. Here was an established car sales site in the centre of Caterham, right next to the station and with easier access to the M25. We could move with no disruption to staff. The negotiations took two weeks."

The new site has a glass-fronted showroom, a 5,000sq ft workshop (which might be used for servicing or the display of Caterham's historic collection of cars). There is also an old theatre to the rear of the site, which Nearn intends to redevelop.

"The new sales and showroom site consolidates what we're doing and moves us on in terms of status. We can have a permanent display of vehicles which people can look in at seven days a week. At the end of the day, it's the *cars* that sell, but premises certainly help.

"We are at an interesting point in our history: the Seven has been developed tremendously over the last few years and will continue to develop under the skin. But we are also moving into a new era with the 21, the first Caterham whose shape strikes out in its own direction. It's a very exciting time."

CHAPTER 5

Racing the Seven

From sprints and relays to 24-hour marathons

The Seven and competition are inseparable. Conceived by Colin Chapman as a dual-purpose car for road use during the week and at race meetings on weekends, the Seven was perfectly suited to its role. Here was a car which could be enjoyed on the way to the circuit *and* be competitive on the day.

Indeed the Seven's first ever appearance was at a competitive event. In September 1957, Edward Lewis drove the new Lotus Mark 7 prototype at the Brighton Speed Trials (and came second in class). A day later he won the 1,100cc class at the Prescott hillclimb and before the year was out he was circuit racing, too.

Circuit racing was, of course, Chapman's passion. One of the reasons for creating the Seven was to build a car which could be bought cheaply and raced competitively. He specifically targeted the successful Bucklers, which were basic sportscars sold as a simple chassis by Dick Buckler from premises in Berkshire. When John Derisley won the Buckler Challenge Trophy in 1958 in a Seven, Chapman's attention was well and truly caught. Derisley went on to drive a works Seven with great success.

But despite its obvious competition potential, Chapman soon lost real interest in the model. His sights were set on higher things with the Mark 8, Mark 9 and Eleven.

For the average amateur racer the Seven seemed heaven-sent. Like the Six before it, it seemed capable of beating just about every other car. It provided the perfect introduction to motorsport for many drivers – as the roll call of famous names who cut their racing teeth in a Seven testifies *(see Appendix E)*.

In an historic first, which has sadly been repeated many times since, the 750 Motor Club reacted to the Seven's success by slapping restrictions on its eligibility: Sevens were not allowed to have the de Dion axle or disc brakes and were restricted to a basic side-valve engine.

Graham Hill cut his teeth on the first Climax-engined Super Seven. At the Boxing Day Brands Hatch meeting in 1958, he stormed ahead of Lotus Elevens, Elvas and the like to win on the car's maiden outing.

Later in the Seven's life, journalist Jabby Crombac effectively started a one-make series in France in 1964 when he created Formula France specifically for the Lotus Seven. Such famous names as Cevert, Pescarolo, Depailler and Servoz-Gavin raced in this formula, which was warmly received by everyone who came into contact with it.

Despite Chapman's essential indifference to the Seven, Lotus still supported the model competitively. One factory-modified car, the so-called 7½, had independent rear suspension and an adjustable double-wishbone set-up at the front. It was in this car that Chapman had his last race in a Seven in the Six Hour Relay at Silverstone in 1962.

Another factory special was the 37 (or Three-7), a car created in 1965 to do battle with the dominant Mallocks in Clubmans racing. But because of the pressures of Lotus' other involvements, it did not enter production. Instead, Lotus sales manager John Berry campaigned the prototype with great success, followed by Tim Goss, to whom the Three-7 passed. The idea developed fully in 1969 when Tim Goss asked the factory to build a very special Seven called the 7X. This had Formula 3-type front suspension, an independent rear and very low bodywork. With semi-factory backing, it was convincingly victorious in its first outing and ran away with the Clubmans title in 1970.

The Lotus Seven had certainly made its presence felt. So much so in fact that, when production of the Seven passed to Caterham, the RAC was reluctant to admit the car on to the Modsports or the newly created Prodsports grids. The BRSCC's objections to the Seven were rather inconsistent.

Had it not been for the Lotus Mark 6's competition exploits the Seven might never have happened. Here POP 444 (the ex-Ian Smith Mark 6) slides out of Druids at Brands Hatch in the hands of B R Millbank.

Extract from an early Seven brochure advertising the model's first clutch of competition wins. Note the preponderance of hillclimb entries, the penchant of Edward Lewis, who campaigned the very first Seven.

By special Customs concession, the completed Seven, as an amateur-assembled car, is not subject to Purchase Tax. The resultant low overall cost of the car affords outstanding value.

Visit your Lotus centre today to inspect the Seven and make an appointment for a demonstration.

Your Lotus Centre will be pleased to advise you on any points before and after you buy your Seven, and can provide full servicing facilities for the completed car.

Lotus Seven Recent Results

BUGATTI OWNERS CLUB NATIONAL OPEN HILL CLIMB PRESCOTT 2.5.59
(Sports Cars up to 1100cc)
FIRST Seven 'C'

MAIDSTONE & MID KENT CC NATIONAL RACE MEETING SILVERSTONE 9.5.59
(Sports Cars up to 1500cc)
FIRST Seven 'C'

BARC HILL CLIMB BRUNTON 6.9.59
(Sports Cars up to 1100cc)
FIRST Seven 'A'
(Novices Award)

BARC HILL CLIMB FIRLE 31.5.59
FIRST Seven 'C'
Robe Down Autocross 24.5.59
FASTEST TIME OF THE DAY
Seven 'F'

BUGATTI OWNER'S CLUB NATIONAL OPEN HILL CLIMB PRESCOTT 13.9.59
(Sports Cars up to 1100cc)
FIRST Seven 'C' (and F.T.D Sports Cars)
THIRD Seven 'A'

THAMES ESTUARY AC SPEED TRIAL BRANDS HATCH 7.6.59
Class M
FIRST Seven 'C'

SHELSLEY WALSH NATIONAL HILL CLIMB 14.6.59
(Sports Cars up to 1500cc)
FIRST Seven 'C'

NOTTINGHAM SPORTS CAR CLUB RACE MEETING SILVERSTONE 13.6.59
(Sports Cars up to 1172cc)
FIRST Seven 'F'
SECOND Seven 'F'
THIRD Seven 'F'

BUGATTI OWNERS' CLUB HILL CLIMB PRESCOTT 20.6.59
(Sports Cars up to 1100cc)
FIRST Seven 'C'

BARC MEMBERS' MEETING GOODWOOD 27.6.59
(Sports Cars up to 1200cc)
FIRST Seven 'F'

ASTON MARTIN OWNERS' CLUB "ST. JOHN HORSFALL" RACE MEETING 11.7.59
(Sports Cars up to 1300cc)
FIRST Seven 'C'

HERTS COUNTY HILL CLIMB WEST-BROOK HAY 10.7.59
(Sports Cars up to 1100cc)
FIRST Seven 'C'

GREAT AUCLUM HILL CLIMB 8.8.59
(Sports Cars up to 1100cc)
FIRST Seven 'C'
(Sports Cars over 1100cc)
FIRST Seven 'F' and new record

Graham Hill was the first racer to try the new Climax-powered Super Seven at the Brands Hatch meeting of Boxing Day 1958. He won the 1,100cc event outright against streamlined opposition.

This was Lotus' Series 2 development car, here admirably demonstrating the Seven's dual-purpose role as a fine road and circuit sportscar.

Sevens were modified where necessary, as with Tony Goodwin's GT-prepared Series 1 side-valve car, seen here racing at Brands with its special hardtop in 1963.

Peter Brand assembles one of a series of 14 Sevens built especially for the Formula France one-make race series in 1964.

Sevens dominated Clubmans racing in the mid-Sixties, as can be appreciated from this BRSCC meeting at Cadwell Park.

The rather special Lotus 7 1/2 built by Lotus employees Hugh Haskell and Don Gadd featured independent rear suspension and disc brakes.

Lotus Three-7 as campaigned by John Berry, driving. This was to have been an official Lotus racing Seven, but it never made it as such, although it was raced successfully by John Berry and later by Tim Goss.

Tim Goss leads this Clubmans race in his highly modified Seven, dubbed the 7X. He won the 1970 championship outright.

First it said that Prodsports cars had to be listed in *Autocar* – but the Seven *was* listed. Then it said that, as a kit-car, the Seven was ineligible – but the Ginetta G15, also a kit-car, was admitted. Eventually Graham Nearn's persistence paid off and, in late 1974, the *RAC Blue Book* finally admitted the Seven into the Modsports category for the 1975 season.

Former Clubmans racer David Bettinson in a Caterham prepared by Reg Price literally walked away with the first race of the season. The car was highly developed, with a lightened and strengthened chassis, a Holbay engine resited further back in the chassis, a close-ratio gearbox, double wishbones at the front and a Panhard rod at the rear.

Reg Price recalls the Seven's first event at Thruxton: "It was in torrential rain. We were running on the latest F3 rubber and, from about seventh position at the start, the car took the lead after four laps and just pulled away for the rest of the race."

But a protest had been received about the Seven. It turned out that the car's eligibility had only been published in an addendum to the *RAC Blue Book* and this was adjudged to be strictly against the letter of the law, which stated that eligibility depended on the car being *in* the *Blue Book*. So for the rest of the season, the car could only race if everyone else in the field agreed to sign it in! Since the Caterham was so fast, not everybody always wanted to sign, notably some exponents of the Morgan and Lotus Elan…

The following year, Bettinson scored third overall and a class win in the Modsports series and went on to a further three seasons of successful racing.

Towards the end of the 1979 season, Bettinson had agreed to sell the Reg Price-modified car to Rob Cox-Allison, but on the very last race of the season at Thruxton the car was destroyed in a spectacular accident.

Not to be dissuaded, Cox-Allison bought the written-off racer along with a new chassis which Reg Price had been building. Using this as a basis, he created the Black Brick, so called because it had the aerodynamics of a brick and a thumping brick-like hardtop. His machine proved to be highly competitive in Modsports and GT racing. In his first season, he took 3.5 seconds off the existing lap record at Thruxton!

Three versions were built in total, spanning some six seasons. One version had a 300bhp Formula 2 engine fitted! Another had Chevron Formula 2 suspension, a Quaife LSD and a Leeson straight-cut gearbox. As Black Brick developed it began to look less and less like a Seven, sporting side pods, a deep front spoiler and a Maurice Gomm biplane wing on the back! Pretty it was not, but it certainly won its fair share of the spoils, notably a class win in the 1982 STP Modified Sports Car championship, followed by an outright win the following year, victory in the 1984 Donington GT championship and again in the BARC GT championship.

However, the Seven was still ineligible for BRSCC Prodsports. Graham Nearn instituted a concerted campaign to get the Caterham in, culminating in a run of T-shirts being printed with the slogan 'Too Fast to Race'. Prodsports champion Chris Meek drove a Super Seven at a demonstration drive in the lunch break at a Donington Prodsports meeting and gave Caterham a useful

In the Seventies, the astonishing Black Brick (seen here at Donington in the hands of Rob Cox-Allison) notched up win after win in the Modsports series, making it virtually unbeatable.

In 1978 a Lotus Seven S4 won the RAC and BTRDA Autotest championships in the hands of Stephen Stringer, while Felicity Kerr won the women's title.

bargaining chip when he said: "It has more right to be accepted in Prodsports than some of the cars racing of which only a few were made... It is ideal for experienced and novice drivers alike. I do not understand what the ban is about."

Eventually the RAC's ban on Caterhams so incensed Graham Nearn that in 1980 he contacted his local MP, who happened to be Sir Geoffrey Howe (later Chancellor and Foreign Secretary). His letter emphasized the fact that a British production car was ineligible for a British production car race series, while Japanese cars were happily admitted. Geoffrey Howe responded, saying he would look into the matter, while he also wrote to Sir Clive Bossom, head of the RAC.

"Suddenly it all happened," recalls Graham Nearn. "We were accepted at long last, albeit in the tougher Class B. This meant the Caterham was up against Morgans, TVRs and other cars with engines up to 2.3 litres, but we accepted the compromise to get our foot in the door. The Seven had to run with a windscreen fitted and a standard 84bhp Ford 1600 engine."

Caterham ran a works Seven that first season (1980), but it was hopelessly outclassed. Driven by various Caterham employees and associates, including Clive Roberts, David Wakefield, Dave Bettinson, Chris Meek and Jeremy Walton, its success rate was negligible.

Reg Price also began his racing career in the works Seven despite being 40 years old: "You're not supposed to start a racing career at that age, but Fangio did, so I thought there was hope. I managed to pass Chris Meekin's Panther Lima 2.3 on the bends, but he always caught me on the straights."

The following year, 1981, the Seven was allowed

to race in the more suitable ranks of Class C. The works entry was joined by several privateers, recreating the atmosphere of the early days of Lotus Seven racing after an absence of many years.

The Seven immediately began to make its dominance felt. John Mayne won his class in the championship in 1981, while John Stenning did the same in 1982. Also in 1982 Gary White campaigned a Sprint in the Donington Production GT championship and won it outright. Then in 1983 Maynard Soares won the Prodsports title outright, only to be penalized on a technicality and so lose the title to a Porsche.

In both 1983 and 1984, Sevens took part in Britain's only round-the-clock motor race, the Willhire 24 Hours at Snetterton. In the first year, Maynard Soares, Clive Roberts and Jeremy Coulter (author of MRP's first book on the Lotus and Caterham Sevens) survived 900 laps of the circuit to finish eighth overall and second in class after losing almost an hour during the night to change a split fuel tank.

In 1984 the Super Seven Drivers Team of John Stenning, Maynard Soares and Gary White finished second in class again after being assaulted several times by saloon cars and having the fuel tank fall out! The car, driven by Caterham's own team of Clive Roberts, Richard Cleare and Jeremy Coulter, was punted off the track and did not finish. Even-

For several years in the mid-Seventies, ShellSport ran a Caterham Seven as a parade car, seen here doing its duty at Snetterton in 1976.

Pole positions and Sevens went side-by-side. This Caterham has beaten a host of exotic machinery to pole in a late-Seventies event for production sportscars.

tually the Seven could no longer compete in the Willhire event because sportscars became ineligible.

Another Caterham success came in the 1983 Six Hour Relay, run by the 750 Motor Club at Silverstone. The team consisted of just two cars and five drivers (Reg Price, Clive Roberts, Gary White and *Classic Car* staffers Jeremy Coulter and Tony Dron). One car circulated totally reliably for five of the six hours, so that it was only really necessary for the other car (Gary White's) to go out when the primary car came in for fuel and a driver change. Since the Seven is so light and therefore so economical, the technique of running a heavy fuel load worked: so well, in fact, that the team won the event on handicap. Clive Roberts' daughter was born just after this win and he named her Lauren (after the laurel wreath of victory).

The workforce at Caterham began taking an increasing interest in racing from the mid-Eighties. Jez Coates and Simon Wheeler (who had joined Caterham as an assembler and quickly graduated to sales manager) built up two Post Office red racers and established what Coates described as a 'syndicate', which they called Last of the Summer Wine Goes Racing, which would eventually encompass four members: Jez Coates (Cleggie), Simon Wheeler (Foggie), Reg Price (Compo) and Jeremy Coulter (Nora). The first car was built in their own time and was loaned by Caterham on the understanding that if it was damaged, the benders would be the menders.

Fitted with pushrod engines, the syndicate became seduced into building more and more powerful versions, in conjunction with Jeremy Coulter, whose own car was in effect the second 'official'

'Last of the Summer Wine Goes Racing' was the name under which Caterham employees raced at sprints and relays. Pictured here after a relay race at Oulton Park in 1985 are (left to right): Jez Coates, Joe Main (mechanic), Simon Wheeler, Reg Price and Jeremy Coulter.

Caterham car. The tuning reached ridiculous levels: the compression ratios went as high as 12:1 and the engines were developing in excess of 170bhp, all using the most basic of parts. With such machines the works syndicate had a busy – and often exhilarating – time competing in events such as Jaguar Drivers Club races.

In July 1985 there was a one-off Colin Chapman Memorial race at Brands Hatch especially for Sevens. The Caterham syndicate raced their car while as many other cars as possible were gathered for the grid: racers even came from as far afield as Germany, with Detlef Schwarz arriving in his distinctive Seven. The line-up totalled about 25 cars and the whole event was a tremendous success, Bob Sands emerging victorious in a Lotus Seven Twin Cam.

At the same time, Prodsports racing was being phased-out by the BRSCC and in its place a variety of one-make race series were being substituted. Alfa Romeo and Porsche were already slated for their own one-make series and John Nicol, the competition director of the BRSCC, suggested at the Chapman Memorial meeting that a one-make series should be created for Caterhams. Nicol and Graham Nearn discussed the possibility in detail and agreed that it had great potential.

Caterham duly drew up a set of regulations for the 1986 season. Graham Nearn: "To keep a lid on the running costs, we decided that only road-going cars would be eligible. If there were any disputes, we would refer to the standard catalogue specification to resolve them."

There would be three classes, loosely based around the road-going models Caterham was selling at that time. Class A would be for Lotus or

On the Seven's return to Prodsports racing, Maynard Soares all but won the 1983 title, coming second on a technicality. Here he touches wheels with an on-the-limit Scirocco.

Robin Gray campaigned his Lotus Twin Cam-powered Seven with tremendous success in 1985, after sportscar racing regulations were relaxed to cover road-going cars.

BDR twin-cam-powered cars or pushrod cars with a free tuning specification, allowing them to reach around the same power output as the twin-cams. With a high-lift cam, bigger valves and so on, a Ford crossflow engine could be pushed up to around 170bhp. Class B was based around the 135bhp Ford 1700 Supersprint engine with specified valve lifts, duration and so on, with a realistic maximum of about 150bhp. Class C was for less highly tuned Ford 1600 pushrod cars developing up to about 120bhp.

A man who was to be significant in later years of Caterham racing, Jim McDougall, was one of the early racers in a Class B car he had just built up from a kit. He remembers receiving the regulations for the 1986 season: "There were basically one-and-a-half type-written pages of rules and that was that! They outlined the three engine classes and

gave indications as to what could and could not be fitted: LSD and dry-sumping was acceptable and a roll-over bar and road legal tyres of a maximum of 6in width were mandatory. There wasn't a lot else!"

There was no prize fund and some people asked what was the point of racing. Competitor Ian Cornick summed it up: "Just personal satisfaction. That's the way it should be. It keeps it as a sport." A further attraction was that a whole season could cost as little as £2,000.

It was a tentative beginning. Some 23 competitors registered for the first season, but not all of them in fact raced. The first races of the season had small grids and almost all interest was in Class A. Many of the entrants were directly related to Caterham – Coates, Price, Wheeler and Coulter for instance, but as the year progressed, privateer interest began to grow.

During the 1985 Colin Chapman Memorial Race exclusively for Sevens: German Detler Schwarz's wide-shod Seven fends off a challenge from Reg Price (14) and Jeremy Coulter (18).

The first race of 1986 was at Mallory Park on March 30. Nine cars finished the event (the winner being Kevin Musson, who was the only man who finished in Class B). The average grid through the season's racing (some seven meetings) hovered around a dozen. Some of the season's events were held together with a fledgling Kit Cars and Specials series, a liaison which did not last long.

The racing was very slow by today's standards (even a fast circuit like Castle Combe was completed at an average speed of only 87.3mph) but the flavour was right: finishes were nearly always very close and the type of person attracted to the event was typically an enthusiastic amateur clubman. Jim McDougall explains another attraction of Seven racing: "The Caterham sold itself to me because it was so cheap to buy and yet so fast – and you could use the car on the road between meetings. I even managed to sell my car after the first season for a modest profit. I doubt if you could do that in any form of motorsport today!"

Ex-Mini racer Kelvin Foy and Fergus Oakley were neck-and-neck for the championship by the final round at Donington, Oakley being ahead by just one point. In the failing October light the 10-lap race was cut to just five laps. Foy led for most of the first three laps, but on lap four he was passed by an out-of-control Coulter, forcing him to a stand-still, only to be severely shunted by Oakley. Amid the drama, it looked like Oakley had taken the championship. But then the organizers announced that, because of the encroaching darkness, the chequered flag had been waved at the end of lap three and no-one had seen it!

So Kelvin Foy won overall in his Class A car, with Fergus Oakley second. Graham Sykes was third overall and winner in Class C, while Jim McDougall was fifth overall to win an under-represented Class B. The series was well and truly established.

Andy Noble joined Caterham Cars in 1986 and was destined to become the racing lynch-pin of the organization. The first race which he attended was at Cadwell Park and he was immediately struck by the fact that, of the 11 starters on the grid, six were cars owned by Caterham. "From that moment, my crusade became getting people involved in Seven racing."

So for the 1987 season, Noble became racing co-ordinator, virtually running the series from home on an Amstrad PC, compiling race results and producing a newsletter after each event.

There were some rule changes for 1987, prepared by Jez Coates and Simon Wheeler, with input from Jim McDougall. These sought to control camshafts by specifying valve lifts and also limiting carb sizes, choke sizes and capacity. Shock absorbers were also standardized and there were further restrictions on suspension.

Entries were up slightly on the previous year with, for example, 16 entrants at the second meeting of the season at Donington. The first race at Snetterton was won by Jeremy Coulter in a monster of a Seven powered by an ex-hot rod 1700 crossflow engine reputedly developing 190bhp! After another win at Oulton Park and a third at Brands Hatch, Coulter stopped racing in the series.

That left the door open for the others. There

The Brands Hatch race of the inaugural year's Seven racing in 1986 was run in dreadful conditions. Reg Price lines up in pole in front of Caterham's Simon Wheeler; Price went on to win the race.

were really only two serious contenders who stayed in the series for the whole season: Kelvin Foy (Class A) and George Cubitt (Class B) who scored points in virtually every round to win the championship overall by a clear 15 points. HPC instructor John Lyon won in Class C. Although he was sometimes the only starter in that class, he was the class victor in every single round in which he entered – a portent of things to come.

The 1988 season was the first to attract outside sponsorship. Andy Noble agreed a deal with *World Sportscars* magazine whereby they publicized the series and offered some prize money. The entry numbers began to build up as a consequence.

There is no question who dominated the series in 1988. Despite racing in Class B, one up from the previous year, John Lyon was overall winner at the first three meetings of the season at Mallory Park, Cadwell Park and Snetterton. He and Cliff Watts basically swapped positions at the top of the table for the rest of the season, but Lyon held sway, finishing the year with 80 points against Watts' 56, who won Class A convincingly. Class C was won by Graham Sykes, narrowly ahead of Len Unwin and Tim Seward. Graham Nearn's son Robert finished equal fifth in Class C in his debut year. 1988 was also the first year that another significant newcomer raced: Magnus Laird, who won Class A at

Jim McDougall battles with the conditions at Brands Hatch, 1986. That year he came fifth overall and won Class B. McDougall would return to run the series during 1990.

Castle Combe, July 1986: Reg Price defends his position on his way to winning this mid-season event. Caterham Cars' own team made up much of the grid during the first years of the series.

The line-up for the start at Castle Combe in 1987. By this time, grid sizes were rising gradually but surely, typically around 15 drivers starting each race.

Donington in August.

Back with the Caterham works syndicate, there was a feeling that the tremendous preparation effort required for a typical club race at Mallory Park which lasted just 10 minutes simply wasn't worth it. Far more enjoyable, it was reasoned, to go for the long-distance endurance races and relays.

This approach culminated in Caterham taking a car to the Nurburgring 24-hour race in 1987. For the lads at Caterham, this was near enough the ultimate race on perhaps the world's finest circuit. Coulter called it "the most complete motor race in the world" and was baffled by the fact that only one other British team made it over. The Caterham team comprised Coates, Price and Coulter, with Andy Noble as team manager.

For Caterham, the event was a disaster before it had even begun. For a start, the team's Escort XR3i was shunted from behind at high speed on the autobahn by a VW Golf whose driver had fallen asleep at the wheel. Jez Coates: "Our car pummelled into the barrier and the tailgate opened up like Jonah the whale, emptying out all our race gear on to the autobahn. We were all dazed, but Reg was running around picking up helmets and bits of iron saying, 'Come on, we've got a race to get to in five hours!'"

Even when they finally arrived at the 'Ring, there were problems: to get through scrutineering, a coke can had to be added to the exhaust to make it quiet enough. In qualifying, there was a sudden panic that the team had not done enough to qualify (out

Nurburgring 24 Hours, 1987: Andy Noble and Jeremy Coulter consult driver Reg Price about a continuing misfire. Note the extra lights on the front which cooked the battery during the hours of darkness.

A cloud of smoke betrays the fact that the Seven's run at the 'Ring is all but over. One of the cylinders had been lost.

of 216 entrants, only 180 would be allowed to start). Price went out in the last 10 minutes to make sure of qualification. He didn't realize he had a full tank of fuel on board (some 20 gallons) and that the car was seriously overweight. A third of the way around the circuit, he suffered a big crash which bent the chassis. "We'd trashed two cars before even getting to the start line!"

However, the team had done enough to qualify. During the race, Caterham were pitting next to a team driving a Suzuki Swift, whom they nick-named Team Panic. "They were always in a state of panic," remembers Andy Noble. "They wore white paper suits and looked like the sperm out of the Woody Allen film. Once their car rushed into the pits and sandwiched my legs between their car and ours. 'Sorry', said the driver, rather pathetically. Then they jacked their car up with an over-long extension pipe. When the car dropped back down, the pipe flew over the roof, crumpling the B-pillar as it went, and almost knocked one of their guys out!"

There were more problems with the Caterham's electrics because too many extra lights had been fitted and the battery was slowly cooking. At night, Jez Coates was driving and actually on the pit radio when he span off the track. "Where are you?," asked Andy Noble. "In a field," replied Coates, who was unable to restart because of the flat battery. "I haven't got a clue where I am." So the team set off across the 14-mile long track to try to locate the stricken Seven – which took about half-an-hour. Unable to bump-start the car on wet grass, they had to hook up a spare battery with jump leads to get back into the race.

About 17 hours into the race, the overworked pushrod engine began releasing long plumes of smoke into the air. Andy Noble said they should cut their losses and bring the car in, just going back out for the last few laps at the end of the race. But Reg Price would have none of it, crying: "If the car will run, I will race it!"

Within a lap, the car was running on three cylinders and virtually using more oil than fuel, remembers Price: "I had oil spurting on to the pedals and I stopped, emerging covered in oil in front of a crowd of people. They cottoned on to what I needed and began throwing hundreds of tissues down like confetti!" But by now it was too late and there was no alternative but to retire. The Seven was able to come back out and limp around the track in the dying minutes of the race just so that the team could say 'we finished', even if it was in 92nd place!

For all that, it had been an encouraging experience, remembers Jez Coates: "The response from the crowd to the car was tremendous. Even at 100mph with the hood up you could still hear the people cheering."

In 1988, Caterham returned to the Nurburgring with not one but two Ford pushrod cars. The first was driven by Coates, Price and Andy Noble, while the second car, a factory-supported private entry, was piloted by ex-BMC driver and ex-Touring Car champion Alec Poole, plus Simon Wheeler and John McLean. This was another massive event, with 244 entries, of which only 180 were allowed to start. The event took place over both the old and new tracks (a total of some 16 miles).

This was tough racing. The drivers took stints of 2 hours 40 minutes at the wheel, often with no stops at all because the car was running a heavy fuel load to stay out as long as possible. This proved so gruelling that John McLean in the second works-supported car ended up on oxygen.

It was hoped that by running reasonably low-spec engines, they would prove reliable. First the McLean car dropped one of its valves and severely damaged the engine. Then the other car developed a misfire, but both problems were put right and both cars finished, fourth and fifth in class.

Despite all the troubles, the event was a great success from the point of view of publicity and enjoyment. The response from the crowd was so rapturous that, on his final stint and with nothing to lose, Jez Coates lowered the roof to return the German crowd's applause.

Sadly, the following year Caterham was ineligible for Nurburgring – very disappointing for everybody at Caterham. The next appearance of a works Caterham at the 'Ring would be in 1995…

Back with the domestic race series, the profile of the series was raised still further in 1989 with a new sponsor (*Cars & Car Conversions* magazine). Entry levels were running at a new high point. The regulations had developed, but were still very open, so that anyone who owned a Seven could come along and race in the appropriate Class. The number of entries became so strong that, from the third race of the season at Mallory Park, two separate grids occasionally had to be run: Class A in one grid, Classes B and C in another.

It was during 1989 that a fateful new competitor arrived on the scene, a man called Alex Hawkridge, who raced in a specially built Class A Seven. Hawkridge's history included running the Toleman

The works car campaigned again at the 1988 Nurburgring (one of two Sevens racing) and finished fifth in class in this gruelling event.

Formula 1 team and he was still chairman of the Toleman transport firm. During the year, with support from his racing contacts, he developed his Class A racer into the quickest in the field. By the end of the season, his car was on a winning streak.

But he didn't win the championship – not this year at any rate. The man to beat in 1989 was HPC instructor John Lyon. Moving up from Class B to Class A, he was obviously going to be a formidable force. It was not all plain sailing, however, and he had strong opposition from Magnus Laird and Andy Crockett early in the season. Later on it was

Musician and singer Chris Rea became a passionate advocate of Caterham racing from the late Eighties when he began competing in the series.

Alex Hawkridge who was taking the advantage, but not enough to stop Lyon winning the overall championship by a comfortable margin.

Steve Hammond and Mike Chitty shared the spoils in Class B after a season of close racing, while Graham Nearn's son Robert scored his first racing success by scooping up Class C.

The following year, 1990, Hawkridge changed the character of Seven racing forever. As a competitive character he naturally wanted to win. He also wanted to race in the safest possible scenario, so, using his experience and the contacts he had made through Formula 1, he embarked on a programme of modifications which improved his car's safety. The fact that these were also performance-enhancing was irrelevant from a legal point of view because none of the (fairly lax) regulations was broken.

It was rumoured that Hawkridge spent as much as £100,000 on his car that season with mods like Kevlar wings and F3-style magnesium wheels. Crucially, he enhanced safety by increasing the torsional stiffness of the tub, shipping his chassis to Reynards of Bicester. They bonded carbonfibre inserts into the sides of the car, making it much more rigid. Jez Coates remembers being helicoptered up to see the car: "As he was adding something to the car which was notionally safety-related, it was impossible to outlaw it."

One side-effect of this technological experimentation was that Caterham adopted additional side protection in road and race cars. Not carbonfibre inserts – they would have worked out at around £500 – but an aluminium honeycomb, which cost considerably less (around £60).

Alex Hawkridge spent very large sums of money on his Seven in the 1990 season and dominated Class A. The experience changed the face of Caterham racing forever.

The first corner of the first race of the 1990 season at Cadwell Park witnessed this huge accident. No-one was seriously hurt, probably due to the new side-impact protection.

So for the 1990 season, Caterham offered new chassis with the honeycomb protection. At the first race of the season, at Cadwell Park, there was a monumental accident on the start line. One car, driven by Colin Ridley, was shunted from behind into the tyres, swiped again from behind and then T-boned at more than 70mph, exploding into flames. Luckily he was one of six starters to have a new honeycomb chassis and, although the car was severely squeezed, the driver walked away with just a couple of cracked ribs. In subsequent seasons, honeycombing became mandatory (honeycombing was later fitted to floors as well).

There was some concern that BRSCC scrutineers might react hastily to such a dramatic crash and prevent further racing. But Caterham acted swiftly to make sure that it satisfied all the scrutineers' recommendations, keeping safety the number one priority. These moves included the free issue of a cover for the battery master-switch, and the voluntary inclusion of a flush-fit fuel-filler and honeycomb boot floor. All of these features would be incorporated into the following year's regulations.

On the race track, Hawkridge was partnered in 1990 by ex-world hot rod champion Barry Lee in a second car. Lee effectively staved off the opposition from challenging Hawkridge by driving tight behind him and acting as a sort of 'minder': if anyone looked like coming too close (generally speaking Magnus Laird), Lee would ease back and prevent them getting into a position where they might threaten the lead.

Despite keen competition from Laird, Hawkridge duly won the 1990 series in his highly developed Seven, with Lee coming second in Class A. This is a fairly familiar scenario in club racing: someone with a lot of money to spend wins hands-down. Equally familiar is the reaction of the other drivers: they just give up, unable to compete with the financial clout. And so it was in the Caterham series and the format was all but killed-off. For Graham Nearn, the scene was very reminiscent of what had happened in Modsports, where the well-financed Black Brick virtually killed that formula in the late Seventies.

Because of the large field in 1990, Class A and C had begun to be run together at some circuits (Classes B and C ran together initially, but the numbers involved swung it around to an A/C combination). This was obviously not very satisfactory because Class A was so much quicker than C and indeed changes would be made the following year.

The dominant figures in Class B that year were Ian St John, Mike Chitty and Andrew Haddon (in that order), with Clive Richards performing well, too. Robert Nearn convincingly won Class C for the second year running.

One interesting aside in the 1990 season was an 'extra-curricular' Caterham race at Zandvoort for British racers which did not count toward the series. This took place over Mardi Gras weekend – not ideal for sober racers! One well-known competitor, Peter Hansen, had rather too much to drink at the party on Saturday night. At about 4am he held his keys aloft and asked: "Who wants to drive my car?", and promptly fell unconscious. Come 9am, however, he duly lined up on the start grid. The whole event was a great deal of fun, which is what Seven racing is all about. The race winners were Magnus Laird (Class A), Mike Chitty (Class B) and Robert Nearn (Class C).

John Barker tests the Vauxhall racer prototype at Snetterton prior to the first season (1991).

At the end of an eventful 1990 season it was obvious that major changes needed to be made. In addition to the 'Hawkridge effect' on grids from 1990 – effectively Formula 1 technology being applied in a series designed for amateur dual-purpose racers – Class A was becoming increasingly extreme: Caterham still insisted on the cars being road-legal, taxed and insured, but drivers were turning up with mega-tuned pushrod engines which could never have been used on the road, sporting rock-hard suspension and no trim. The cars only ever saw race-track use, which made a mockery of the 'road-legal' requirement.

In the light of all this, the regulations evidently needed to be changed. Class A would henceforth become a bespoke racing class, and to prevent another Hawkridge scenario, the regulations were tightened up vastly.

The 1991 season was also the first where the new Vauxhall-powered cars could race. Jez Coates opined that these cars should have their own class and be tailored as racecars, albeit convertible back to road use because the standard chassis was used. The idea was to have cars designed to go as quickly as possible.

Therefore the Vauxhall race series was populated by cars with no windscreen, fewer instruments, a special wiring loom, cycle wings, no lighting apart from a foglamp, no spare wheel or wheel carrier and no interior trim. They came with an FIA roll-over bar, brake balance valve, standard Vauxhall engine with larger 48mm Weber carbs, remapped ignition and modified exhaust (so power shot up from around 175bhp to 188bhp with no internal mods). These units were sealed and not allowed to be touched, just as with the Vauxhall-Lotus engines

used in the single-seater formula created the previous year. Running tight controls on the engine also made cars in this series reasonably cheap to run.

Additionally, the specification included a standard close-ratio straight-cut gearbox, LSD, masterswitch, plumbed-in fire extinguisher system and F1-style bag tank with a honeycomb boot board above it. Caterham also spent 5,000 miles on the track developing special Bilstein dampers for the Vauxhall racer and setting the car up with the correct anti-roll bars, adjustable front end, correct castor angles and so on. Eventually, Caterham would also develop its own quicker racing steering rack in response to comments from experienced racers such as Gerry Marshall.

Just about everything was now under regulatory control. Drivers could change only the rear-view mirrors, steering wheel, seat, windscreen, brake friction material and spring rates, while there was a choice of anti-roll bars (three front, three rear), all available from Caterham. You could paint your car, but that was that as far as modifications were concerned. You had to run the specified wheels, and the tyres were controlled slicks and wets from Avon. All this strictness was designed to stop anyone out-budgeting the others.

Caterham wanted the Vauxhall racers to be one of the fastest one-make series in Britain. Given the constraints – standard chassis, largely unmodified engine, hard slicks – this was no mean feat. But on a twisty circuit, the Caterhams proved a match for any car at that time and the series quickly gained a reputation for being the quickest around. On fast circuits like Thruxton, other more powerful machines possibly had the edge, but on balance

'Harlequin' was the Vauxhall race car shown to the press at the launch of the HPC in August 1990. Note the Perspex bubble screen which was later rejected because it tended to deflect air directly at the driver's head. 'Harlequin' was raced by Robert Nearn.

the Caterhams were quicker, as was proved in 1993 by a shoot-out at Cadwell Park. A Caterham was pitched against a TVR sitting 100 yards ahead. Both cars were driven by expert drivers (BTCC racer Tim Sugden in the Caterham and *Fast Lane* road-tester Mark Hales in the TVR), and the Caterham caught the TVR in three laps!

Andy Noble had been struggling to keep abreast of an increasingly unwieldy co-ordination job, so for 1991 he enlisted the help of Jim and Belinda McDougall, of Entreprix. At that time Jim was financial director of Team Lotus and had formerly been with the Williams Grand Prix team, while Belinda had previously run the Honda CRX series. As such they seemed ideally positioned to take over the running of the Caterham series, assuming the co-ordination role, while Andy Noble continued to make the decisions on matters of policy, and there was a committee which agreed the regulations each year.

From day one, the Vauxhall series was sponsored and there was prize money for the winner, plus money for the fastest lap and for pole position, so the racing was always highly competitive. That strict 1991 formula remained the trademark of the Caterham series henceforth. The championship rulebook had a stipulation which effectively read: 'If it doesn't say you *can* do it, you cannot.' The events were also closely policed, with proper scrutineering.

This had the effect of putting people's raw driving ability in sharp focus. There was no room

for getting an edge by using trick pushrods, for example. What it did mean was very exciting racing for spectators. Competitors ran very close to each other, constantly trading places, pushing their cars to the limit all the time. There were spills as well as thrills – always a crowd-pleaser!

Initially, the Vauxhall concept was difficult to sell to drivers because the recession hit just as the series was launched, but over the first few years Vauxhall racing established itself and became a very successful series. It was consistently shown on TV, both on satellite and terrestrial channels, which attracted sponsorship and some very good drivers, making the series extremely competitive.

The first Vauxhall Challenge season was won by Magnus Laird (who was Caterham's first official motorsport agent as MD of Hyperion Motorsport, and a man truly dedicated to promoting the ideals of Caterham racing). He finished comfortably ahead of Robert Coates and Robert Nearn, and was able to boast an impressive string of five wins in a row near the start of the season.

As for the other classes in the 1991 season, they had to start from a different grid. Class A continued, but because of the Hawkridge experience, there were only four regular competitors (Milicevic, Lumley, Jones and Ridley). Jez Coates was in favour of ditching Class A to concentrate on the Vauxhall series, but he felt that it was unfair to those competitors who had spent time and money preparing for the season. However, Class A would be dropped in 1992.

Class C was totally dominated in 1991 by Bart Hayden. He failed to come first in class only twice out of 12 races and he finished the season the winner by a huge margin; indeed with 85 points to his credit, he comfortably beat Jonathan Milicevic in Class A.

Class B attracted a record entry in 1991. No less than 42 racers scored points that season, but the

Brands Hatch, 1991, and the famous Paddock Bend sees Magnus Laird leading from Robert Coates, Robert Nearn and Robin Rex.

racing was really between two people: Howard Cramer and Art Markus. They jostled positions right through the season and the class was still wide open up until the last race at Donington. Cramer was leading by two points and managed to finish ahead of Markus to clinch the Class B title.

A good example of the level of support Caterham racing engendered was the letter that Art Markus of *Cars & Car Conversions* wrote to Andy Noble at the end of the 1991 season, after having competed successfully for three years. It said: "I believe there is no better racing series in Britain. Thanks to you and everyone at Caterham Cars for providing me with my best years in motorsport."

With Class A now dropped because of the low level of interest, for 1992 there was the Vauxhall Challenge, Class B and Class C, the latter two now sponsored by *Performance Car* magazine. The Vauxhall series was won by a clear 20 points by Ben Edwards, the Brands Hatch Racing School instructor (and later an Indycar and Formula 1 commentator for the Eurosport satellite TV channel).

As it transpired, 1992 proved to be a vintage year for Class B. With no less than 47 people registered to drive that year, the grids were full to bursting and the racing was competitive and exciting to watch. The class turned into a three-horse race for the title between Nigel Smith, Nevil Smith and Michael Wright, the latter clinching victory at the last race of the year at Castle Combe.

Because there were too many Class B cars, the overflow raced with the Class C category. For the first time, K-series cars were available to line up on the grid under Class C regulations and about 10 cars did so. They were at a significant disadvantage

Magnus Laird leads Chris Strakosch, Robert Nearn and John Wilson on his way to victory at Donington Park in July 1991. Laird would be the convincing winner of the inaugural Caterham Vauxhall Challenge championship.

because they only pushed out 110bhp compared with a typical 120–130bhp from the pushrod engines.

Class C was also very closely fought between two drivers: Rupert Douglas-Pennant in a Ford-engined car and, in a K-series, John Barker (road test editor for *Performance Car*). The 1992 season was Barker's introduction to Caterham motorsport and he proved to be very quick. Because he was driving one of the new K-series cars, the sparring for the lead developed into something of a battle royal between the Ford traditionalists and the new 'factory preferred' Rover cars.

With one race to go, there were just four points in it, Barker just ahead of Douglas-Pennant. During a very quick race over Castle Combe's flat straights, the superior power of Douglas-Pennant's Ford-engined car triumphed and he clinched the class by a two-point margin – much to the factory's chagrin!

Perhaps the greatest international triumph for Caterham came on Midsummer's Day, June 1992, when the works team took on the might of America. At that time, Caterham was again looking seriously into the possibility of marketing the Seven as a road car in the 'States, so an American race fitted in perfectly with company plans. Clive Roberts, who was now based at General Motors in America, brought to Caterham's attention the existence of a 24-hour race called the Nelson Ledges, an event run by the Sports Car Club of America (SCCA), who were very keen for Caterham to be involved. This sounded ideal.

The car stood every chance of doing well: it was lightweight, had a modern 16-valve power unit of proven reliability and a strong background of experience from the domestic Vauxhall race series.

A specially-conceived Vauxhall-powered HPC car was put together, with an engine left in essentially bog standard tune in the interests of reliability. There was only enough time for a single day's testing prior to the car being flown out. The organizational back-up was taken care of by Simon Nearn and Adam Sharp.

Graham Nearn spoke to Frank Bolton, Caterham's importer for the USA, and he found someone to deal with transportation and the support crew in the form of Delaware-based distributor George Alderman. The deal was that Alderman would be one of the drivers. No-one at Caterham knew his racing form, but he was described as a very experienced racer.

When the team arrived at the Ohio track, they found it had more troublesome bumps than a road cursed with sleeping policemen. The finely-honed suspension just couldn't cope: "I couldn't breathe because the air was getting knocked out of my lungs," recalls Jez Coates, "and I had double-vision. We had to tell the two mechanics coming over from Britain to bring standard road dampers with them!"

The Ohio circuit was a pretty basic affair, as Graham Nearn remembers. "There was no computer timing, virtually no toilets, everything was rough and ready. The circuit owner was a large, abrasive man who even had his own oil well on the site! He told us in no uncertain terms that he was in charge, there were no ambulance or fire facilities during practice and that if anything happened, it all came through him. At one stage, he said: 'Get that support truck moved or I'll tow it away myself', but returned, gave me a bear hug and said:

Defeating works Mazda RX-7s and Honda CRXs, the Seven blasted to victory in the Nelson Ledges endurance race in Ohio, America. This was perhaps the Seven's greatest international triumph.

American East Coast distributor George Alderman lines the Seven up – late! – on the grid at Nelson Ledges, sandwiched between a Mazda RX-7 and a Consulier. Note the indicator light mounted on top of the roll-cage.

The support crew rushes to fit a replacement front wing during the race. Trouble was, a wing was not ready and the team had to improvise with cardboard! A dubious marshal looks on (far right).

This nosecone was nicknamed Dolly Parton for obvious reasons…

'Don't worry, Limey, I speak to everyone like that!'"

A team consisting of Coates, Price, Robert Nearn and George Alderman readied themselves for the campaign, which included opposition from 63 other entries, including works teams from Mazda and Honda and a strong entry from American supercar makers Consulier. Graham Nearn recalls his impressions of George Alderman: "We were a bit taken aback when we found he was about 60 years old and was a rather sleepy sort of guy. We put him straight in the car and he made no fuss, just went out on the track and in no time at all he was going round within the lap record! He also brought a huge, fully-equipped rig along and a whole team of volunteer helpers – we were certainly not expecting anything so grand."

Caterham qualified an encouraging third. The team was a little nervous that the American racers might gang up to edge the little Caterham off the track. Certainly there was a legitimate concern over being seen and a flashing orange light was placed on top of the roll-over bar. In the end, the worries were unfounded, as virtually everyone was extremely friendly.

At the start of the race, all the cars lined up – with the exception of the Caterham. It transpired that the first driver was Alderman, and true to form, he was fast asleep! He inserted himself in the grid just in time before the start. Within the first hour, the Seven was in the lead.

Caterham's main opposition was from the works Mazda team and the all-American Consulier. Mazda always appeared to be upset about the Caterham and even lodged a protest about failed brake lights. What they didn't realize was that the Seven was taking corners flat-out and was not using its brakes. Caterham had to demonstrate that the lights *were* working by applying them down the straight!

Consulier was better set up for long-distance racing thanks to its purpose-built fuel tanks, and the race became a head-to-head between Caterham and Consulier. At one stage, one of the Consulier team (an ex-Indianapolis driver) came up to Graham Nearn and said: "Our boss has just told us to drive to finish second, but we think this is the greatest race of our life. May the best team win!".

With about two hours to go, the Consulier broke a driveshaft and had to come in for repairs. By that stage, the Caterham's lead was unassailable. Reg Price kept the car going and finished first. The race went to 990 laps (or 1,980 miles), by which time the Caterham was leading by seven laps. Its average speed had been 85mph. Coates estimated that they had done about 7,000 overtaking manoeuvres during the race. "With so much opportunity for altercation, I was frankly amazed that we didn't get knocked off the track by one of the lumbering yank tanks. That's why we have never returned to the event."

Still, there was no hiding the winning team's glee at the victory and the corporate pride which awaited their return. Graham Nearn: "It was one of those wonderful events that just happened. It's not so much a case of having good luck as avoiding bad luck, and that's what we did."

There was then another discovery: that Caterham was eligible for a 24-hour event for modified production cars in 1993 in Zolder, Belgium. The

The lap of honour for the winning team, with drivers Reg Price, George Alderman, Robert Nearn and Jez Coates.

trouble was, it was only a matter of days before the race when this fact was confirmed. The question of whether there was enough time to get a realistically prepared car together was swept aside in a wave of post-Nelson Ledges enthusiasm and a 190bhp Vauxhall-powered car was hastily assembled.

The car was still being finished in the pit lane at Zolder when qualifying began. "I suppose we were quite bullish," admits Coates. "We had done seven or eight endurance races successfully and had the recent win in America in our minds. But the Zolder car was diabolical. We had to run a special roll-cage and hardtop, but neither of them fitted the car, and neither did the wheels. The fuel tank leaked, the handling was horrible, the brakes were inadequate, the fuel consumption was desperate."

Robert Nearn, Price and Coates were the drivers. With luck, the team qualified 18th out of 72 starters, but the midnight oil had to be well and truly burnt to get the car into a raceable state. Amazingly, from the start line, everything went almost like clockwork. Fifth gear was lost after only eight hours, then fourth as well, but that one came back and the car was nursed home. After 1,664 miles, the team finished seventh overall and first in the 2-litre Class. Considering the problems and the opposition (which included Le Mans-spec Porsche 911s), this was an extremely pleasing result.

Back in Britain in the 1993 domestic series, Class B and C were again sponsored by *Performance Car* magazine. Nothing was done to the regulations and the size of the Class B grid promptly nose-dived to about half the 1991 level. The Ford pushrod engine was simply not as popular as previously, having been eclipsed by the 16-valve Vauxhall series.

But the racing was as good as ever. Over the 12

The entire Caterham entourage with all back-up personnel, partly from Britain and partly from Alderman's own racing support team. Graham Nearn is far left, Alderman third from left.

US distributor Chris Tchorznicki salutes the rather obscenely large Nelson Ledges trophy.

events, Peter Fiddes and Jeremy Rollason were consistently close, Fiddes emerging victorious. Incidentally, Clive Chapman, son of the man who conceived the Seven and then part of Team Lotus, raced in Class B over six meetings (and still finished the season in 12th place). He concluded that "the Seven is a powerful testament to my father's approach to high-performance engineering".

The K-series Supersport package was now on line and available for racing in Class C (that year dubbed the *Performance Car* Caterham Seven Challenge). The 128bhp Supersport engine was now on a roughly equal footing with the Fords and about 16 Rover-engined cars made the grid in 1993.

Jack Newland in a Ford-powered car again fought off the Rover cars, beating Shaun Balfe and Danny Audritt to take Class C by a small margin – once again much to the factory's chagrin.

In the Vauxhall series (sponsored by Vecta Immobilisers) Robert Nearn sharpened his performance to win by 18 points over David Walton, with Guy Parry a further point adrift. The first five events of the year were won by Nearn and he also won three further events to emerge as the dominant force in 1993.

After 1993, a lot of people began asking what Caterham was actually doing to promote the series: a lot of other names like Entreprix, Hyperion and all the sponsors had been cropping up. It was obvious that Caterham needed to promote itself more: after all, it was still organizing the series, paying for it and doing a lot of work behind the scenes. As well as this, Caterham owned several of the cars being raced. Contrary to popular belief, television coverage was not free: indeed, the cost of this alone was over £60,000 a year!

So Andy Noble conceived the Caterham Motorsport name and a logo was duly created. Everything to do with racing was now promoted under that banner, which worked to unite all the disparate parts of the competition organization.

In 1994, attempts were made to rekindle interest

Following the Nelson Ledges victory, IMSA asked Caterham to attend a meeting at the Atlanta Speedway. Robert Nearn was the driver.

Long-time campaigner Jonathan Milicevic, here at Cadwell Park, won Class A of the road-going series in 1991, the last year in which it was run.

Howard Cramer fends off a challenge from Jeremy Rollason during his successful assault on the 1991 Class B title.

Just as it had done the previous year with the Vauxhall racer, Caterham launched the K-series racer at the same time as the road car, this time in Docklands, London, in 1991.

Eventual winner of the 1992 Class B championship, Michael Wright, leads Keith Farrance in appalling conditions.

in Class B by finding a sponsor (Arrowstar) and having some prize money. Despite this sponsorship, the 'B' grid was practically non-existent in 1994, an eventuality which sealed the fate of this particular series. In its last year under the auspices of Caterham, Class B was won by Patrick Havill, followed by Graham Griffiths and John Schneider.

Class C, meanwhile, was made exclusively K-series and was sponsored by Rover through Rover Sport, the series now being called the Caterham Rover K-series Challenge. The remnants of the Class C Ford group (about half a dozen) ran with the Class B cars.

The new K-series class was run along similar lines to the Vauxhall class: rigidly controlled with sealed engines, fixed gearboxes, tyres, differentials and so on. The difference was the K-series cars were road-going. Clive Richards dominated the K-series with 10 race wins out of 12. His Seven credentials went back to racing in Class B in the 1990 Caterham series and in hillclimbs and sprints in a Caterham Vauxhall in 1992/93, and he went on to be competitive in Caterham Vauxhalls in 1995.

For the first time the Vauxhall series was sponsored by Vauxhall itself. It was won in masterful style by Paul Milligan, who was aged just 19, with six clear race wins and six fastest laps. He

beat Caterham 'veterans' Keith Farrance and David Walton by a sizeable margin.

A number of changes were instituted for the 1995 season. For the previous four years the Vauxhall grid and B/C grids had been split up and run on different circuits, so there were double the number of races for Caterham to attend, in addition to all the international events, which were ever-increasing in number. Resources were being stretched to the limit and it was felt that factory support for the races was suffering. So Andy Noble took the decision to run all Caterham races at the same venue. That made the races much easier to co-ordinate and easier to promote.

Also in 1995, Class B was handed over to the 750 Motor Club. Caterhams had been racing in 750MC road-sports for some time, so this was a sensible move. There would always be interest in racing Ford-powered Caterhams, but it no longer sat comfortably within Caterham's race programme.

In terms of regulations, the Vauxhall Challenge was largely unchanged for 1995. Shaun Balfe took an early lead in the championship, which was characterized by the close competitiveness of the top half-dozen drivers. In the end, David Walton proved victorious after four previous tries, and despite the fact that he scored no points in the first

In 1993 a works Seven lined up alongside Porsches, Astras and other quick machines in a 24-hour event at Zolder, Belgium. Nearn, Price and Coates scored a notable success by finishing seventh overall and first in class.

The Zolder success was all the more impressive considering the haste with which the car was prepared, its use of a never-before-tried hard-top and a host of mechanical glitches.

race. "This was the most competitive season yet," he concluded. Keith Farrance was second, ahead of Shaun Balfe, Clive Richards, Bart Hayden and Guy Parry.

The K-series racing went from strength to strength, taking Caterham racing back to the good old days. There were reserves on the Rover-sponsored K-series Challenge grid for 1995 – for example, 35 cars turned up at Silverstone with only 34 places on the grid. With 41 registered K-series cars, Caterham was *still* building more K-series racers through 1995.

The cars were marginally quicker than the previous season thanks to a switch to 021 Yokohama tyres rather than 001 Yokos. Simon Harris emerged as the leading driver in the early part of the season,

and consolidated his leadership by being the only driver to finish in every race of the season. He won by a comfortable margin from Daniel Eaves and Warren Gilbert.

Sponsorship had grown over the last five years, so that both Rover and Vauxhall were official sponsors of their respective series and a host of other sponsors were supporting the events. Another unique feature of the Caterham series was the creation of the Caterham Race Centre, run by Tangent Motorsport, one of Caterham's competitions agents. Competitors would use it for information, practice times, free refreshments and as a social gathering point.

A further significant development was a new race programme sponsored by the BBC's *Top Gear* magazine. With the Ford series now in the hands of the 750MC, Graham Nearn was keen on Caterham making an 'official' return to the budget Ford racing days. Andy Noble and Jim and Belinda McDougall of Entreprix sat down at a dinner at the October 1994 Motor Show and came up with the idea of a low-cost series for novices. By February 1995, the package had been put together and the series would be known as the *Top Gear* Caterham Sport Scholarship, with publicity in *Top Gear* magazine.

The idea was to introduce novices to motorsport and ultimately to Caterham racing. Novices were invited to buy a car specifically built down to a price – incredibly, just under £9,000. This included the purchase of the kit, racing medical, articles, race licence and entry fees. In effect, the competi-

1992 was the first year when K-series cars competed and leading 'K' driver John Barker (car 1) chases Danny Audritt (8) and Jez Coates (27). As a Caterham employee Coates was not allowed to score points.

Robert Nearn outside the Dartford factory after comfortably winning the 1993 Caterham Vauxhall Challenge.

A spectacular shot of the field at the start of the Silverstone K-series Challenge in 1994. Championship winner Clive Richards is away first, closely followed by the *Autocar* car (68) and Martin Burley (83).

1994 K-series champion Clive Richards, son of Lotus Seven Fifties racer Jack Richards, winner by a clear margin of some 35 points.

A 19-year-old Paul Milligan indulges in a spot of low flying on Cadwell Park's Mountain as he storms to victory in the Vauxhall series of 1994.

Milligan leading David Walton and Keith Farrance at Cadwell Park in 1994. These would be the three top-placed drivers at the end of the championship, albeit with the positions of Walton and Farrance reversed.

tors' hands were held throughout the season: an important point, because Caterham insisted that, to take up the scholarship, you should never have held a competition licence before. The whole essence was to bring motorsport to people who had never tried it.

Rather than dump competitors who had never circuit raced in at the deep end, Caterham eased them into the process with an introductory programme of two events each of karting, autotests, hillclimbs, sprints and finally circuit racing in their Caterhams.

These cars were specially conceived for the series with 1600 Sprint 100bhp Ford pushrod engines, reconditioned five-speed gearboxes from the V6 Ford and live rear axles. It was initially intended to use four-speed 'boxes, but after building one, supply worries led to choosing the five-speed. To keep costs and weight low, the cars came with an aero screen and no weather gear, but you did get all the bits needed for racing, including a roll-over bar, fire extinguishers and so on. Additionally, the cars were road-legal.

The series was limited to 25 cars for several reasons: firstly, certain events such as hillclimbs and sprints could not cope with more than 25 entrants; secondly, there was a severe time restraint preparing the cars; and thirdly, there was a limited amount of sponsorship. For the first time in Caterham's history, the cars were built without having first been ordered by a customer. If there had been any concern about the risk (it had been suggested that, if any cars didn't sell, they would be parked at Andy Noble's house…), they need not have worried: all 25 cars were sold within three

weeks. One of the 25 cars was loaned as a prize in a *Top Gear* magazine competition which was won by ex-ballet dancer David Sorrell. Another car was lent to *Auto Express* magazine and raced by journalist James Mills.

The major sponsors were *Top Gear* magazine, which provided coverage and an umbrella for the series, BP (lubricants), Arch Motors (fabrication) and Perry Engineering (supplier of all Ford components).

The overall winner emerged as Miles Moorhouse, with Simon Lambert taking the runner-up prize. The Top Ladies trophy went to 18-year-old Hazel Garner.

The *Top Gear* Scholarship proved so successful that it was repeated in 1996 with 25 new cars. No car from the '95 season could be taken through to the next, but owners of '95 cars could part-exchange for a K-series or Vauxhall racer. Alternatively, they could sell their car back to Caterham, use it as a road car, or continue competing in any of the events they tried in 1995.

One cannot ignore the importance of other forms of motorsport. Caterhams compete extensively in hillclimbs, sprints and autotests. Although Caterham has no official involvement with this sort of racing, it does encourage it and helps individuals from time to time. "Privateers can be very good ambassadors for Caterham," acknowledged Andy Noble, "and we always try to encourage them."

Hillclimbing is particularly suited to the light weight and cornering agility of the Seven. Caterhams won the Midland Championship five years in a row: Allan Warburton (1989), Robert Stevens (1990–91), Rob Fradley (1992) and Clive Kenrick

(1993). Caterham Cars even supported one Scottish driver, Alan Nicol, in his Caterham Vauxhall's assault on the Scottish Road Car Hill Climb championship. He won the title in 1993 and 1994 and with the opposition getting tougher he uprated his engine to JPE specification and won again in 1995! A fantastic record, particularly as the car is driven to every event.

Colin Goodwin of *Car* magazine summed up the appeal of the Seven as a hillclimb car when he tried a K-series Seven up Prescott in 1992. "The ideal vehicle, if you want to have fun and stand a chance of winning, is a Caterham Seven… [Its] fantastic power-to-weight ratio and amazing handling make it a great car for lobbing up a twisty hill in a hurry."

Relays were another area where Caterham became involved. Andy Noble's first ever competition drive was in a Class A racer at the Jaguar Drivers Club relay at Donington, and the works team attended several of these events. Sevens were eligible for a variety of other relays including the Birkett six-hour, which grew out of the Ann Hamilton Trophy. Andy Noble competed four times in this enjoyable relay with drivers like Tim Seward, Mike Dixon and Simon Leighton. Caterhams succeeded in scoring five successive victories, from 1991 to 1995.

In 1994, Andy Noble took the Nelson Ledges-winning Seven to the Birkett, where it lined up against about half a dozen Sevens and various Porsches. After the first hour, the Caterham was in third place behind two other Vauxhall-powered Sevens, while two of the Ford pushrod cars did not finish. The following year, these two drivers switched to Vauxhall engines!

The 1995 Birkett was again won by a Caterham, that of the privateer team of Tangent Motorsport, driving Vauxhall racers. They fended off Ferraris, Porsches and a very strong BMW CSL 'Batmobile' to take the event comfortably. Helped by five other drivers, Dave Walton notched up his fourth win at Birkett. Another team of Sevens called Team Bedlington came second, some four laps behind and, remarkably, two of the three team cars were road-going. One of them, driven by Tim Seward, lost fourth gear, which handicapped him to the tune of just one second per lap.

Yet another area of growing importance is international Seven race events. A number of one-make series grew up in the Nineties, including Japan and France. The Japanese series (with exclusively Vauxhall-engined cars) was launched in 1992 and proved to be even better supported than that in the UK. Caterham also ran a number of 'shop window' races in Europe to generate interest in Sevens in what was a very important market for the car. For fuller details of international Seven racing, see *Chapter 7.*

The question of what actual benefit the racing programme has on sales is constantly in the minds of everyone at Caterham. You only have to look at the story of the BTCC Alfa Romeo 155 to realize that having success on the track does not necessarily mean success in the showroom.

Despite the fact that only about 80 cars were racing each year (out of total annual domestic sales of 300), it was felt that the exposure the racing received on a national and international level did have a significant and positive effect on sales of cars and parts. Graham Nearn: "The main point is that we make a sports-racing car. It's important for the

Scotsman Alan Nicol proves the suitability of the Caterham for hillclimbing, winning the Scottish title in 1993, 1994 and 1995 in a Vauxhall-engined car.

An 'extra-curricular' event during the 1994 season was a highly enjoyable race at Zandvoort, in Holland. Here a mixed field negotiates the Heugenholtz Hairpin.

David Walton leads Verney Wood during the early part of the 1995 season.

136

Sevens dominated the Birkett Relay for years. This is the 1991 event at Snetterton, where Caterham's works entry won its class.

Caterham Seven events are among the best-supported in British club racing, with – typically – two full grids like this one at Cadwell Park.

Lotus Sevens, with the odd Mark 6, enjoy their own race series in Britain, organized by the Historic Sports Car Club. These early Lotus Sevens are competing at Mallory Park.

Seven to be seen racing. Competition does lead directly and immediately to benefits in road cars. We get instant feedback because there is always a company representative at every meeting of the Caterham series, unlike club events."

Certainly, the number of people watching and enjoying Caterhams race is pleasingly large, reflecting its status as probably the best one-make racing series, certainly in the UK and probably in the world.

LAP RECORDS IN CATERHAM ONE-MAKE SERIES

CATERHAM-ROVER K-SERIES

Brands Hatch (Indy)	0:53.10	Daniel Eaves, 1995
Cadwell Park	1:43.27	Daniel Eaves, 1995
Castle Combe	1:10.94	Clive Richards, 1994
Donington Park	1:24.69	Daniel Eaves, 1995
Lydden Hill	0:47.10	Martin Burley, 1994
Mallory Park	0:53.30	Shaun Balfe, 1993
Oulton Park	1:59.68	Warren Gilbert, 1995
Silverstone (International)	1:39.58	Neil Delargy, 1996
Silverstone (National)	1:12.31	Tom Clarkson, 1995
Snetterton	1:25.64	John Barker, 1992
Thruxton	1:31.47	Tim Fuller, 1995

CATERHAM-VAUXHALL

Brands Hatch (GP)	1:35.72	Magnus Laird, 1991
Brands Hatch (Indy)	0:47.66	Howard Walker, 1995
Cadwell Park	1:33.07	Tim Sugden, 1992
Castle Combe	1:03.65	Steve Parrish, 1994
Donington Park	1:16.46	Russell Morgan, 1995
Donington Park (GP)	1:43.11	Jason Plato, 1993
Knockhill	1:00.73	Robert Nearn, 1991
Mallory Park	0:48.08	Keith Farrance, 1993
Oulton Park	1:47.67	Clive Richards, 1995
Pembrey	1:01.09	David Cook, 1994
Silverstone (International)	1:29.64	Peter Matthews, 1996
Silverstone (National)	1:04.12	Simon Jackson, 1995
Snetterton	1:15.39	James Matthews, 1995
Thruxton	1:22.46	Robert Nearn, 1993

CHAPTER 6

Buying and restoring a Seven

Choice, value and performance

The most attractive option for a prospective owner of a Seven is, of course, to go to Caterham Cars and buy a brand-new car. This will be *your* car, tailored to your requirements and cared for as you would wish it. But naturally, not all of us can afford to buy a new car; neither is everyone looking for the characteristics of a new car; or perhaps you are unprepared to join the waiting list for a new Seven. Buying secondhand is therefore often the most practical route into ownership of a Seven.

With over 3,000 Lotus Sevens and well over 6,000 Caterhams built to date, there is an ever-expanding choice for potential initiates of Seven motoring. There are Sevens to suit every taste, from the classic early Lotus Series 1 with an asthmatic charm to the scorching GTi-bashing catalytic HPC from Caterham. The purchase of a Lotus Seven is covered admirably in Jeremy Coulter's *Lotus Seven: A Collector's Guide*, so in this book it

suffices to list the main points to look out for in the purchase of a Caterham-built Seven.

The best news is that, unlike many classic sportscars, a Seven is both easy and cheap to run, very well supported by dedicated specialists and passionately promoted by the owners' club. The downside is that there are always fewer Sevens than there are people who want to own one, so often a long search is necessary and purchase prices are often very high. At least this means that, when it comes to letting your Seven go, you will get back roughly what you paid for it.

The first question to address is what exactly you want from your Seven. Are you going to use it as an everyday car? If so, are you aware of its limitations? Do you intend going racing? If so, in what sort of races? Do you want a car which you can work on, like a restoration project or a new kit from Caterham, or do you just want to get in and drive?

The Seven's structure is very simple. Unlike with almost every other car, rust is really not a problem. The integrity of the structure and originality are much more important considerations.

Lotus Seven or Caterham Seven? It is often hard to tell unless you examine the badge because so many of the earlier cars have been updated with modern Caterham components. The most important thing is condition, and this car is absolutely immaculate.

Are you looking for performance and ultimate handling, or are you content to derive your pleasure from simply being in a Seven? Perhaps most importantly of all, what is your budget?

Having raised all the questions, deciding exactly which model and specification you want may be a luxury you have to forego. Firstly, there is the scarcity of used examples compared with most sportscars. Secondly, many cars over 10 years old will have been restored in a fairly major way, often using different and often non–original parts. There are almost as many varieties of Seven as there are cars built. As long as you have a basic idea of what you want from a Seven and are aware of the various types built, persistence will usually reap its own reward, even if you don't end up with precisely your ideal specification.

Choice of models and identification features
Your first decision should be: Lotus or Caterham? Each has its own advantages. Many diehard enthusiasts insist that the Lotus Seven is the true Seven, the original Seven, and there is undoubtedly a mystique about the Lotus name. But Caterhams certainly have the edge dynamically: they all have stiffer chassis, better suspension, more direct steering and the later you go the better the dynamics become. The heart may be tempted by the Lotus badge, but the head surely has to follow Caterham.

Generally speaking, the early Lotus cars attract a loyal and fanatical diehard following. Series 1 and early Series 2 cars command prices which far exceed what their raw ability could ever justify, but they are undoubtedly charismatic and genuinely

historic. Series 3 Lotus Sevens are relatively scarce and, in any case, a Caterham S3 is a far more practical proposition.

The S4 may have a reputation as the poor relation of the Seven family, but even so it is well appreciated by those who own one. It is probably the most practical Lotus Seven for everyday use. Who knows, the return of such Seventies fashion icons as flares, platform soles and Gary Glitter in the Nineties may herald a sudden resurgence of interest in orange and lime green S4s. There is certainly no mistaking an S4 for any other type. Its glassfibre body and reworked chassis are substantially different from all earlier Sevens. It is impossible externally to distinguish a Lotus S4 from one of the 38 S4s which Caterham built in 1973 and 1974; only the badging is different, and many Caterhams have since been fitted with Lotus badges anyway. The only reliable method is to check the chassis numbers: any number from 3501 upwards is a Caterham-built car, but you will be hard-pushed to find one.

The Caterham S3 built from 1974 onwards used a modified version of the strengthened S3 Twin Cam SS chassis – a much stiffer affair that gave superior handling characteristics. All Caterham S3s that might be confused with Lotus cars can be identified by their 'CS3' prefix on the chassis plate.

From 1981, Caterhams came with a Morris Ital rear axle (an item which is still fitted to some new Sevens even today). If you are a tall driver (6ft or over), it would be advisable to find a long-cockpit Caterham (offered as a popular option from 1982 and standard from 1992).

Little trouble in identifying this 'Q-car' as a Caterham with its bold '7' grille. This is another illustration of a pristine example, seemingly as well prepared for a concours as a race track.

Chassis became progressively stronger throughout the Eighties. De Dion suspension, available on Sevens from 1985, provides a much improved ride while a five-speed gearbox (from 1986) gives better cruising ability. Rear disc brakes (1988), honeycomb side impact protection (1990) and Bilstein suspension (1991) were all significant advances which enhanced the appeal of the Seven.

Perhaps the widest degree of choice comes in the engine department. Virtually all early (pre-1980) Caterhams will have a Twin Cam engine fitted. More recent cars favour the Ford pushrod range. It's a question of what you want from your Seven. A basic 1600 Ford engine is quite sufficient for a bit of fun at weekends, but more dedicated performance enthusiasts will probably prefer a Sprint or Supersprint version. The Cosworth BDR-engined Seven is a rare and sought-after beast (therefore rather an expensive option), while the ultimate performance Seven is the later Vauxhall-powered HPC.

It's worth mentioning the Rover K-series engine, too. Quite a few of these can now be found secondhand and they make a practical and rapid alternative to the more common Ford engine. Indeed, many regard them as the sweetest of all Sevens.

General condition
Because of their inherent value, generally speaking Sevens are well looked-after by owners. Even thrashed examples tend to be nursed back to health by doting enthusiasts. As a result, it's rare to come across a Seven which is genuinely shabby. The days of neglected old wrecks are long gone.

That said, the Seven has its weak points like any other car, and condition does play an important part in pricing – simply not as much as with other cars. One of the main reasons is that a Seven can be brought back to pristine condition fairly easily. The only exception would be a write-off where the chassis has been severely distorted.

It is also essential that you check the car's identity. Is it what the seller says it is? Does it have the correct engine? Has it been modified? Perhaps most importantly, is it actually a Seven? There have been plenty of lookalikes over the years and it has not been unknown for sellers to pass them off as real Sevens. Since 'replicas' are normally of inferior quality and therefore of far less intrinsic value, take care to check the chassis and other identifying details against the registration document. This will also help you spot a stolen car. If in doubt, refer to Caterham for advice.

Later Caterhams (post-1984) were available for sale in basic kit form and most of these will have been built up using secondhand parts (in which case the car will have a 'Q' registration). Inevitably, more care needs to be taken when looking at a kit-built Seven. You will need to satisfy yourself that the car was properly screwed together in the first place. Did Caterham check the car after build? Also bear in mind that some of the secondhand parts used may have been almost shot when fitted, so budget for repairs and replacements.

CHASSIS
The condition of the chassis should be at the top of the list in any buyer's mind when he looks at a

You need to check carefully for accident damage. GRP panels (*ie* wings and nose-cone) simply unbolt. Chassis front ends are available in long and short sections from the factory.

Seven. Although replacement chassis and repair sections are available for all types, having to do this is a skilled and involved job. Arch Motors, which has built chassis for the Seven for over 25 years, can repair any chassis to 'as new' condition quickly and cost-effectively.

Accident damage – Well over half of all accidents involve frontal impacts, so particular attention should be paid to the engine bay area. First and particularly second suspension legs are likely to be damaged in any impact on a front corner. Chassis tubes should be straight and without joins, except at the nodes.

Chassis sections are available from the factory to replace the 'short front' (first 12 inches of the chassis with all the front suspension pick-ups, ending immediately behind the second suspension leg), or the 'long front', which extends to the rear of the pedal box. Both sections – if fitted correctly – can constitute a good-as-new repair, except for the disturbance of the protective powder coating finish, which will be burnt away where the brazed joints are made. Air drying paint is usually sprayed over these areas on factory repairs, which is inevitably less durable. Look out for sprayed repairs as a sign of a pukka factory repair.

Checks should also include all areas for bent tubes and breaking joints. Take the nosecone and bonnet off and look for evidence of repair work, including a creased undertray. Drive the car and feel if there is misalignment from a previous repair. Be aware of the car pulling to one side and/or bad creaking under acceleration and be suspicious of uneven tyre wear.

Rust – This often begins inside the chassis tubes and works its way outwards. Check the tubes surrounding the suspension pick-up points front and rear and the lower side tubes, which are crucial to rigidity (look for an additional riveted panel on the aluminium side panels, which could indicate that rust is being concealed).

Stressed aluminium panels – Look at the floorpan and around the transmission tunnel for ripples, cracks, tears and loose panels. More involved repairs can be expensive because the work is best left to professionals.

BODYWORK
No rust is one of the powerful fringe benefits of owning a Seven. Aluminium exterior panels can dent easily. The glassfibre nose and wings on Caterhams are susceptible to accident damage, but on all Sevens except the S4 they are detachable in next to no time and very cheap to replace.

ENGINES
Twin Cam – Initially, the Twin Cam engine in Caterhams was a genuine Lotus unit, but from the late Seventies these were constructed by Vegantune and quality was variable. Later units used a Ford 1600 block, taking capacity up from 1,558cc to 1,598cc.

All Twin Cam engines need looking after. If they are properly serviced, they can be reliable and consistent, but once neglected, power and performance can drop significantly and the cost of overhauling a Twin Cam is much higher than for any of the pushrod Ford units.

For example, changing the troublesome water pump requires removing the cylinder head, while the camshaft drive chain and tensioner wear quickly and, because of the sealless valve guides, oil consumption tends to be high. On the parts side, the only problem with the Twin Cam is a shortage of cylinder heads.

Ford pushrod – Practical and reliable with plenty of spares back-up and masses of tuning potential. Be aware that engines tend to get much harder use in a Seven than in an old Escort/Cortina banger (although there's less weight to carry around). Listen for piston slap and watch for blue exhaust smoke. Also be sure that any tuning that has been carried out has been done professionally. The more highly tuned the engine, the more hassle it will give. Race-spec engines might sound attractive in an advert, but the pain of actually running something as temperamental as a full-race engine will far outweigh the pleasure it gives when it's on song.

If you want a more powerful Ford engine the best course of action is to find a Seven Sprint or, even better, a Supersprint. These Caterham-modified engines are reliable and widely known. The Sprint unit, introduced in 1980, is a mild reworking of the Ford Kent 1600 engine to produce 110bhp. The Supersprint unit, available from 1984, is bored out to 1.7 litres and has more goodies (larger valves, fully-worked head, Kent cam and twin Webers). Producing 135bhp, it is probably the most practical way to reach the upper echelons of what the Seven can achieve. It's also the most commonly-fitted engine among cars built by the factory.

Cosworth BDR – Somewhat more temperamental. In 1600 form, the engine develops 150bhp; in 1700 guise, the output is 170bhp. Weeping head gaskets were a common problem even when the units were new. Constant adjustment is needed to keep these highly tuned engines in the peak of performance. But there is no denying that a Cosworth-engined Seven is one of the most desirable of all, and prices reflect this.

Vauxhall – The Vauxhall 2-litre engine which superseded the Cosworth as the standard HPC engine in 1990 is undoubtedly the most reliable of the high-powered engines. Its 175bhp (or 165bhp in fuel-injection form) is extracted from a virtually standard Vauxhall powerplant (as fitted to the Calibra), so reliability, spares and servicing are not a problem.

Rover K-series – Equally practical is the Rover K-series engine, launched in 1991. Several hundred cars have been fitted with this power unit (although only recently has it approached the popularity of the Ford), so it is becoming more common to find a used one. This is a standard Rover engine (as fitted to the Metro GTi) and can even be serviced by Rover dealers thanks to an agreement between Caterham and Rover. There are unlikely to be any problems with any K-series engine. Pre-1993 engines will almost certainly be non-catalyzed. Later engines may well be catalyzed, identified by a rear-exiting exhaust or side-mounted exhaust with an extended heat shield. The catalyst is large and made of a high-tech metal substrate, so power loss is minimal; but beware of damaged units as replacement can be costly. The soundness of cats is now part of the MoT test.

The K-series Supersport engine, a 128bhp tweak of the standard 1.4-litre unit, was jointly developed by Rover and Caterham. It has become very popular, being fitted to 75% of all K-series Sevens. Since the Supersport option has only been around since 1993, it is too early to comment on weaknesses, but the unit has been successfully raced without reliability problems. Its maintenance should be entrusted to Caterham.

Non-standard engines – Generally speaking, don't be tempted by a Seven fitted with a non-standard engine. Caterham does not recommend alternative engine choices and will not service non-sanctioned engines. There are examples of Sevens running with all kinds of units from Alfa Romeo to

Choose your engine carefully. A Lotus Twin Cam like this may be one of the most desirable, but it is not necessarily the most practical in everyday use.

143

The Vauxhall 2-litre HPC is the most powerful engine in a Seven that you are likely to come across. It's also completely practical to run.

Toyota twin-cam, Mazda rotary to Ford CVH, Ford Zetec to Rover V8, but the used value of a car so fitted reflects what most people think of them. The weight difference of alternative engines can upset the handling balance and can even affect safety. If you are tempted by the cheap asking price of a non-standard Seven, make doubly sure of the soundness of areas like engine mounting points, suspension set-up, ignition and exhaust systems, plus stress on the chassis and the rear axle.

SUSPENSION

On Caterhams, the rear axle changed over the years from the original Ford Escort axle to an Escort RS (1977). More common will be the Morris Marina/Ital rear axle used from 1981; most likely is a Sierra-based de Dion rear end (optional from 1985).

Check for oil leaks from the diff and drums on the Ital axle. Also, if the car has a powerful engine fitted (say above 150bhp), you should be aware that live axles are not ideal. Again look for oil leaks as a sign of axle distortion. Reconditioned rear axles (both Ford and Ital) are quite easy to find. Indeed, Caterham still builds some of its basic models with reconditioned Ital axles.

The de Dion rear end has proven almost unburstable in use and can handle very much higher power outputs than either of the live axles. The rubber bushes in the rear A-frame are very hard-worked and can start to knock out after only a few thousand miles. These need to be replaced regularly, but thankfully the exercise is cheap and simple (post-1994 cars used a more robust bush so this should not be a problem). Wheel bearings all round tend to get a pounding and can affect handling.

GEARBOX

On early Caterhams (1974–80), the gearbox is the Ford 2821E unit. From 1980, Ford Escort Sport Mk2 unit took over and an option of the close-ratio Sierra XR4-type five-speed was available from 1986. All are very reliable and, in the event of malfunction, cheap to repair and replace.

The only exception is with the K-series and Vauxhall-powered HPC models, both of which have their own special bellhousings in aluminium, but the gearboxes themselves are standard (the Vauxhall engine requires that 10mm be cut at the input shaft). Clutches can suffer under the heavy use associated with driving a Seven, but again replacement is not expensive.

The six-speed gearbox is too new to comment upon. However, since most of the insides are derived from Ford parts, the long-term practicality of the 'box should be assured.

WEATHER EQUIPMENT

Hoods on Sevens are very simple in design. They are all held in place by popper fasteners and do deteriorate with use. Faded Perspex screens, hood shrinkage, tears, leaks and missing fasteners are all common and screens can be fiddly to erect. If not folded correctly, they are prone to damage. However, they are well-made and the cost of replacement is low compared with most soft-top sportscars.

The improved visibility weather protection introduced in 1988 is much more practical than the earlier type, in particular by providing better elbow room as well as visibility and the opportunity to stow the sidescreens in the boot. However, the rigid folding sidescreens cannot be fitted to the original-type hood; if you want to upgrade, you must change the whole hood.

Interiors are often tatty because of frequent exposure to the elements. Cloth seats fade, so vinyl or leather is preferable. Finally, don't worry about carpets as these are cheap to replace.

CHAPTER 7

Sevens around the world

A sportscar with international appeal

Almost from the moment the Lotus Seven was announced in 1957, international markets have had a tremendous importance for the model. America was probably the first foreign export market, and the specially-modified Seven sold there was even called the Seven America.

However, in terms of sales volume, it was primarily the British enthusiast who supported the Lotus Seven through the Sixties. Customers abroad were never in short supply, but Lotus was not always keen to exploit them. It was not even keen about keeping the Seven in production for much of the Sixties!

As soon as the news of Caterham's 1973 deal with Lotus broke, there was a barrage of inquiries from potential overseas agents, proving that its appeal worldwide was undiminished.

Almost all of the Caterham-built S4s of 1973 and 1974 went abroad, mostly to Germany, but also to Portugal, Switzerland, Italy, America, Eire, France,

Holland and – significantly – Japan. In fact Caterham was not the only company to whom Lotus granted the right to produce the Seven. By its nature the Seven was simpler to put into production than more complex machines like the Elan or Europa. Plenty of overseas parties approached Lotus over the years with proposals to enter licensed production. Very few, of course, ever came to anything, but in the Sixties and Seventies Sevens were also made in New Zealand (Steele Brothers), Argentina (Boschi, Mutio & Vignoles) and Spain (Hispano-Aleman).

After the first year, when Caterham switched to the S3 Seven, overseas interest was even more intense. The first production S3 – something of a one-off special with several non-standard parts – went to Hong Kong and then on to Hawaii, but most of the early production was snapped up by Japan and America. Indeed, British customers sometimes had difficulty even seeing a car as

The Seven was represented in an increasing number of countries. Behind this Seven HPC is Hong Kong's famous harbour.

145

initially about 95% of production was exported.

However, as production increased, the proportion of cars sold in Britain began to rise. In purely numerical terms, foreign sales rose almost without let-up through the Seventies and Eighties, extending into new areas like the Far East, Middle East and Eastern Europe.

In 1989, some 37.5% of production was being exported. But overseas markets became crucial when the recession of the early Nineties hit domestic sales. Caterham redoubled its efforts overseas: in 1992 new agents were appointed in Thailand, Taiwan, Hong Kong, Macao, Singapore, the United Arab Emirates, Korea, Indonesia, Malaysia, Brunei, Venezuela, the Czech Republic and Portugal. In the same year, exhibitions were held in Frankfurt, Essen, Paris, Melbourne, Taipei and Thailand. The result was a big increase in foreign sales: some 55% of production was exported in 1992. In recognition of the fact, Caterham was presented with the Queen's Award for Export Achievement in 1993.

At the time of writing Caterham is represented in more countries than at any time in its history, from as far afield as Australia and Brunei to Venezuela and the Czech Republic. No-one within the organization underestimates the importance of these overseas markets, just as the customers abroad who buy Caterhams appreciate the significance and value of the Seven.

JAPAN
Caterham's first export market was Japan. David

Wakefield dealt with the many early Japanese inquiries: "This was a market I couldn't wait to get my hands on – it was time to turn the tide of Japanese imports. We had an inquiry from the then Lotus and Lamborghini dealer, Atlantic Trading, but they wanted us to homologate the car for Japan. We got the compliance requirements through and just laughed. They were several inches thick and all in Japanese. We hadn't a hope of trawling through

Off to America: a batch of very early Lotus Sevens on the first stage of a very long journey. However, the American market was always a fickle one for the Seven.

Production of the Seven S4 was also licensed to Steele Brothers of New Zealand. This is their prototype fitted with the Lotus 907 Elite 2-litre engine, but creeping legislation ended production in 1979.

146

that lot, so that was the end of Atlantic Trading!

"Then I got a letter in impeccable English from a man called Hajimu Tanaka, of Kiwa Trading in Tokyo. He wanted to buy some used Lotus products and also asked about representing us with the Seven. He bought several used Sevens from us and operated faultlessly, so we had a gut feeling that he was the right man to go for."

This began as early as 1973 with three Series 4 cars. Kiwa had gone to all the trouble of providing a Series 4 for test in all the major Japanese magazines, so David Wakefield was apprehensive about breaking the news that production was ceasing in favour of the Series 3. But the reply came back: "We don't care. Just send us Super Sevens!"

Japan was instrumental in keeping Caterham going through the desperate economic wasteland of the mid-Seventies. The excellent working relation-

Graham Nearn in Tokyo with the Japanese importer of the Seven, Hajimu Tanaka of Kiwa Trading. Tanaka was instrumental in making Japan the most important export market for the Seven.

Flying helmet and goggles were obligatory costume for the Tokyo suburbs! A happy-looking owner needs no interpreter to convey his feelings to Graham Nearn.

Graham and Jane Nearn meet Mr Saito, vice-president of the Seven Owner's Club of Japan, who is also the Emperor's official photographer.

147

Japanese Seven owners are tremendously enthusiastic, spurred on by the Seven Owner's Club of Japan. Here is one of a regular series of track tests.

ship just flowered and Kiwa eventually ceased selling used Lotus products and other British cars exclusively in favour of Sevens.

Homologation in Japan was a sensitive issue. Every tenth car of each version had to be presented to the equivalent of an MoT test station to check that it complied with agreed guidelines. Japanese-spec catalysts had to be fitted to get them through the tests, plus wider front wings. Once transport and import duties were added on, this made the Seven very expensive in Japan – typically around twice the cost of a car in Britain – but then Japan is used to paying dearly for imported cars (as an illustration, a Fiat Panda cost £12,000 in 1993!).

From the start, Japan was consistently Caterham's most important export market. Over the years, the number of cars Kiwa took steadily increased to the extent that, in the Nineties, 20% of Caterham production (around 120 cars per year) ended up in Tokyo. "Mr Tanaka is a very dedicated and professional enthusiast," said Graham Nearn. "We have an absolutely confident relationship with him. He is extending the borders of the Seven's market with seven sub-dealers around the country."

The Japanese importer was insistent that the Seven remain as British as possible. That is part of the reason why some 95% of components have been sourced in the UK throughout its production life at Caterham. Tanaka also wished to keep the car as original as possible. For example, when Caterham switched from toggle switches to rocker switches on the dashboard, there was the sternest deputation from Japan to return to the traditional toggles!

Japan was also the source of some development advice. Minor design faults would sometimes crop

The typical Japanese Seven is highly specified and plays on its racing appeal.

The inaugural meeting of the Japanese Seven race series took place at Suzuka in 1992, initiating the first race series for a non-domestic-made car in Japan.

up on Japanese cars which might have looked like one-off glitches in the UK. Occasionally, there would be specific changes required by Japanese law, such as dual-circuit braking.

In 1992, the Japanese importer set up a domestic race series especially for Caterhams. The series immediately attracted a fanatical entry. One of the most powerful attractions was the fact that this was the first instance of any imported car gaining a one-make series in Japan.

Based around the Vauxhall-engined Caterham, some 68 cars regularly took to the tracks – far more than the equivalent British series, in fact. The regulations were a little more relaxed in Japan than in Britain, allowing a certain amount of modification – the lifeblood of the technologically-minded and

performance-mad Japanese competitor. One major difference was that since no slicks were allowed, many of the Vauxhall racers were actually road-legal!

Since the Japanese Vauxhall race series started in 1992, a large proportion of the Vauxhall race-car production has been shipped out to Japan. Interestingly, the JPE is classified as an uprated Vauxhall racer in Japan for legal reasons, and Tanaka has additionally imported around 20 of these.

Today, the Japanese market is as strong as ever. There is a one-year waiting list for delivery because Caterham and the importer have been careful to keep the Seven exclusive. That's one of the reasons why the Caterham has been so durable where other copy cars have faltered. The Seven Owners Club of

Caterham always has an official presence at the important Geneva Motor Show in association with the Swiss importer Kumschick Sports Cars. This was the Swiss debut of the Classic in 1994.

Graham Nearn pilots the German-spec Seven with its cycle wings, relocated indicators, wing mirror and a host of other minor changes.

Japan is probably the most highly regarded one-make club in Japan, since many other marques are represented by fragmented owners' clubs.

EUROPE

The early export markets for Caterham in Europe were Switzerland and Germany, both of which were steady importers from the Seventies onwards. Germany in particular was an enthusiastic market and at times rivalled the number of cars being exported to Japan. The market became so important that a special German-specification Seven was created in 1984 to pass local construction laws allowing the car to be sold fully built. The full story has been recounted in Chapter 3.

Caterham has always made a point of attending international motor shows, ever mindful of the necessity for exposure. An early example was its attendance at the 1977 Amsterdam Speedshow. These days Caterham always has a stand at the Frankfurt and Essen shows, while it also attended Brussels one year. Geneva is another show at which there has been a consistent official presence in recent years in conjunction with Kumschick Sports Cars, the Swiss importer.

Fredy Kumschick was a very enthusiastic exponent of the Caterham. For example, when the Swiss authorities began insisting on emissions-controlled engines (well before the rest of Europe), special Ford XR-powered Caterhams had to be built. Kumschick restored the performance record of the Seven by turbocharging many of these engines locally, going on to offer Sevens with an incredible 300bhp turbocharged Opel engine.

The Dutch Seven had a special chassis widened at the rear to create a wider cockpit (note the slimmer rear wings). This example also had a Lotus Elite 2-litre engine fitted.

Literally hundreds of Caterham and Lotus Sevens descend on St Moritz each year for the biggest international Seven meeting.

Another early market was Holland. Willem Boterman was the first Dutch agent. He asked Caterham to build a special Dutch chassis called the 3B. To allow extra cockpit width (a minimum width was required by Dutch law), the chassis tubes from the front bulkhead back tapered outwards to the rear frame as opposed to running parallel. That also made the rear end wider and the whole cockpit slightly longer.

Graham Nearn remembers he and Clive Roberts going to meet Dutch officials. "We discovered that the minimum cockpit width law was based on an example of an old truck where a large degree of elbow room was required to turn the steering wheel. It was also not clear where the width should

be measured, but it seemed logical it meant at elbow height – so we removed the sidescreens! The Seven was modified to pass these tests, but the law in Holland was changed soon after as a result of our discussions."

Boterman adapted a 3B chassis to accept a Lotus 907 2-litre engine and Elite five-speed gearbox in the late Seventies. This was actually displayed at a show in Holland, but it was never made as an official model.

France was a difficult market. Even following the Seven's successful barrier crash test in France in 1989, allowing it to be sold fully-built, and even with the very successful race series of the Nineties, road-car sales have always been disappointing.

Sevens go even further afield: here German chemist Peter Bergmann is pictured during his epic journey with two other Seven owners to the Sahara desert.

Basic GT and HPC as imported to Italy await service at a Milanese pizzeria.

A Seven at the Drei Eechelen, near the city of Luxembourg.

152

Geneva Salon, 1996: the Caterham Cars stand boasting importer Fredy Kumschick's inter-galactic turbocharged 300bhp Seven, on sale for the equivalent of no less than £65,000.

Canadian Seven: the Caterham sits in front of the Toronto skyline dominated by the CN Tower, the world's tallest free-standing structure.

However, that situation may well be changing as awareness of the Seven increases.

In the Nineties, Type Approval in Europe has become easier for the simple reason that everyone is now clearer what the laws actually mean. Many countries are bound to accept Type Approval passes in other markets as the basis for approval in their own country.

Up to the historic presentation of the Queen's Award for Export in 1993, Caterham had obtained National Type Approval for the Seven in Germany, France, Holland, Belgium, Luxembourg, Switzerland, Portugal and Norway, with a personal import service available for Italy and Spain.

Eastern Europe was a fresh market opportunity following the collapse of the various Communist regimes. In particular, the Czech Republic looks promising, having taken four cars by early 1996.

AMERICA

"The United States is a curious market," comments Graham Nearn. "It has tremendous potential, but remains a very grey area. We have always been at a disadvantage because cars are so cheap over there. It's a very hard market to operate in and has always been something of a monkey on our back. I really feel that we are two countries separated by a common language.

"It's not that people are not aware of what the Seven is: most customers still remember the Lotus Seven, even though Sevens hardly ever appear in the American motoring press. It's mostly the confused legislation and the difficulty of finding reliable outlets. California is still our main US market."

Now at least there is a definitive policy which

states that you can import a kit-car as long as it doesn't have an engine and transmission. That way, the expensive Federal Type Approval regulations are avoided. Buyers then have to source drivetrains themselves; Caterham recommends the 1600 Ford unit.

Perhaps the future looks more rosy as a race series is being set up at the time of writing. This is ironic since, way back in 1963, the Seven made news because the US racing organization, the Sports Car Club of America (SCCA), had banned the Lotus Super Seven from racing in standard guise because it was 'contrary to the spirit' of the regulations. Some people took that to mean just too fast, including some parts of the British press, who were apparently incensed that exotic machinery

was being allowed to race but the humble Seven was booted out. However, in 1977 the Seven returned to the US racing scene when Tom Robertson drove a 1963 Lotus Seven to victory over far more modern competition in the SCCA National Championship – 14 years late!

The racing publicity helped make the Lotus Seven a popular car in the 'States until federal laws in 1968 meant the Seven was no longer possible to market. But Caterhams have always made it to the 'States, and always in kit-form.

Other parts of the American continent are represented, too, with agents in Canada and Venezuela, the latter represented by Stephen Goss, the brother of Tim Goss, who won the 1970 Clubman's championship in the Lotus 7X. Small world... The way

Racers from all over Europe converged at Le Mans in 1991 for a well-attended one-off race for Caterhams. It was so successful that the event was repeated in 1992.

Action from the French race series, in which Ford-powered cars raced along the lines of the Class C series in Britain.

Nurburgring 1995: a pre-race gathering of all the Sevens which would be competing at this historic one-make event.

he sells cars is to gatecrash local Ferrari and Porsche high-speed events and trounce all the exotics with the little Seven!

PACIFIC BASIN
The very first Caterham Seven S4 was exported to the Far East and, ever since, there has been a consistent flow of Sevens in that direction. In addition to Japan, Caterham Cars is represented in Thailand, Taiwan, Hong Kong, Macao, Singapore, the United Arab Emirates, Korea, Indonesia, Malaysia and Brunei, while personal import services are available in New Zealand and Australia.

Australia was a brand-new market in 1992. Despite having to contend with import duty at 40%, Monarch Motors of Melbourne successfully began selling the Seven in Oz. Initially only K-series cars were available as they were in the best position to comply with Australian rules.

"We don't expect Australia to be a big market," says Graham Nearn, "but we'd hope to sell around 20 cars a year."

INTERNATIONAL RACING
Caterham's works team attendances at international events such as the Nurburgring and the Nelson Ledges in America have been covered in the racing chapter. The Seven's suitability for racing has not been lost on enthusiasts abroad,

either, and many events have been organized on foreign shores. In addition, the well-written regulations help sell the idea of full race series abroad.

In Australia, importer Monarch Motors entered an HPC in the Targa Tasmania five-day event in 1994. After qualifying in 16th position, Robert Nearn and navigator Andrew Smith worked up into the top 10 before hitting a tree. They went on to complete the race – which took place over 1,250 miles of closed roads – in 38th place out of 290 entrants.

In 1991, a Caterham race on the Le Mans Bugatti circuit was organized by enthusiasts in France. There were various classes for the racers and overall winner was Robert Nearn. Reg Price remembers driving out of the pit lane on to the circuit and found himself shaking: "I thought to myself, I'm getting too old for this. But it wasn't that at all, it was the fact that I was driving out on to the circuit at Le Mans, something I'd dreamed of all my life."

All the cars were lined up prior to the race for photographs and, remembers Graham Nearn, "there wasn't a dry eye in the house". The event proved such a success that it was repeated the following year.

There was also a French Ford racing series from 1991, which roughly equated to Class C in the UK and proved very successful. That was supplemented in 1994 by a Vauxhall series, and today both series are very professionally run by an organization called TOP and recognized as a National championship. The leading drivers take it very seriously, but most enjoy their racing in typically French style – large transporters and grand hospitality. As a measure of its impact in France, the series has been featured in the programme of the French Grand Prix.

In 1993, the first of the Caterham races at Spa was organized by the Belgian importer of the time. There were 68 starters, including entrants from Belgium, France, Germany and Britain. On the Friday night before qualifying, the police closed the road between Francorchamps and Spa (about 10km) and everybody drove their cars into town – whether they were road-legal or not – which turned into a big racing parade and party. The carnival atmosphere even fell over on to the circuit, with a jazz band playing on the line before the start. The categories were for Vauxhalls, K-series, French Vauxhall racers, French Ford racers and standard and modified road cars.

The Spa event took place again in 1994, 1995 and 1996 with even larger turnouts; Caterham's new Belgian agent, Johan de Bolster, organized the 1995 event. Extra events were added in 1995 as the precursor to a proper racing series in Belgium, since it is a market which is well supported and boasts healthy sales.

Yet another new chapter in Seven racing was opened at the Nurburgring in November 1995 when a Sevens-only meeting was held in conjunction with the German Caterham importer. The authorities were reportedly extremely keen for the Caterhams to appear, accommodating their special requirements within the track regulations. The race was run over the short Grand Prix circuit and the general level of enthusiasm was extremely high. These days, racing a Seven is truly an international activity.

British driver Danny Audritt joined dozens of continental enthusiasts at the fabulous Spa circuit in Belgium for the special Caterham race, which has proven immensely popular.

CHAPTER 8

Sevens under scrutiny

A shot of adrenalin for road-testers

Road-testers always relish the chance to get behind the wheel of a Caterham. Perhaps that is why the marque occupies so many column inches in proportion to its sales volume. There is something about the Seven which inspires wizened old hacks to dispense with their cliches and tap into a super-conscious store of superlatives to describe their experience. That is just one of the joys of driving a Seven: it is unlike any other car, any other experience. Here is a representative, model-by-model sample of the best of what the press has said about the Caterham Seven.

Lotus Twin Cam

Autocar ran one of the first road tests of a Caterham S3 in September 1975. The Big Valve Twin Cam test car, registered JPE 946N, provided the testers with a happy opportunity to take a rest from Austin Allegros.

"Only a handful, and a tiny handful at that, of cars can match the performance of the Super Seven in accelerating from rest to 100mph in 22sec, and none that we have ever tested reach 30mph in only 2.3sec... No less impressive is the acceleration in each gear, especially in third, in which only the 20mph increment from 50 to 70mph occupies more than 4sec."

As for road behaviour: "The roadholding is marvellous, the ride is diabolical and the handling on the nervous side of reassuring... Light steering with plenty of feel tells you exactly what is happening and allows instant correction of the result of any careless or excessive use of the right foot."

In *Motor Sport*, September 1975, it was said of the Twin Cam: "You don't really drive a Super Seven, you think it along... The Super Seven is

The author re-acquainted himself with the Seven in the form of this 1995 K-series. Driving it from Caterham to Aberystwyth and back, he became convinced that this was surely the best all-round Seven.

This prophetic number-plate graced the first Caterham press car, a dark blue Twin Cam, chassis number 3592, built in 1975. Here *Autocar* staff member Chris Goffey confirms that the Seven was then the fastest car ever tested from rest to 30mph.

crude, uncomfortable over long distances and thoroughly impractical, but its magical performance and handling would make it a 'must' in my mythical stable of ideal cars. The Super Seven is not *just* a sports car, it's the definitive article."

Doug Nye in *Road & Track* tested a Twin Cam in 1977. "From standstill it's simple to drag away with spinning wheels and the engine pulling hard from around 3,000rpm. The Elan Sprint gearbox has the shortest lever I've ever seen and you just blink to snatch 2nd, blink again for 3rd then top with the tires chirping with wheelspin in each intermediate cog!

"This little car is fun – so much fun you just can't believe it's still allowed… It's crude, it's uncompromising, but it's also sheer, unadulterated, unbelievable fun."

In *Autosport*'s road test of July 1979 (one of the last contemporary tests of a Big Valve Seven), John Bolster pronounced: "The whole point of the Super Seven is that it's marvellous fun to drive. There's nothing difficult about it and almost anyone would enjoy it, but only a competent *conducteur* can make it display its full magic. In the hands of a real coachman, there is practically nothing on wheels that can look at it on a winding road. This combination of roadholding, quick steering and immense acceleration adds up to about the safest car that's made anywhere. When you flick past a mimser who is wandering all over the road, you are past him and gone before he has time to hoot his pathetic little horn in his fury… Although I suppose I am old enough to have reached years of discretion, I reckon that the Super Seven is the ultimate for fun on wheels."

Caterham Cars' test car for 1977 was a blue Twin Cam with a roll-over bar.

1600GT

Tests of the basic 84bhp GT version of the Super Seven were rarities because Caterham Cars seldom had a 1600GT available for test. In the Seventies, virtually no-one bought one; why should they, given the ready availability of the Lotus Twin Cam? Well, perhaps they should have looked again, as John Miles of *Autocar* did when he tried a 1600GT alongside a Twin Cam in January 1980; indeed these were the first Sevens he had ever driven.

He was immediately struck by the unique experience: "You are sitting near the ground, seemingly *wearing* a generously tyred road racer with 120bhp per ton laden on tap... The steering is superb... about perfectly weighted and wonderfully direct – the Super 7 cries out to be flicked around. I had forgotten what open air motoring was all about."

Of the GT he said: "In the dry the standard Super 7 does not have the power to kick out the rear, whereas in second gear the Twin Cam one just does... In most respects I found the Kent-engined Super Seven most fun. Where it lacks the Twin Cam car's ultimate performance it has much better low down acceleration bite in the gears... [The Twin Cam] has to be turning at around 1,500rpm before it will accept full throttle without hesitating and does not even begin to pull hard until turning over at 3,500rpm, *ie* precisely where the Kent motor is giving peak torque. In cars that have the same overall gearing this makes the more prosaic model far nicer to drive round town, neither does it have to be 'rowed' along like the Twin Cam on the open road. In fact acceleration in third and top below 60mph actually proved somewhat better in the standard Super 7."

Vegantune VTA

Autocar's John Miles got behind the wheel of a Vegantune Twin Cam-engined Caterham in 1983, being pictured in the magazine opposite-locking the car around a roundabout on public roads!

Miles reckoned that the Vegantune Twin Cam was every bit as lively as the old Lotus version. "It would take a supercar to squirt past slow-moving trucks with such a complete lack of fuss." He described the 0–60mph time of 6.2 seconds as "staggering" but was surprised to find that a 1600 Sprint version sampled at the same time "felt very nearly as quick through the gears as the VTA car, and perhaps even more responsive at low to middle rpm".

He concluded: "There were times when I hated it. So much would be gained by quietening the inlet system and improving the seat further. There were times when I suffered for it (the wet). But give me a Caterham Super 7, a dry road, and the world seems a rosier place."

Brian Laban broadly concurred in *Automobile Sport* dated November 1982. "Muted burbles as the VTA catches instantly on the key do nothing to suppress the Walter Mitty streak, the lurid tail slide from mixing hurried take-off with wet, leaf strewn road does... All this adds to an Honest-to-God real live motor car, with straight-line performance in the Wham-Bam-Thankyou-Ma'am league – as the Inn sign says: 'Take Courage'!"

Sprint

Again, the 110bhp Sprint version of the Seven was not commonly available for press road tests. In June 1981, John Miles of *Autocar* pitted an example

Suspension expert John Miles, then of *Autocar*, complete with testing machinery stuck to the windscreen, pushes a Twin Cam hard in 1980: "It corners very securely, very fast, and with a trace of understeer."

After his first drive of a Seven, John Miles became a firm advocate, even if his 6ft frame was a tight fit.

against various sportscars up Harewood hillclimb in Yorkshire. The Seven Sprint came second to a Porsche 911 SC and beat off such rivals as a TVR Tasmin, Lancia Montecarlo, Morgan Plus 8, Reliant Scimitar and Panther Lima. Miles said the Seven "would be an easy winner with limited slip differential – or even without, given another couple of practice runs."

John McCormick in *Car* of July 1982 tried a Sprint and concluded, "Despite the passage of time the Seven remains as crude, uncomfortable, uncivilized and downright exhilarating as the day it was born." Of the Sprint engine it was said that it "might look mundane, but it packs 110bhp of Webered power to push the Caterham beyond 110mph. Acceleration is terrific."

The author tested a Sprint for *Component Car* magazine in 1984 when the kit-built Seven was launched and, being my first experience of Sevens, I found it to be every bit what it had been cracked up to be. The Sprint engine was lively enough for near-supercar performance (0–60mph in under 7 seconds), while its power delivery was both smooth and flexible. Of the kit-built version I concluded: "The same devastatingly fast, superbly agile, charismatic little sportscar which enthusiasts idolize is now just a little closer to being the sportscar for the common man."

The Ford-engined Seven continued to enchant testers well into the Nineties.

160

Caterham Cars and the Seven have been inseparable almost from the very beginning. This Seven has come full-circle: it is Graham Nearn's early Lotus Seven S1, pictured outside the redeveloped Caterham sales office.

A very early Caterham-built S3, which the company began making in 1974 to replace the more complex and unloved S4. Externally, only a few differences identify it from a modern one: old-style wheels, narrow rear wings, no roll-over bar, basic sidescreens and a bench seat.

A Seven as it should be seen: overtaking at speed. This is a press/demonstration car pictured in 1977. Virtually all Sevens were fitted with the Lotus Big Valve Twin Cam engine at this time, which provided fabulous performance in that pre-hot hatch era.

The Caterham team pictured in 1983. From left to right: Graham Nearn, Roy Crane, Jez Coates, Neil Whitford, David Wakefield, Clive Roberts, Johnny Johnstone, John Payne, Reg Price, Ian Cowdrey, Peter Cooper, Isobel Forster and Alex Davids.

Sevens always needed an element of home construction to circumvent Type Approval laws (at least until the passing of Low Volume Type Approval in 1993). Here ex-*Classic Cars* writer and author Jeremy Coulter builds his Seven in 1981.

A major advance for the Seven was the development by Caterham of the 1700 Supersprint engine. With an output of 135bhp, it was the engine which finally had enough 'go' to replace the revered old Twin Cam.

In response to changing times, Graham Nearn saw the need to introduce more basic Seven kits in late 1984. Because the customer did so much more of the build-up, the price of the car could be greatly reduced with no loss of the traditional Caterham level of quality.

CATERHAM CAR SALES

The Seven has always been a dual-purpose car. Although most are in fact bought strictly for road use, customers are very well aware of the Seven's competition role.

The new Dartford factory, occupied in October 1987. Compared with the cramped old Caterham site, the new 25,000sq ft unit was spacious, airy and much more thoughtfully planned out.

This Supersprint looks just as much at home in the city as on twisting country roads.

Patrick McGoohan's "I am not a number" speech has long since passed into cult status. As a free man in the *Prisoner* TV series, he drove a Seven. From 1989, so could anyone, with the Prisoner special edition, pictured in 'The Village' (Portmeirion, in North Wales).

Patrick McGoohan was flown over from Hollywood to endorse the Prisoner special edition at the Birmingham Motor Show in 1990. He was presented with the keys to this very car, chassis number 6 of the special edition, echoing his name in the TV series – 'Number 6'.

The Vauxhall-powered HPC launched in 1990 was the fastest Seven yet: it could do 126mph and reach 60mph from rest in 4.8 seconds. Wider wheels and tyres were specified to give much-needed extra grip, although some testers bemoaned the resulting loss of on-tap over-steer around bends!

The heart of the new HPC was a Caterham-branded Vauxhall 2-litre 16-valve engine. This one has big twin Webers and a very tractable and reliable 175bhp. Fuel injection was fitted later on.

The interior of the Seven was traditionally a very stark place to be, but by the 1990 HPC, things were looking much more comfortable: plenty of dials and rocker switches, and separate seats with optional leather upholstery.

Caterham turned to Rover for its latest engine, the K-series unit. The K-series-powered Seven was launched in London's Docklands in 1991. Graham Nearn is straddled by the Mayor of Bexley and Sir Graham Day, chairman of the Rover Group.

Undoubtedly the wildest Seven ever made was the JPE. Ex-Formula One driver Jonathan Palmer endorsed and helped develop this ultimate Seven, which had 250bhp on tap and was, at the time, the world's fastest-accelerating car, capable of reaching 60mph from rest in under 3.5 seconds.

The set of JPE gauges which caused such controversy: the rev-counter had virtually no markings below 6,000rpm and the speedo was unmarked beyond 70mph! It all added to the very special character of the JPE.

Everything was either fluorescent yellow or black on the JPE, including the Kevlar seats and the webbing of the Luke six-point harnesses.

Jonathan Palmer was a confirmed fan of the Caterham Seven, several examples of which he used on his Motorsport Experience corporate days. He commented that his Seven was "more fun than anything else I have driven".

The dedicated Research & Development area at Dartford allowed Caterham to pursue its own engineering solutions to the fullest extent. In the foreground is L7 VXT, the experimental Vauxhall Turbo car, while in the background work is in progress on the composite 21.

Full roster of staff at the Dartford factory…

…and at the sales and administration office at Caterham. Standing, left to right, are Andy Noble, Mike Thodesen, Belinda McDougall, David Wakefield, John Brigden, Peter Haynes and Jean Mallery; in the car is Kerry Ricketts and squatting in front is Paul Kite.

One-make racing for Sevens started as early as 1986 and has grown rapidly since then to encompass three classes. This is the top end: a Vauxhall Challenge meeting (at Thruxton in 1994, where Guy Metcalfe leads ex-Euro Truck Champion Steve Parrish).

A huge variety of drivers raced in the Caterham series. Here, the road test editor for *Performance Car* magazine, John Barker, sprints on at Cadwell Park during his 1992 debut season. He just failed to win the Class C crown in this K-series-powered car.

Racing was always spectacular to watch, as very closely-matched cars continually passed and re-passed each other. Here two cars touch wings as they dash for a corner.

Victory! Against all odds, Caterham won the 1992 Nelson Ledges 24 Hours in America, perhaps the Seven's greatest single competitive achievement. Reg Price is driving, American George Alderman is waving the stars and stripes, Robert Nearn the Union Flag and Jez Coates sits behind. All four drove in the race.

Caterham racing has taken off in a big way in Japan. Here a large field takes on the famous circuit at Suzuka. *[Photo by Saito]*

Lotus heritage: the new all-aluminium Caterham 21 prototype pictured outside the Dartford factory alongside two historic aluminium-bodied Lotus forebears: Seven S1 and Eleven. 21 designer Iain Robertson cited the Eleven as one of his main influences.

This is the production-ready 21 with painted composite bodywork and Rover 1.6 K-series power.

The distinctively styled and beautiful interior of the 21, which drew such favourable comment at the car's debut at the 1995 London Motor Show.

Part of the 1996 specification for the Seven are these classic Caterham-branded gauges.

176

Getting in and out with the hood up was an art invariably commented upon by testers.

Supersprint

Soon after Caterham launched the Supersprint, *Autocar* ran a full road test of the new car in 1985. They opened up by calling it "this masterpiece of a lightweight motor car".

"The engine's spread of power is surprisingly good, considering its rorty character, and one can certainly let it get on with the job unaided by wheel or clutch slip from comparatively low rpm. And get on with it, it does – and how... Considering how, when accelerated in anger from a low speed, the power does not come in until 3,000rpm, and not truly strongly until 4,000rpm (whereafter it is evenly if raucously frantic all the way to 6,500rpm and beyond), we were pleasantly surprised how, with a little care, one could pull away from below tickover speed."

Test figures indicated a top speed of 111mph and a 0–60mph time of 5.6 seconds. Of the "superbly accurate" steering, the testers said: "This is *so* refreshing after the number of examples of wandery, over-responsive front-drive steering we have encountered lately."

Their verdict? "The Caterham is an enthusiast's car: we know of no other that comes close to offering the sort of buzz the 1700 Supersprint has to offer for the price."

Motor Sport also tested the same car, A530 FPJ. Of it they said: "Harmony is perhaps the word which best sums up the Seven: it's noisy to be sure, it vibrates, the ride is hard (but not harsh) but all its characteristics combine to present a unity of style... It is the phenomenal acceleration, the sure-footed handling, the precision of the steering and

John Miles demonstrates amusement potential of the Vegantune VTA engine in this 1983 test for *Autocar*.

the overall sense of harmony which gives so much pleasure... Acceleration is extraordinary, even if you have to fight the car on a quick getaway."

Cars & Car Conversions tried the white Supersprint de Dion show car in September 1986 and enthused: "We unreservedly recommend the de Dion option. The legendary Seven roadholding and precision are still there, but the ride is totally transformed. It is not just far better than before: we would go so far as to say it is good, very good for a car of this type. It is firm, of course, but never harsh; just as it should be... Every now and then, all motoring enthusiasts should drive a Caterham Seven, if only to remind themselves... how a car can *really* go, stop and handle; the Seven's capabilities are really on a different plane to more mundane vehicles."

In 1987, two years after its first test, *Motor* revisited the Supersprint, this time fitted with the de Dion rear end and five-speed gearbox. The engine came in for the same sorts of praise: "[It] works best in the 4,000–6,000rpm range hinted at by the high revs at which the peak torque is developed [4,500rpm]."

The de Dion rear end was praised: "Traction is superb... Such are the car's immensely quick reactions, particularly to steering inputs, that seldom can the man/machine relationship be more intimate. Every bump, ridge or mere loose chipping is felt precisely, even though minor suspension deflections are well-absorbed by the chassis... The de Dion rear suspension has certainly enhanced the Sprint's sheer gripping ability, especially when traversing mid-corner bumps. The minus side is that with such a well-controlled pair of rear wheels,

understeer can become a mite too strong. Only sharp provocation will prompt the car to move into a satisfying balanced drift."

The Supersprint was also voted one of *Car* magazine's Top Ten cars of 1987. "What impresses *Car* about the Seven is the way it sticks out, more and more, from the common sports car herd... The car hits peaks and stays there... No other sports car of under £10,000 – no other *car*, in fact – can come within a bull's roar of its capabilities... The essence of the Caterham... is this: it is a unique driving experience. Even the special attributes of a Rolls or Mercedes can be found in other cars, but if you want what a Caterham has, there's nowhere else to go."

In the American *Automobile* magazine's test of a Supersprint in 1988, William Jeanes stated delightfully: "Unless you had lived through the years I think of as the Era of Flopping Side Curtains, when men were men and sports cars spent a lot of their time acting cranky, the Caterham may not make sense to you. It's loud, it rides about an inch off the road surface and, with its top erected, it has the visibility of a body bag... Unless you are British – a race of motorists who enjoy breaking up the monotony of driving with hypothermia and pneumonia – the Caterham is a fair-weather friend... It has the single-minded utility of an elephant gun and the irresistible attraction of free champagne."

Cosworth BDR

The first Cosworth BDR-engined Seven arrived in 1984. This was the 150bhp 1600 version which, strangely, hardly appeared in the press. An early test was that of *Sporting Cars* magazine in October

Richard Bremner, then of *Motor*, beats the mud as he pilots a Seven up Harewood hillclimb in Yorkshire.

The Supersprint test car in 1986 had the new de Dion suspension fitted and was universally praised for its improved ride and control.

1984 – even before the de Dion rear end was a standard feature. Their Japanese-spec BDR was "*really* quick and incredibly agile" and they revelled in a car which offered a power-to-weight ratio of around 300bhp per ton.

The very first Prisoner car of 1989 was also fitted with a 1600 BDR engine, one of only 50 to be so equipped. Darren Styles, editor of *World Sportscars* magazine, drove it and commented on the "explosive acceleration". He added: "The handling responses are pin-sharp, the road adhesion akin to a fly on treacle and the exhaust note and exuberance of the BDR enough to awaken even those in eternal sleep. Savour, too, the almighty crackle, the banging and popping and pyrotechnic display from the pipe at the passenger's side on the over-run."

Of the Prisoner edition specifically, he was amazed at "the curious effect four letters and three numerals on a number-plate can have on the public perception of a car... Virtually everybody who expressed interest recognized KAR 120C as *the* Prisoner car sooner or later, and I was cross-examined countless times about Portmeirion in Wales, setting for the series, and a big, bouncing weather balloon called Rover."

World Sportscars was also one of the few magazines to test a Cosworth 1700 BDR. Despite the model's introduction in 1986, the first test did not take place until 1989, the reason being that Caterham hardly needed the publicity – or frankly the accident risk – of a magazine road test.

Darren Styles described the experience: "Imagine, if you will, jumping from Beachy Head in a sitting position with your arms at ten to two... The tired old adjectives can be swept away by the HPC because what semblance of logic the Seven may once have possessed no longer applies. Who honestly would ever want to move quite that quickly in something weighing as little as 640 bags of Tate and Lyle?

"Caterham are genuinely close to Utopia for the hardened enthusiast. Sure the car is a little twitchy in the wet, sure the ride remains as knobbly as an old man's knees... Ultimately, however, it will be worth your while as you eat into that slab of torque, maximum 140lb.ft at 5,500rpm, and unleash the 170 horses at 6,500rpm as an inane grin fixes itself across your frozen countenance."

Vauxhall HPC

Car magazine had already voted the Caterham Seven as its Sports Car of the Year in 1987 and 1989. In 1990 it happened again, when Mark Gillies explained the charms of the then brand-new HPC. On its performance: "It goes like a Rottweiler after a rabbit... Because you're sitting so low, the trees rush towards you at what feels like 220mph."

On its handling: "The footwear gives outrageous grip in the dry, which is a shame because I enjoy the more slip-slidey style of lesser siblings. I can think of only three ways of getting the HPC's tail out in the dry: booting it hard in second gear (and then it only just steps out of shape); arriving at crested bends at speed, when the car skips sideways a little; or being brain dead."

On the concept: "It's a marvellous antidote to the bigger, bulkier, more comfortable school of car design."

Autocar & Motor conducted the seminal test of the HPC in August 1990. "It's loud and lusty, raw and raspy," it said. "Give it the gun and it will stay with anything this side of a Ferrari Testarossa up to around 100mph: 0–60mph in 5.2secs (same as Testarossa)… The in-gear times give the 7 an opportunity to show a clean tailpipe to the super-cars… Indeed, running through our complete listing draws a blank when attempting to find anything that will match the Caterham's top gear 50–70mph time of just 5.7secs.

"Driving the 7 hard and fast to achieve those figures is a rich, sensory experience of total driver involvement… Even once aware of the high power achieved from Vauxhall's lusty 2-litre, the breadth and the intensity of it still astonish.

"Contrary to most testers' preconceptions, the 7 HPC isn't the twitchy and unruly beast imagined. Going hard through a corner, the 7 assumes a state of steady balance bordering on mild understeer… But if gratuitous power-induced oversteer is the aim, razor-sharp driver reflexes are essential to avoid an over-correction… The 7 corners as flat as a racer, with bitingly sharp turn-in and continuous, finely detailed feedback through the tiny leather-rimmed wheel… Dynamically, only the high-speed stability demands criticism. The engine and chassis otherwise share equal billing for the starring role… For the ultimate thrill on four wheels, a 7 is still king."

Ian Kuah sampled an HPC in the September 1991 edition of *World Sportscars*. "In full cry, the HPC has plenty of grunt. 60mph comes and goes in around five seconds and the car storms quickly onwards to its drag limited 120mph top speed. With a 20.6 top gear ratio, the 0.6 plus drag coefficient slams the car into a brick wall of air when the rev-counter is still two grand from its screaming 7500rpm rev-limiter in top."

Performance Car's John Barker managed to extract a 0–60mph time of 4.9 seconds for the HPC in his test of September 1991. He concluded: "The HPC is a well-rounded, complete performer… There really is nothing quite like it, comparable cars lacking the Caterham's integrity."

Of the same machine *Motor Sport* said: "If the

Good Lord has a 'grin machine' for recreational purposes, it must be a Caterham 7 HPC… The Vauxhall engine has provided the most potent of arguments for fresh air speed and rear drive handling."

Autocar & Motor pitched the HPC against Gordon Murray's lightweight Rocket in May 1992. Both got five stars overall in the test, but which one was better? The £38,000 Rocket was dynamically a slightly quicker machine but "for us, the Seven and the thick end of £20,000 in the bank is harder to resist."

In February 1993, the then-leading British motoring monthly, *Car*, again included the 7 HPC as one of its top 10 cars. Paul Horrell stated: "If an open sports car is a psychiatric restorative then a Caterham is a miracle cure… Driving it is sensory saturation… Perhaps for one mile in a hundred, a Diablo might be more exhilarating than an HPC. For the other 99 miles I'll be happier in my Seven."

The same month the American magazine *Car and Driver* tested a US-spec HPC with a 150bhp version of the 2-litre Calibra engine. They had some reservations about the cramped cockpit, the noise of the engine and its skittery behaviour on rutted bends. But overall they were stunned: "There may not be a better player around: the Caterham's steering is sharp and properly weighted. We'd be hard pressed to find a better set of non-ABS brakes. Throttle response is instantaneous and the engine always rewards prods of the pedal with a surge in the back and a trombone-like blast from the exhaust… Sometimes the package seems so goofy, it's hard to stop grinning."

K-series

Autocar's test shared Jez Coates' view that the K-series was probably *the* Caterham to have: in value terms, it outshone the HPC at almost £5,000 cheaper: "As it stands, the K-car is still arguably the most enjoyable car Caterham makes.

"What the 1,396cc motor lacks in flexibility – even in the ultra-lightweight Seven it struggles to pull with any real conviction until 4,000rpm – it more than compensates for with its fantastic response at the top end combined with outstanding fuel economy… Over the final 2,000rpm, it's smoother than a pint of Guinness."

The five-speed gearbox came in for some criticism because it, "severely blunts progress and comes disturbingly close to spoiling the car. It also demotes the Seven's flexibility to levels occupied by vastly heavier rivals." Small wonder that Caterham's own six-speed gearbox was subsequently developed.

As usual, *Autocar* was glowing about the Seven's handling: "Alongside rivals of a similar girth and weight, the K-car is way out in a class on its own… It's not the grip that makes it so special – that's a commodity the HPC specialises in. Instead it's the combination of its steering – the most informative, involving helm we've come across on a road car – its incredible directional adjustability via the throttle, and its propensity to drift, foursquare, around any corner you choose."

In March 1992, John Barker tested the K-series for *Performance Car*. He commented: "The K-series Seven is the most responsive Caterham in the last two decades." But he was less impressed by refinement: "The K-series is not the smoothest, most eager-sounding of engines… in a space-framed, aluminium-clad semi-racer it sounds like a clockwork mouse in a biscuit tin." His conclusion? "Seriously addictive."

The author's own experience of the K-series confirmed how right the Rover engine is for the Seven. Inevitably, drivers do tend to chase you across a well-known country route; equally inevitably they are lost – whatever their pursuit vehicle – if you keep the Rover engine high in the rev-band and trust the Seven's phenomenal ability to negotiate corners. It was only when I had to return to London from Aberystwyth at night that I tired of the Seven's delights. Let's just say that, if you aren't wearing earplugs, drive with the roof down if you possibly can unless you like whistling ears for two days. Then again, even if you *are* wearing earplugs, still drive with the top down.

Autocar & Motor returned to the K-series car in 1993 when the Supersport engine came on stream, inspiring the magazine to buy a Supersport as a long-term test car-cum-racer. Through 12,000 miles of hard road use, sprinting, hillclimbing and racing in the K-series Challenge, the Supersport hardly missed a beat. Peter McSean concluded: "Nothing's perfect. But I'm beginning to wonder if our Caterham is as close as it gets."

Performance Car's first impressions of the Supersport were very favourable. David Vivian felt attracted to the concept because he recognized that the standard K-series was probably "the purest and most rewarding Seven of them all", but "if I'm brutally honest, the K doesn't have quite enough in the go department…

"Take [the Supersport] above 4,000rpm," he said, "and suddenly the light [to change gear] is

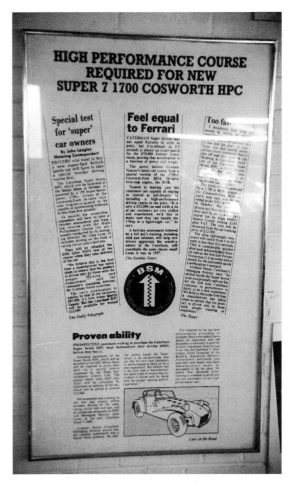
Press cuttings on Caterham's wall following the launch of the publicity-generating HPC in 1986.

winking at you, hedgerows have become a fluid grey-green blur and it's time to change gear. That doesn't take long either: the 'box is as delectably snappy as ever and the ratios absolute perfection… The best news of all, though, is that the extra urge doesn't corrupt the essential intimacy and accessibility of the car. If anything, it makes it easier to exploit."

Autocar & Motor sampled the new six-speed gearbox in a K-series Supersport in November 1993. They commented: "If anything the stubby gear lever has an even shorter throw than before… Palming the lever comes about as second nature, although the gates are close and the lever requires a little bit more guidance than before…

"But just look what the ratios do for performance. Compared with a non-Supersport K-series fitted with the five-speed gearbox, the improvements are startling… The in-gear incremental figures are rather good as well... Clearly the ratios have done their job well – the engine is unlikely to be let off the boil and rapid forward motion is virtually ceaseless. It also makes it the third most accelerative Caterham after the full-house JPE and the Vauxhall-engined HPC.

"As far as we're concerned, though, this is the best Caterham yet... At £16,995 fully built, the six-speed Supersport is pricey but unquestionably worth it. There, I said it. Six into Seven does go."

Classic
Since the Classic was merely a stripped-down old-style version of the standard GT, no full road test was ever published. However, *Which Kit?* magazine built a Classic during 1994 with a live rear axle, aero-screens and single-carb engine. Editor Ian Stent reported on the completed machine in August 1994.

He said: "With the simple aero-screens in place, cruising on the motorway is nigh on impossible without the aid of some flying goggles... I'm almost certain that the use of aero-screens also increases the top speed... Even the humble Classic can kick out its back end at will. Combined with the light weight, sensible engine performance, good weight distribution and decent rubber, the Classic is a beautifully, sumptuously predictable roadster to flick around the back roads...

"If I was to order one myself, I certainly wouldn't worry about the full windscreen, alloy wheels or twin carburettors. However, I'd make sure there was a tonneau cover and also some of the important gauges that are not normally included in the Classic package... It's a cracker and the company should make the most of it."

Mark Dixon of *Performance Car* drove a Classic SE in February 1993 and concluded that "it's a bargain and it's living proof that you don't need mega-horsepower to enjoy driving in its purest form."

In the February 1996 edition of *Car* magazine, one of the Top Ten best British cars was a Ford-powered Seven Classic ("sparse but sprightly," it said. "This, make absolutely no mistake, is ALL you need"). Part of the tribute read: "Nothing falls off or breaks. Nothing gets in the way of sheer amusement. There is no heater that doesn't work, no dodgy computer aggravation, no jammed electric windows, just noise, fresh air and hilarity."

JPE
The near-luminous yellow JPE was the stunning cover car for the November 1992 issue of *Performance Car*. As the coverline trumpeted, John Barker managed to record the phenomenal 0–60mph time of 3.5 seconds, which apparently caused Caterham's Jez Coates to "dance a jig and whoop with joy".

Barker enthused: "This fluorescent yellow Seven offers to redefine your perception of 'bloody quick' for little more than a tenth of the price of the [Bugatti] EB110.

"Performance is quite good low down, though you sense that all the way up to 5,500rpm the twin cam is just clearing its throat... When the needle hits [6,500rpm], the engine goes bonkers, rocketing the JPE forward on a truly breathtaking wave of power. Grab second and you're on top of the wave again, third and the acceleration is still flooding your senses, fourth and it still pulls like it's just hit the power band in first.

"Remarkably the chassis never feels overwhelmed – far from it... Traction is superb and lateral grip from the Yokohamas never less than outstanding. The brakes are, quite simply, brilliant, among the very best I've ever tried... It will oversteer, naturally, but feels so much like a race car that you find yourself driving it like one, picking out lines, keeping it neat and working hard at the gears to keep it in the power band. As Palmer said, it is a real 'driver's car' – you get as much out as you put in."

Car magazine's Brett Fraser also got his hands on the JPE in time for the November 1992 issue. His description was as dramatic as the car: "Blip the throttle hard – no, harder – and the Evolution yowls like a single-seat racer on the final qualifying lap of the session. It's ear-pluggingly loud, rippling with raw energy... The engine pops and grunts and babbles, its bad attitude ripping to shreds the veneer of sophistication the engine management tries to impart.

"There isn't a red line on this car – it's a green one, starting at 6,500rpm and ending on the other side of the 8,200rpm rev-limiter. What's available in the green zone is what you've slapped down all those readies for.

"Your senses have trouble keeping tabs on how fast everything happens when you floor the throttle, and your reactions need a while to recalibrate. It's pretty scary, but in the same addictive way that stopped you turning off the telly as a kid when the Daleks attacked Dr Who."

When *Autocar* did its famous 0–100mph–0 test with Jonathan Palmer in the JPE, it said: "This car is fast with a capital F... The F40 is going to get stuffed out of sight... The Seven JPE is unequivocally the world's fastest-accelerating production car."

Mark Gillies drove the JPE for the leading Japanese magazine *CAR* in February 1993. His testimonial was going right to the people who would buy almost all of them, so it is no surprise to hear how he enthused: "It is simply mega-fast and mega-exciting... From 6,000 revs, there's forward urge that's almost unbelievable in its ferocity... Of all the road cars I have driven, this one has the best brakes... You won't find a gearshift this sharp on any other road car... You'd have to say that this dainty little car offers the highest level of useable performance in the world, for a fraction of the cost of the barnstormers from the great names in the industry."

The Australian magazine *Wheels* got behind the wheel of a JPE in February 1995 and led with the strap-line: "It was terror. It was torture. It was everything I'd fondly imagined." They elaborated: "Driving the JPE hurts. The noise is ferocious. The induction rasp... is amazingly loud. Exhaust noise is tremendous... On a steady throttle at middling revs, in every gear but direct fourth, gear whine is dominant... The JPE is capable of instant, furious acceleration... The Seven's steering is beautiful, but the JPE's handling on the public road is well balanced only in the sense that both ends bump steer."

In 1995 *Autocar* revisited the JPE for a special supplement to decide its choice of the greatest sportscar ever. Andrew Frankel commented: "In pure power-to-weight terms, if you put one of this season's more powerful Formula 1 engines in a

Performance Car's cover of November 1992 after they had accelerated the JPE from 0–60mph in just 3.5 seconds.

Vauxhall Calibra Turbo, the effect would not be dissimilar... It felt the fastest thing any of us have ever driven on the highway. Not even the McLaren [F1] seemed so swift."

21

When it first appeared in 1994, only the priceless

The completed composite 21. It is almost impossible to tell the difference between a painted Clubmans composite car and a painted aluminium Lightweight.

aluminium-bodied prototype of Caterham's new-generation 21 existed in road-going form, and even at the time of writing the 21 has still to enter production. It is therefore not surprising that a full road test has not yet appeared. However, Caterham had been brave enough to lend the car to BBC TV's *Top Gear* programme at the time of the car's 1994 Motor Show debut. Tiff Needell drove the car and was extremely favourable in his comments.

Shortly after, the JPE-engined prototype was loaned to *Autocar*. Andrew Frankel was enthusiastic: "Thanks to the doors and new cockpit, jumping in and out is easier, yet you sit in the same snug channel as a Seven provides and, even before you move off, the feel of the car is unmistakably Caterham. It attacks corners with the same eagerness, changes direction with the same alacrity...

"It handles the power of an engine that's not materially different to the one fitted to a BTCC Vauxhall Cavalier with ease, resisting wheelspin and staying firmly planted to the road despite a power-to-weight ratio almost identical to that of a Jaguar XJ220.

"It is pulverizingly quick and, I am sure, would reach 60mph in 4 sec. Its top speed is unknown, but... it seems reasonable to expect that it wouldn't stop accelerating in top until the rev-limiter intervened. Which equates to 8,000rpm and 171mph...

"There is much less buffeting [than a Seven], much better visibility and a greater sense of security from the wraparound bodywork, and vastly improved elbow room... It is, if you like, a Seven without the strings. It has a big boot and blots out the elements well enough to make a two-week European tour not simply possible, but natural and appealing."

Great Seven Quotes

"An exhilarating touring car ideal for starting one's racing career..."   *1958 Lotus 7 sales brochure*

"If you're tired of Caterhams, you've surely begun to tire of driving..."   *Autocar, June 17, 1992*

"I have more fun driving my Seven than anything else I have driven..."   *Jonathan Palmer*

"The Seven was very much an English car – had it been any more English it wouldn't have been a car at all..."
Allan Girdler, Road & Track, November 1984

"I doubt even Colin Chapman could have foreseen the JPE but, if he had, he would have smiled. It's his kind of car..."
Andrew Frankel, Autocar 1995

"Whoever was the first to describe the Super Seven as 'a four-wheeled motorbike' all those years ago was, in fact, a cretin of a liar... For a start, your bottom is but six inches from the floor in a Seven and if that's how you ride a motorbike then I harbour a suspicion you will be feeling a great deal of pain very shortly. Equally, sit astride the fuel tank in a Seven and not only will you have trouble reaching the pedals but your view of the traffic will be impeded somewhat by the fact

you're facing sideways..."
Darren Styles, World Sportscars, March 1989

"The most fun thing on four wheels..."
Auto Express, 1995

"Take your shoes off. Then take all your clothes off, smear yourself liberally with Vaseline and you still won't be able to get in..."
Mark Graham, Car, February 1996

"If the journey is more important than the destination, if you're tired of the sanitized plastic cocoons that modern automobiles have become, then there is no better car, Ferraris and Porsches included..."
Ross Benson, Daily Express, December 30, 1995

"Oh yes, other cars... might provide higher speeds, stronger forces, a sharper tang of exhilaration, more fluid and elegant motion. But if you simply want to climb out at the end grinning like a rock-ape, this is the way to go... There's a certain sort of fun which only it can supply. Original and best. Accept no substitute..."
Paul Horrell, Car, April 1996

"A Seven is a Seven is a Seven, and if you don't bloody well like it, you don't bloody well buy one..."   *Cars & Car Conversions*

CHAPTER 9

The Caterham 21 story

A slippery son of the Seven

Caterham Cars has always been known as a one-model manufacturer. The Seven has not only sustained itself over the years at Caterham, it has redoubled its popularity. With the Seven proving a consistent seller it was not surprising that Caterham should consider producing another model.

Intriguingly that other model might have been one of three other cars already produced by established European manufacturers. The most exciting would have been the Lotus Elan – the first-generation one, and not (as was reported in the press) the 1990 Elan which Lotus was forced to abandon. Unfortunately it was not to be. The other two possibilities were well-known small cars which had both been in production for a long period and were about to be axed.

However, Graham Nearn's real passion had always been to tackle an all-new project from the ground up. He and Jez Coates would talk about such a possibility from time to time. But throughout the early Nineties, there was such a weight of development work that the time was never right to undertake such an ambitious project.

Jez Coates and his team had been devoting their energies towards getting the Seven through the legalities required by the early-Nineties legislation – Low-Volume Type Approval, noise tests, emissions and so on – and only when this was finally complete could they contemplate tackling such a big project as a new car.

Such was the amount of development that Caterham had carried out on the Seven that literally the only item left from the original Lotus Seven in the Caterham's underpinnings was the hand brake lever (and even this was changed for the 1996 model year). Such a complete overhaul of the Seven was an impressive feat and it was this realization that finally persuaded Nearn that he had within Caterham all the engineering expertise he needed to tackle a new project.

He had always wanted to do something like the Lotus Eleven (which was the original enveloping-bodied Seven), but a specific 'replica' would not have met European legislation. Instead, an original project was launched, initially with the codename '35', but quickly changed to C21 to reflect the fact that it would appear in Caterham's 21st year as a car manufacturer.

"This was like a Boy's Own story come true," said Coates. "The opportunity to be working on a new car for a company with the legendary credentials of Caterham was the stuff that my boyhood dreams were made of. I felt it was my job to put together a proposal as to what we should be doing.

"So Reg Price and I sat down and we agreed that we would like to do a mid-engined car. We could lift out a complete front-wheel drive package from a current production car and site it amidships. That would be both effective and cheap to buy in. We would like to have revisited the composite monocoque pioneered by Colin Chapman in the Lotus Elite. Again, that would make it very lightweight and, because there is no chassis, economical to manufacture.

"But as Clint Eastwood would say: 'A man's got to know his limitations'. This may have been our ideal scenario, but it was frankly too big a step for us to take. It would have been a complete new car, a major project. Even with our 60-plus employees, we still have only a very small engineering team whose time will always be largely devoted to the Seven."

Instead it was decided to build on the race-proven mechanical package of the Seven and put a new body on that. If it was an enveloping body, there would certainly be enough space to develop the chassis. For reasons of packaging and simplicity, it was decided to keep the same wheelbase and rear track. The wheelbase was generous by class standards and to increase it would have added

185

weight and bulk, both of which were highly undesirable. Keeping the rear track identical also meant being able to stick with the existing axle and driveshaft configuration. Having a wider body would mean more interior width anyway.

So all the rear suspension, engine and gearbox transferred straight over. The front track was widened by three inches to match the rear (on the Seven, there is a mismatch of front and rear tracks). This would have benefits on handling and on the oft-criticized footbox width. So the chassis was actually simplified at the front by making the longitudinals run straight back. There was now enough space for the luxury of a clutch foot rest! In addition, what Caterham called 'Toblerones' were added into the chassis sides to increase torsional stiffness – indeed, by up to four times – and also to enhance side-impact protection. However, as understanding of the composite body structure increased during the development process in 1995, the tubular-steel 'Toblerones' were deleted and the torsional stiffness gain recovered by exploiting the stiffness of the tub.

"We toyed with the idea of dropping the sill," recalls Jez Coates, "so that we could make the door aperture bigger, but we didn't want to compromise the stiffness of the chassis. Caterhams are about driving, not about how easy it is to get into them."

The front suspension hardly had to be altered, either: the only item which connected the two sides was the anti-roll bar, which had to be altered. The passengers would actually sit in the same positions within the 21 chassis as they did in a Seven chassis. The only difference was, the cockpit was a lot wider.

Reg Price built a 1/10th scale balsa model of the chassis with the extra side 'Toblerones', a pyramid structure under the windscreen and a cat's cradle over the engine. Arch Motors built the prototype revised chassis during February and March 1994.

In a way, the 21 project was the opposite of the Caterham philosophy not to touch the exterior shape of the car but to do anything underneath to improve its dynamics. By contrast, the 21 would retain the underpinnings of the Seven largely unchanged, but adopt a completely different body style.

But the 21 project did sharpen what Caterham cars were all about for the team at Caterham. Everyone was clear what a Seven was about, but it was an instructive exercise deciding what elements should be retained for the new Caterham.

"Interestingly," says Coates, "our most important deciding factor was quickly established: that all the compromises should fall in favour of driving pleasure. That's why we kept small doors and high sills and resisted the temptation to make the windows drop. We even built the first car with no carpets. There is no pleasure to be gained from these fripperies as you pilot your 21 down your favourite road."

Who should Caterham use to design the all-important new body? There was one very obvious choice: someone who used to work for Caterham

The four proposals submitted by designer Iain Robertson are carefully scrutinized by a young member of the Coates family.

186

Proposal A was the one that received universal approval.

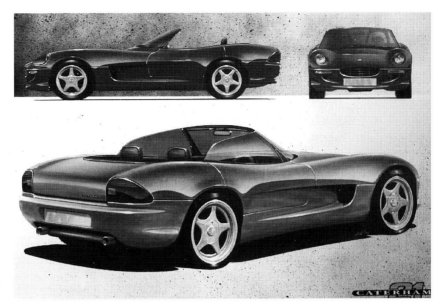

The difficulty of selecting the ideal front intake shape is illustrated by these six renderings of alternatives by Iain Robertson.

Cars in sales, actually lived in Caterham, was a graduate of the Royal College of Art in automotive design and long-term illustrator for *Autocar* magazine.

That man was Iain Robertson. Both Coates and Nearn liked the work he was doing for *Autocar* and Robertson was familiar to Graham Nearn, too. Another point in his favour was that he would not charge a Pininfarina-scale fee!

So three days before Christmas 1993, Jez Coates approached Iain Roberston with the suggestion. He naturally agreed and was called in to meet Nearn, Coates and Noble informally. Together, they came up with a set of defining words for how the new car should look. Nearn favoured "a traditional English sports-racing car, pure, light and uncomplicated", while Coates added the adjectives "taut, lithe and agile – as if the body were stretched over a skeleton".

"It was crucial to get the car to look right," said Coates. "I believe that a sportscar must look sexy first to attract the customer, who can then be informed of its other qualities. If it doesn't instantly inspire a desire to own, the engineering excellence is all for nothing. I always point to the Reliant Scimitar SS1 – a good car in terms of value and dynamics but pig-ugly. That's why people bought MX-5s, not Scimitars."

Robertson submitted four proposals based on these ideas. These were shown to various internal people and to key overseas dealers, whose response was very encouraging. It was quickly apparent that his first proposal was the favourite. Indeed Robertson admitted he had struggled to produce second, third and fourth proposals. So Proposal A virtually chose itself.

Iain Robertson: "I deliberately allowed function to determine the 21's main visual features. The skin stretches membrane-like within a few millimetres of the spaceframe chassis to emphasize the 21's squat stance. The wing lines draw inspiration from the Lotus Eleven."

Once the body style had been agreed and the chassis had been finalized, it was time to begin full-scale modelling of the bodywork. It was decided to

187

Compare the nose on the finished car with the alternatives in the previous photograph.

adopt the TVR approach of sculpting the shape from blocks of polystyrene.

In April 1994, Arch Motors' chassis was despatched to Jez Coates' barn-cum-garage and nine blocks of 2ft x 4ft x 8ft polystyrene blocks were ordered and taken (one by one!) to the barn. Chopped into 6½in wide slices, Jez Coates and Iain Robertson set about getting the shape.

Entirely by eye, the pair wielded nothing more delicate than a chain saw, hacking pieces off. "I felt like Michelangelo," said Coates. "There was a sculpture in there somewhere, all Iain and I had to do was release it!" First the left-hand side was cut to size and fine shaped with a wire brush by Robertson. Then Coates measured it up and duplicated the shape on the opposite side.

Not that it all went smoothly. There had already been a problem with glueing the slices of polystyrene together. Then the front end had to be cut off three times before it looked right (and even then, Jez Coates did a bit of final fettling).

To create bespoke lighting for a car needs a budget running into the millions of pounds, so that was never an option. Initially, inclined Porsche 911 headlamps were used, but eventually 7in round lamps were selected. At the rear end, several light clusters were considered, including Mazda MX-3, but Robertson's first choice of Ford Mondeo hatchback units was the best. Front indicators considered included Ford Probe, MR2, Escort RS2000 and MX-5, but eventually it was decided to go for the seemingly obscure option of Suzuki Cappuccino units. Internal door handles came from a Vauxhall Astra – superseded by Rover 100 handles on all subsequent cars – and mirrors from a Metro (on production cars, the new Rover 200). Likewise, the prototype was built around a Marcos windscreen. Coates promised Jem Marsh of Marcos at the time that the screen had been donated to the project and that Caterham would tool up its own glass. Triplex made the windscreen and side glass, but this was retooled for the composite cars in the light of development. Production side glass, which unusually required curvature from front to back, were to be made in Spain.

Coates and Robertson wanted to paint the car red, but Coates' father-in-law returned from Do-It-All with a faintly nauseating pink! The car was repainted grey, then Duluxed in mid-electric blue. In this form, it was presented to the staff at the Dartford factory and pictured in *Autocar* some months before its public debut.

Another area in which the Caterham team felt justly proud was the car's interior. This was a quantum leap up from the ultra-simple treatment of the Seven. Iain Robertson's vision called for individual nacelles for each of the passengers (which co-incidentally made it easy to convert over to left-hand drive). The dials may have been transferred directly from the Seven, but they were arranged in a novel way, with the minor dials and switches grouped vertically within a narrow

The basic modified Seven chassis on which the first 21 shape would be created. Reg Price designed the modifications and Arch Motors built it.

From humble beginnings... The body was sculpted out of polystyrene blocks.

Designer Iain Robertson (left) and Jez Coates work their body with nothing more delicate than a chain saw.

The completed polystyrene full-size mock-up next to the latest Super Seven.

Through the headlamp aperture can be seen the revised chassis with its straight-ahead front extensions.

is an unlucky number in Japan and so there was talk of renaming the car C23 (because the car would actually enter production in Caterham's 23rd year), but then the Japanese importer said that 23 pronounced in Japanese sounds rather like Nissan. Eventually, the tag chosen was simply 21, to reflect a progression from the Seven.

There was one final trump card up Graham Nearn's sleeve. Although details of Project C21 had appeared in the press, no-one knew that he intended to body the first car in aluminium. "I wanted to mark it out as a quality product," he said, "and having an aluminium body distanced us from everybody else."

There were very few companies skilled enough to undertake this job but, of three names who were short-listed, Coates chose Roach Manufacturing Ltd, of Ower in Hampshire, whose more usual business is to recreate the vintage masterpieces of designers like Figoni & Falaschi.

The foam mock-up was duly transported to Keith Roach, who was extremely enthusiastic about the project. "The ability of Roach Manufacturing to make shapes in aluminium is just amazing," said Coates. "They are a very talented team."

More than just talented, as it transpired. With less than 16 weeks remaining to the 1994 Birmingham Motor Show, Roach finished the bodywork *and* was able to complete opening doors, bonnet and boot, something which no-one was expecting. *And* the car had all its mechanical components in place (skimping nothing, a JPE engine and six-speed gearbox). In the early hours of the morning before the show press day, the car was made a runner.

The 21 was revealed at the Motor Show in an

console. Another character feature was the way the body colour extended into the dashboard.

"We are not setting out to compete with established sportscars," said Jez Coates. "The 21 will never be as practical as a mass-produced sportscar. What we want is a car which extends the qualities of the Seven, but has an appeal outside the usual frames of reference for Seven buyers."

As its debut approached, there was some debate over the car's name. The project was continually referred to as C21 to reflect Caterham's 21 years as a manufacturer. There was some comment that 21

The 21 was launched at the Birmingham Motor Show in October 1994 to universal acclaim. Its rapturous reception shed any doubt that the 21 was anything but a viable proposition.

Shapely lines evoked Lotus' classic period of the Sixties, but were modern, individual and harmonious.

Bold interior design made use of individual nacelles for driver and passenger and a unique centre console with vertically stacked dials. Elbow room was significantly greater than in the Seven.

impressive display which actually brought tears to the eyes of Jan Russell, PA to Graham Nearn. No-one was ready for the amazing sight which emerged from under the dust covers: the car was resplendent in its natural polished aluminium finish. "The response was incredible," said Graham Nearn. "Overwhelmingly positive."

One reason why the car was made a runner in such a short space of time was that BBC TV

wanted to film it in motion for *Top Gear*, with Tiff Needell at the wheel. Immediately after the show, it was taken to chosen composite body suppliers Rawlsons of Dover for a plaster of Paris mould to be taken. The very next day, it was tested by *Autocar*'s Andrew Frankel. He said: "The basic feel of the car is right... unmistakably Caterham." Three days after the *Autocar* road test, the 21 found itself in Essen, Germany for the international motor show.

It had always been the plan to offer the 21 with a composite body as standard, and in aluminium as an option. Rawlsons had been selected to do the moulding work for the 21. They were responsible for the composites in Gordon Murray's Rocket, the Chrysler Viper hardtop and aeroplane wings among other projects, so their credentials were impeccable. Rawlsons digitized the aluminium show car's body and discovered that it wasn't symmetrical in the process – the entire aluminium car had been created by eye, so it was hardly surprising that the rear lights were slightly cross-eyed and had to be moved an inch out (a major exercise as it meant changing all the rear wing profiles).

After four months with Rawlsons, during which time some fine-tuning was applied to the body styling, the styling buck was signed-off. The future home of the aluminium car lay in Japan, as it was bought by Caterham's Tokyo based importer, Mr Tanaka. He was so enthusiastic about the styling drawing that he insisted on buying the first car unseen!

At the time of writing, a second aluminium car

191

has been finished (each body takes 1,000 man hours to complete!) and the composite moulds have been completed. Chassis numbers 7 and 8 of the production-ready composite 21 were unveiled at the 1995 London Motor Show and everything was set for a launch in May 1996 in both fully-built and component forms. Logistically, the 21 posed new challenges for Caterham. It had to deal with factors it never had to face before: curved glass, panel gaps, hinges, locks, opening panels, doors, windscreen bonding and so on.

And then there was the actual process of production. Arch Motors were to build the chassis and deliver them to Dartford as per usual. But now Caterham would have to deal with extensive composite bodywork delivered from Rawlsons in Kent. It was estimated that the 21 would require more than three times the floor space needed to build a Seven.

The maximum production capacity of 21s was estimated at around 250 units a year (with Seven production steady at 600), but no-one presumed that this number would actually be built. More likely was a rate of between 10 and 20 in 1996, building up to about 100 a year. At the time of writing, Caterham have 25 orders for the car – even before it has become officially available.

The launch price was set at £18,750 in component form (dubbed Clubman). The Supersport engine package was priced at an additional £999, while other options included the six-speed gearbox, 1.8 VHP engine, special paintwork and lightweight aluminium bodywork.

"It's very much up to the buying public to decide how the 21 will develop," comments Nearn. "Customers will be able to choose between a composite car which they can build themselves or a more upmarket fully-built product."

The 21 arrived in a flurry of sportscar activity. At the same time as the 21 was announced, British buyers were already aware of the Lotus Elise, Renault Sport Spider, MGF and BMW Z3. But the 21 was intended as something much more exclusive, being built at a rate of less than 200 a year.

At the time of writing, some eight 21 chassis have been constructed, each of them differing in detail. Although the prototype was built around a JPE engine, no Vauxhall unit was offered on the price list. Instead the Rover K-series was chosen, in the form of the 115bhp 1.6-litre unit just developed by Rover, also offered in 138bhp Supersport form.

Another definite option announced for launch was a Very High Performance (VHP) version of the 1.8-litre K-series engine, an enhanced version of the engine fitted to the MGF. This was developed by Rover in conjunction with Caterham to provide in excess of 100bhp per litre. Caterham had a significant input in the hardware of this unit; for example, the inlet manifolds and dry-sump equipment.

This VHP engine was slated eventually to replace the 2-litre Vauxhall engine, particularly in Japan, where the 188bhp Vauxhall race-spec engine has been such a popular choice.

The perfect polished aluminium body is covered in plaster of Paris to make the glassfibre moulds for the production 21.

APPENDIX A

BIOGRAPHIES

GRAHAM NEARN

Born September 9, 1933. Grew up in Croydon, Surrey. Served National Service, commissioned in the Royal Signals, then worked for Meyer International, the timber importers. In 1959, accepted an invitation to become a co-director and co-founder of Caterham Car Services, which became one of the first Lotus Centres. Became sole proprietor in 1962, had major input in the development of the Lotus Seven and secured sole concessionaire rights in 1967 before concluding an agreement with Colin Chapman for the world rights to manufacture the Seven in 1973.

Has two sons: Robert, who raced Sevens (and won Class C in 1989 and 1991 and the Vauxhall series in 1993), was a member of the 24-Hour teams at Ohio and Zolder, organized motor shows and was instrumental in appointing the French agent; he currently races a Porsche in long-distance events. The second son is Simon, who became joint works manager in 1994 and spent a year in 1995 running the sales department at Caterham; he now races 18ft skiffs and is chairman of the UK skiff association.

JANE NEARN

Born in England of Scottish parents, spent formative years in South Africa, trained as a journalist, and is an acknowledged artist of modern expressionism. Became a director of Caterham Cars from its formation as a limited company.

Always accompanied Graham Nearn on foreign visits and at exhibitions, particularly in the early days, when son Robert was brought around in a carrycot. Inspired the special show models, for which she selected colours and finishes. She is a mother of four.

DAVID WAKEFIELD

Born November 17, 1936 in Beddington, near Croydon. Left school at the age of 16 by which time he was already besotted with cars. Worked for the Ford dealer, Dees of Croydon, in the service department. Served National Service, then returned to Dees' body shop.

Saw an advert for a bodyshop manager at Caterham Coachworks, was interviewed by Graham Nearn and joined on January 1, 1964. Sprinted and raced with Graham Nearn in the Sixties.

Conceived and managed the introduction of the Caterham Seven Series 3 in 1974. Ran Caterham's bodyshop, then took over as production manager. Was behind the Vegantune Twin-Cam engine.

As well as production and quality control, took on the overseas sales role, particularly developing Japan. As Clive Roberts took over the development and production roles, Wakefield progressed increasingly into exporting.

CLIVE ROBERTS

Born May 14, 1953 in Plymouth, Devon. Graduated in mechanical engineering at Coventry and went to work for Triumph in 1976. Was the first graduate to join Caterham in 1977 as purchasing manager and development engineer. Responsible for design, testing, sourcing, homologation and product support. Developed the de Dion rear suspension, long-cockpit chassis and race derivatives.

Left Caterham in 1985 to join Lotus as Development Engineer. Managed whole-vehicle development for the new Lotus Elan and subsequently went to General Motors in Detroit on electric vehicle programme. At 183.822mph, Roberts holds the world land speed record for electric vehicles.

JEZ COATES

Born October 30, 1956 in Germany, returned to native Britain aged two. Lived in Kirkby Stephen, in Cumbria. Studied mechanical engineering at Warwick university.

Sponsored by Leyland Trucks through university, during which time he owned a Lotus Elan. From 1979, at Leyland he took a full-time job doing testing – durability, noise, emissions, pave, brakes and so on. Worked for four years as "a small cog in a massive organization," says Jez: "I was becoming disillusioned about my opportunities within the company."

Left Leyland to join Caterham in January 1983 in general management capacity, later specializing in purchasing. When Clive Roberts moved on, he assumed his technical and development mantle. Became a director of Caterham in 1988. Raced Sevens, notably forming part of the 24-Hour teams at Ohio and Zolder. Has been responsible for major engineering developments, including Vauxhall and Rover engine installations, emissions and Type Approval work, Vauxhall racer, JPE development, six-speed gearbox and the 21 project.

ANDY NOBLE

Born February 19, 1963. Went to school in Bath. Showed an early interest in motoring with his first motorbike, a Greaves Villiers, at the age of 11.

First engineering project was the creation of a six-wheeled soapbox derby winner (later converted to lawn mower power).

Went to Salford University to study mechanical engineering, sponsored by Leyland Trucks. During his sandwich course, he stayed in the same hall of residence as Jez Coates. With Leyland he worked on a project to put buses on railway lines and became bored having to justify each decision to the nth degree and jumped at the chance when Jez Coates offered him a job at Caterham.

Joined Caterham in time for the Motor Show in 1986. Assumed purchasing and general management roles. Took on control of the race series and became instrumental in securing wide-ranging

sponsorship for racing. This in turn led to a greater input in marketing and publicity, for example donating a Seven to Beaulieu and offering a Seven as a prize through BP petrol stations and introducing the Caterham Seven Scholarship.

Became a director in 1988. Had detailed engineering input, conceived the Seven Classic of 1992 and was responsible for involving Jonathan Palmer in the JPE.

REG PRICE

Born May 31, 1939 in Lewisham, London. Went into medical research as a career, but National Service interrupted (electronics in the RAF). Attended teaching training college at Shoreditch College after RAF, then went on to teach design technology.

Modified John McLean's Lotus Seven for sprinting and hillclimbing, then built two clubmans cars. Prepared cars for David Bettinson when the Lotus Seven was allowed back into Modsports. Bought and modified a very early S3 Caterham in 1974 – which proved a winner. Formed Astap Engineering after French students saw his Seven and howled: *"A se tapper le cul par terre"* (*ie*, so low that you'd hit your backside on the ground).

Asked Graham Nearn about holiday work at Caterham in 1976 as a mechanic. Accepted with a brief to come up with ideas. Many engineering developments including conception of the de Dion rear suspension and race car preparation. Also a successful Seven racer, winning the first Vauxhall race at Brands Hatch and as a member of the winning 24-Hour teams at Zolder and the Nelson Ledges.

Started working full-time for Caterham in 1989 once he had obtained early retirement from teaching. "Although he has no set hours," says Graham Nearn, "I just know that if he isn't working on the cars, he's thinking about them. He virtually lives in a Seven."

MIKE DIXON

Born June 8, 1962 in Liverpool. After graduating, worked for Austin Rover on manufacturing the Maestro/ Montego and Rover 800 lines.

Joined Caterham as production engineer in September 1987 and was instrumental in setting up the new factory and production process at Dartford. Became production director in 1988 and also headed after-sales department. It was his production skills that allowed output to swell from 250 to 800 cars a year. In 1992 – exactly five years to the day after joining – he left to manage the family motor trade business (Ryders in Bootle, Merseyside).

APPENDIX B

PRODUCTION HISTORY

1957 Lotus Mark 7 launched at London Motor Show with Ford or Coventry Climax engines.

1959 Lotus 7A launched using BMC A-series engine from Austin A35 or Sprite.

1960 Series 2 launched with simplified chassis, rear suspension A-frame, relocated steering rack, restyled nose.

1961 Ford 105E engine fitted for the first time. Super Seven launched with Cosworth-modified 1,340cc Ford engine.

1962 Super Seven 1500 launched.

1963 Cycle wings replaced by standard flared wings.

1967 'Series 2½' introduced.

1968 Launch of Series 3 with 1300 or 1600 Ford crossflow engines.

1969 Lotus Twin Cam-powered SS introduced.

1970 Series 4 introduced with all-new glassfibre body, redesigned chassis.

1972 Production of Lotus Seven S4 believed to have ceased.

1973 Production restarted at Caterham.

1974 Caterham Seven S4 replaced by S3 with Lotus Big Valve Twin Cam engine and strengthened Lotus S3 chassis.

1975 Ford 1300 and 1600 engines offered. Rear axle switched from Mk1 Escort to Mk1 RS, then Mk2.

1976 Improved seating, KN 6J alloy wheel option.

1978 Escort Mk2 RS rear axle standard.

1980 Seven Sprint introduced with uprated Ford Kent engine. Morris Ital rear axle launched to replace old Escort Mk2 axle (in cars from 1981). Escort Sport gearbox replaced 2000E 'box. Revised wiring loom and rocker switches.

1981 Silver Jubilee model first seen. Vegantune VTA engine first fitted.

1982 Spring rates increased and front brake pad material upgraded. Long-cockpit chassis offered as an option.

1984 Cosworth 1600 BDR (150bhp) engine introduced in the Seven. Caterham-modified 1700 Supersprint (135bhp) engine introduced. Lightweight radiator installed. Spitfire steering rack replaced by modified Mini rack. Kit-form Seven launched.

1985 Caterham-designed de Dion rear end offered as an option (eventually replaced live axle in production cars).

1986 Five-speed XR4i gearbox first offered. HPC model launched with 170bhp Cosworth BDR engine (first chassis 5LC/4589/BDRD – first official chassis 5LC/4628/HPRD). Symmetrical 'universal' chassis introduced with front cruciform and additional upper engine bay diagonal. VDO instruments and new wiring loom. Radiator upgraded and mounted on front of chassis.

1987 Powder-coated chassis for better corrosion protection. Heated front screen introduced.

1988 Disc brakes all round, revised suspension settings (camber, toe-in, bump-steer, spring rates all modified). Pedal box replaced original bracket. Larger, foldable sidescreens with increased visibility and extra elbow room.

1989 Prisoner special edition first seen. 15in 'Prisoner' wheels and tyres introduced for better

ride, grip and stability. Ignition timing modified to allow use of unleaded fuel in Ford engines. Aluminium fuel tank introduced. Chassis tubes made smaller.

1990 Launch of Vauxhall 2-litre HPC. Honeycomb side-impact protection fitted to all chassis. Improved front suspension location with front half-link added to top wishbone. Inertia-reel seat belts introduced.

1991 HPC entered production. Launch of Rover K-series-powered Seven. Bilstein suspension introduced with adjustable front geometry; revised dampers, spring rates, anti-roll bars.

1992 K-series entered production. Low-cost GTS model first produced, but even more stripped-out Classic quickly became the official budget model. 35th Anniversary model launched. Ultra-high-performance JPE launched.

1993 Fully-built LVTA K-series and HPC launched in UK. Public launch of new six-speed gearbox. Introduction of K-series Supersport (128bhp) engine. New grille with '7' logo for HPC.
1994 Enlarged footbox giving extra legroom. Common chassis for Rover, Ford and Vauxhall engines. Public launch of Caterham 21 at Birmingham Motor Show.

1995 Six-speed gearbox entered production.

1996 1.6-litre K-series and 1.6-litre Supersport replaced 1.4-litre. Revised stiffened chassis, revised suspension, new seats, resited handbrake, Caterham-branded instruments and new lightweight loom. Caterham 21 entered production.

CATERHAM FULLY-BUILT AND COMPONENT PRODUCTION YEAR-BY-YEAR

S4	TC	1300GT
1973	22	6
1974	8	2
Total	**30**	**8**

S3	TC	1300	1600	BDR	MK/GS	SS	VT	H	XR	VX	VI	RI	JPE	None	TOTAL
1974	20														20
1975	47	2	1												20
1976	52	1	3											6	56
1977	46		4											3	59
1978	40		8											6	56
1979	49		9											35	83
1980	30		19	15										25	83
1981	26		10	21		1								22	86
														19	77

S3	TC	1300	1600	BDR	MK/GS	SS	VT	H	XR	VX	VI	RI	JPE	None	TOTAL
1982	2	1	38		23		3	2						12	81
1983	1		22	1	33		24	1	1*					24	107
1984			29	1	41	7	10	2						21	111
1985			25	29	23	29	3							25	134
1986			33	37	13	35			1					10	129
1987			5	26	7	37			9**					13	97
1988			20	47	10	45			15					12	149
1989			31	56	4	42			22					37	192
1990			43	103	11	34			26	3		1		36	257
1991			38	76	11	52			18	39	2	3		19	258
1992			14	38	7	65				57	11	23	3	6	224
1993			11	8	2	54				66	28	36	8	1	214
1994			52	11	5	16				38	36†	53	13		224
1995			33	2	1	24				25	32	73	6		196
Total	313	4	448	435	227	440	41	5	92	228	109	189	30	332	2,893

TC	Lotus Twin Cam	VX	Vauxhall HPC carb
BDR	Cosworth (1600 & 1700)	VI	Vauxhall HPC/VXI injection
MK/GS	Sprint (1600)	RI	Rover K-series
SS	Super Sprint (1700)	JPE	Jonathan Palmer Evolution
VT	Vegantune Twin Cam		
H	Holbay (1700)	*	CVH-powered development car
XR	Ford CVH	**	Includes turbo one-off for Germany
None	Supplied without engine/no engine details recorded	†	Includes turbo car

---

KIT & CKD PRODUCTION BY YEAR

	Kits & CKD
1984	8
1985	82
1986	120
1987	184
1988	331
1989	440
1990	571
1991	424
1992	334
1993	329
1994	357
1995	368
TOTAL	**3,548**

These production figures are as accurate as they can be, given the nature of the production records. Exact year-by-year figures may vary because precise dates of manufacture were not always recorded. However, the overall totals are accurate according to the production log.

COSWORTH BDR PRODUCTION FIGURES

1600cc BDR	**149**
1700cc BDR	**331** (of which **62** were HPC)
Total number of BDR engines	**480**

(Two engines were not fitted to cars and two 1600 units remained in stock at the time of writing. Therefore, the total number of BDR engined cars, including those supplied in kit form, is **476**.)

CATERHAM CHASSIS NUMBERS

Seven S4

First S4	S4/3501TC	1973
Last S4	S4/3538GT	1974

Seven S3

Prototype with Twin Cam	CS3/3550/TCP	1974
First RHD production S3	CS3/3551/TCR	1974
First LHD production S3	CS3/3564/TCL	1974
First 1600GT	CS3/3575/16R	1975
First 1300GT	CS3/3580/13R	1975
First Ford RS axle	CS3/3601/TCRS	1975
First Mk2 Escort axle	CS3/3612/TCR2	1975
First Vegantune-built TC	CS3/3643/TCR2	1976
First S3B chassis	S3B/3735/TCR2	1978
First Mk2 RS axle	CS3/3736/TCRS	1978
First 1600 Sprint	CS3/3938/MKRS	1980
First Morris Ital axle	CS3/4002/TCRM	1980
First Jubilee model	CS3/4060/MKRM J001	1981
First Vegantune VTA TC	CS3/4077/VCRM (engine VTA001)	1981
First 1700 Holbay option	CS3/4110/17HRM	1982
First long cockpit	LCS/4140/MKRM	1982
Last 1300GT	CS3/4154/13LM	1982
Last Lotus Twin Cam	CS3/4164/TCRM	1983
CVH testbed prototype	XLC/4240/XRM	1983
First 1600 Cosworth BDR	LCS/4268/BDRM (engine BDR001)	1983
Last 1700 Holbay	CS3/4295/17HRM	1984
First 1700 Supersprint	LCS/4330/17RM	1984
Last Vegantune VTA	CS3/4397/VCRM	1985
First de Dion suspension	LCS/4477/17RD	1985
First 1700 BDR	CS3/4519/BDRM	1986
First five-speed gearbox	5LC/4577/17LD	1986
First HPC	5LC/4628/HPRD	1986
First CVH engine	5LC/4630/XRLD	1986
CVH turbo one-off	5LC/4659/XTLD (engine RST001)	1987
Last complete car from Caterham factory	4730	1987
First car built entirely at Dartford factory	4742	1987
First Prisoner	5LC/4944/PRI001	1989
Vauxhall prototype	5168	1990
K-series prototype	5198	1990
Vauxhall HPC show car	5253	1990
First production Vauxhall racer	CS3/5365/VXRM (engine VX0001)	1990
Vauxhall EFI prototype	5416	1991
Last Cosworth HPC	5426	1991
K-series launch car	SDKLD/FORIMOOO/5538	1991
Last CVH car	5LC/5589/XRLD	1991
First production K-series	SDKLD/FORINOOO/5602	1991
First production HPC injection	SDKLD/FHVINOOO/5657	1992
First 35th Anniversary	SDKRD/CO17NOOO/5706	1992
First GTS	SDKRL/COGSNOOO/5710	1992
JPE prototype	SDKRD/CJPENOOO/5785	1992
First production JPE	SDKLD/FJVIPOOO/5812	1992
First Classic	SDKLC/FOGTPOOO/5883	1993

Key to codes used on Caterham chassis

A	Alternative (denotes non-HPC/Clubman/race car)	O	Other (denotes non-HPC/Clubman/race car)
BD	Cosworth BDR	P	Prototype *or* built 1993
C	Classic *or* Component-form *or* Clubman	PRI	Prisoner
		Q	Built 1994 (first half)
C6	Cosworth 1600 BDR (post-1990)	R	Right-hand drive *or* Racer *or* built 1994 (second half)
C7	Cosworth 1700 BDR (post-1990)		
CS3	Caterham S3	RI	Rover K-series (pre-1992)
D	de Dion	RJ	Rover K-series (post-1992)
F	Fully-built	RMJ	Japanese-spec Vauxhall racer
GS	100bhp 1600GT	S	Escort RS axle *or* built 1995
GT	84bhp 1600GT	S3B	3B chassis (Dutch market)
H	HPC (post-1990)	SDK	Caterham manufacturer ID code
HP	Cosworth HPC	T	Turbo *or* built 1996
J	Jubilee	TC	Big Valve Twin Cam
JPE	Jonathan Palmer Evolution	VC	Vegantune VTA
K	Kit (post-1990)	VI/VJ	Vauxhall EFI
KS3C	CKD kit-built short cockpit (pre-1990)	VT	Vauxhall Turbo
KLCC	CKD kit-built long cockpit (pre-1990)	VX	Vauxhall Carb
KLDC	CKD kit-built de Dion (pre-1990)	X	Experimental
KS3 etc	Kit-built (not CKD) as above (pre-1990)	XR	Ford CVH
L	Left-hand drive *or* long cockpit	XT	Ford CVH Turbo
LCS	Long cockpit	2	Escort Mk2 axle
M	Marina/Ital axle *or* built 1991	5	Five-speed gearbox
ME	Japanese-spec JPE	13	Ford 1300GT
MK	Modified Kent (Sprint)	16	Ford 1600GT
N	Built 1992	17	1700 Supersprint
NS	Engine not supplied	17H	1700 Holbay

APPENDIX C

SPECIFICATIONS

ENGINES

Lotus/ Vegantune	Big Valve Twin Cam	Tall Block Twin Cam	Vegantune VTA
Bore	82.5mm	81mm	81mm
Stroke	72.7mm	77.6mm	77.6mm
Capacity	1,558cc	1,599cc	1,599cc
Comp ratio	9.5:1 or 10.3:1	8.5:1 or 9.5:1	10:1
Max power	126bhp * at 6,500rpm	126bhp at 6,200rpm	130bhp at 6,500rpm
Max torque	113lb.ft at 5,500rpm	106lb.ft at 5,500rpm	115lb.ft at 5,000rpm
Carburation	2 Dellorto 40DHLA or Weber 40DCOE	2 Dellorto 40DHLA	2 Dellorto 40DHLA

* Claimed by Lotus, but in reality outputs probably varied between 105 and 119bhp.

Ford	1300GT	1600GT	1600 Sprint	1700 Supersprint	1700 Holbay
Bore	81mm	81mm	81mm	83.3mm	83.5mm
Stroke	63mm	77.6mm	77.6mm	77.6mm	77.6mm
Capacity	1,298cc	1,599cc	1,599cc	1,691cc	1,699cc
Comp ratio	9.2:1	9.0:1	9.0:1	9.5:1	9.5:1
Max power	72bhp at 6,000rpm	84bhp at 5,500rpm	110bhp at 6,000rpm (later 100bhp at 6,000rpm)	135bhp at 6,000rpm	140bhp at 6,000rpm
Max torque	68lb.ft at 4,000rpm	92lb.ft at 3,500rpm	105lb.ft at 4,800rpm (later 100lb.ft at 4,500rpm)	122lb.ft at 4,500rpm	121lb.ft at 5,000rpm
Carburation	1 Weber 32DGV	1 Weber 32DGAV	2 Weber 40DCOE	2 Weber 40DCOE	2 Weber 40DCOE

Cosworth BDR	1600	1700HPC
Bore	81mm	83.5mm
Stroke	77.6mm	77.6mm
Capacity	1,599cc	1,699cc
Comp ratio	11.0:1	11.0:1
Max power	150bhp at 6,500rpm*	170bhp at 6,500rpm**
Max torque	125lb.ft at 5,500rpm	140lb.ft at 5,500rpm
Carburation	2 Weber 40DCOE	2 Weber 45DCOE

* Claimed by Cosworth but later revised after testing by Caterham to 140bhp.
** Claimed by Cosworth but later revised after testing by Caterham to 160bhp.

Vauxhall	2.0 HPC Carb	2.0 Racer	2.0 HPC/VXI Injection	JPE
Bore	86mm	86mm	86mm	86mm
Stroke	86mm	86mm	86mm	86mm
Capacity	1,998cc	1,998cc	1,998cc	1,998cc
Comp ratio	10.5:1	10.5:1	10.5:1	12:1
Max power	175bhp at 6,000rpm	188bhp at 6,000rpm	165bhp at 6,000rpm	250bhp at 7,750rpm
Max torque	155lb.ft at 4,800rpm	165lb.ft at 4,800rpm	165lb.ft at 4,500rpm	186lb.ft at 6,250rpm
Carburation	2 Weber 45DCOE	2 Weber 48DCO/SP	Bosch M2.5 or M2.8 Motronic EFI	Weber Alpha EFI

HPC Evolution Options	Stage 1	Stage 2	Stage 3
Bore	86mm	86mm	86mm
Stroke	86mm	86mm	86mm
Capacity	1,998cc	1,998cc	1,998cc
Comp ratio	10.5:1	10.5:1	11:1
Max power	218bhp at 7,000rpm	225bhp at 7,250rpm	235bhp at 7,250rpm
Max torque	170lb.ft at 5,500rpm	180lb.ft at 5,500rpm	180lb.ft at 6,500rpm
Carburation	2 Weber 45DCOE	2 Weber 45DCOE	2 Weber 45DCOE

Rover	K-series 1.4	K-series 1.4 Catalyst	K-series 1.4 Supersport
Bore	75mm	75mm	75mm
Stroke	79mm	79mm	79mm
Capacity	1,397cc	1,397cc	1,397cc
Comp ratio	10.0:1	10.0:1	10.0:1
Max power	110bhp at 6,000rpm	103bhp at 6,000rpm	128bhp at 7,400rpm
Max torque	96lb.ft at 5,000rpm	94lb.ft at 5,000rpm	100lb.ft at 5,000rpm
Carburation	EFI	EFI	EFI

Rover	K-series 1.6	K-series 1.6 Supersport
Bore	80mm	80mm
Stroke	79mm	79mm
Capacity	1,588cc	1,588cc
Comp ratio	10.5:1	10.5:1
Max power	115bhp at 6,000rpm	138bhp at 7,000rpm
Max torque	107lb.ft at 5,000rpm	115lb.ft at 5.000rpm
Engine Management	Rover MEMS fuel injection	Rover MEMS fuel injection

GEARBOXES

1974–81   Ford Corsair 2821E 4-speed
Ratios: 4th 1.00, 3rd 1.40, 2nd 2.01, 1st 2.97, Rev 3.32
Final-drive: 3.89:1 (or 3.54:1) (S4 = 3.77:1)
Speed at 1,000rpm: 17.4mph

1981–date   Ford Escort Sport 4-speed
Ratios: 4th 1.00, 3rd 1.42, 2nd 1.99, 1st 3.33
Final-drive: 3.64:1
Speed at 1,000rpm: 18.5mph

1986–date   Ford Sierra close ratio 5-speed
Ratios: 5th 0.82, 4th 1.00, 3rd 1.26, 2nd 1.81, 1st 3.36, Rev 3.87
Final-drive: 3.92:1 (optional 3.62:1)
Speed at 1,000rpm: 20.2mph
Or optional straight-cut:
5th 0.87, 4th 1.00, 3rd 1.21, 2nd 1.54, 1st 2.04 (Vauxhall)/2.39 (Ford and Rover)
Final-drive: 3.92:1
Speed at 1,000rpm: 19.1mph

1993–date   Caterham 6-speed
Ratios: 6th 1.00, 5th 1.13, 4th 1.32, 3rd 1.59, 2nd 2.01, 1st 2.69, Rev 2.96
Final-drive: 3.92:1
Speed at 1,000rpm: 17.0mph

SUSPENSION, AXLES & BRAKES

1974–77 Independent front suspension with Triumph Herald uprights and lower wishbones; upper links and anti-roll bar form top wishbones. Ford Escort live rear axle located by A-frame and twin trailing links. Girling 9in front disc brakes, 7in rear drums

1977–80 As above but with Ford RS, then RS2000, rear axle plus 9in RS rear drums. Dual-circuit brakes from 1978

1980–85 As above but Morris Marina/Ital live rear axle, Marina 8in rear drum brakes, adjustable Spax dampers. Continues to be offered to date

1985–88 de Dion rear suspension based around Ford Sierra differential. Sierra 9in rear drums

1988–date Rear 9in disc brakes

1990–date Half-link on top front wishbone

1991–date Bilstein suspension with adjustable rear anti-roll bar

1996–date Revised front and rear suspension geometry

WHEELS AND TYRES

S4 and S3

Wheels:	5.5 x 13in pressed steel (Brand Lotus alloy option)
Tyres:	165 SR13 or 165 HR13

Later S3

Wheels:	6 x 13in or 6 x 14in KN/Revolution alloy Optional 6.5 x 15in Prisoner type alloy
Tyres:	185/70 HR13 or 185/60 HR14 (195/50 VR15 on Prisoner)

Vauxhall HPC/VXI

Wheels:	7 x 16in HPC-type alloy
Tyres:	205/45 ZR16

K-series

Wheels:	6 x 14in spoked alloy
Tyres:	185/60 HR14

JPE

Wheels:	Front: 6.5 x 15in Dymag Magnesium Rear: 7.5 x 15in Dymag Magnesium
Tyres:	Front: Yokohama A008R 205/50 VR15 Rear: Yokohama A008R 225/50 VR15

21

Wheels:	7 x 16in alloy
Tyres:	205/45 VR16 Michelin Pilot

DIMENSIONS AND WEIGHT

Caterham Seven S4

Length:	144.5in (367cm)
Width:	60.5in (154cm)
Height:	43.5in (110cm)
Wheelbase:	90.0in (228cm)
Fuel tank:	7.5gal (34*l*)
Kerb weight:	1,276lb (579kg)

Caterham Seven S3

Length:	133in (338cm)
Width:	62in (157cm)
Height:	37in (94cm)/with hood 43in (109cm)
Wheelbase:	88.5in (225cm)
Fuel tank:	8gal (36*l*)
Kerb weight:	1,100lb (499kg) – Twin Cam
	1,200lb (544kg) – K-series
	1,300lb (590kg) – Ford Kent/Vauxhall
	1,168lb (530kg) – JPE

Caterham 21

Length:	153.8in (380cm)
Width:	62.2in (158cm)
Height:	41.7in (106cm)
Wheelbase:	88.5in (225cm)
Fuel tank:	12gal (54.5*l*)
Kerb weight:	1,428lb (648kg)

OPTIONS

1973	Brand Lotus alloy wheels, seat belts
1975	Heater, air horns, full tonneau cover, adjustable dampers, aero-screens, stainless-steel exhaust
1976	Roll-over bar, KN alloy wheels
1981	Silver Jubilee paint scheme/trim
by 1983	Rear wing protectors, oil cooler, electronic ignition, long cockpit chassis, Cibie headlamps
by 1986	Boot cover, locking wheelnuts, headlamps stoneguards, de Dion rear suspension, external mirror, Revolution alloy wheels (13/14in)
by 1987	Stainless-steel brake hoses, full paintwork, wind deflectors, leather seats, LSD, spare wheel cover
1989	Prisoner-type alloy wheels, boot cover, luggage rack
1992	Anniversary paint scheme, Vecta immobilizer
by 1994	S-Type trim, 1/2 S-Type trim, hood bag, luggage rack, Motolita/Racetech/Momo steering wheels, 6-speed gearbox, straight-cut close-ratio gearbox, dry sump system (VXI)
1996	Bespoke Caterham designed luggage for 21

PERFORMANCE FIGURES

Seven performance figures are difficult to be comprehensive about because the specifications of individual models were open to so many variations (*eg* wheel size, final-drive, gearbox type, etc). Where reliable road test figures are available for different variants of an individual model, they are given.

	Caterham S4 TC	S3 Twin Cam	S3 1600GT
Engine	Lotus Twin Cam	Lotus Twin Cam	Ford 1600
Power	115bhp	126bhp	84bhp
Maximum speed	116mph	114mph	100mph
Acceleration (sec)			
0–30mph	2.6	2.3	2.4
0–40mph	4.2	3.2	3.7
0–50mph	6.0	4.5	5.3
0–60mph	8.7	6.2	7.7
0–70mph	11.4	8.3	10.7
0–80mph	14.8	10.9	14.6
0–90mph	19.0	15.0	22.9
0–100mph	24.5	22.0	–
Standing ¼-mile	15.8	14.9	15.7
Top gear acceleration (sec)			
20–40mph	–	6.0	7.1
30–50mph	–	5.9	6.8
40–60mph	–	6.4	7.0
50–70mph	–	6.5	7.8
60–80mph	–	6.7	9.3
70–90mph	–	7.9	13.6
80–100mph	–	11.0	–
Overall fuel consumption (mpg)	18	28.3	27.1
Kerb weight	1,300lb	1,162lb	1,110lb
Price	£1,487 (1973)	£1,979 (1975)	£4,684 (1980)
Test source/date	*Car and Driver 1971 (Lotus S4)*	*Autocar 1975*	*Autocar 1980*

	S3 Twin Cam	Sprint	Supersprint VTA
Engine	Vegantune VTA Twin Cam	Ford 1600 (modified)	Ford 1700 (modified)
Power	130bhp	110bhp	135bhp
Maximum speed	107mph	110mph	111mph
Acceleration (sec)			
0–30mph	2.4	2.3	2.0
0–40mph	3.4	3.4	3.0
0–50mph	4.6	4.7	4.2
0–60mph	6.2	6.5	5.6
0–70mph	8.6	8.3	8.2
0–80mph	10.8	11.0	10.0
0–90mph	16.2	14.8	13.9
0–100mph	26.9	22.9	19.9
Standing ¼-mile	15.0	–	14.6
Top gear acceleration (sec)			
20–40mph	7.0	6.1	7.6
30–50mph	7.8	6.9	7.1
40–60mph	8.9	7.7	7.1
50–70mph	8.8	6.7	6.7
60–80mph	9.5	6.5	6.5
70–90mph	10.5	7.8	7.5
80–100mph	16.2	11.0	10.3
Overall fuel consumption (mpg)	22.2	26.5	23.5
Kerb weight	1,204lb	1,310lb	1,196lb
Price	£7,476 (1983)	£5,638 (1980)	£8,700 (1985)
Test source/date	*Autocar 1983*	*Fast Lane 1984*	*Autocar 1985*

	HPC	HPC	JPE
Engine	Cosworth 1700 BDR	Vauxhall 2.0 16V Carb	Vauxhall 2.0 (modified)
Power	170bhp	175bhp	250bhp
Maximum speed	120mph	126mph	150mph
Acceleration (sec)			
0–30mph	2.0	2.2	1.7
0–40mph	3.0	3.2	2.3
0–50mph	4.1	4.1	2.9
0–60mph	5.0	5.2	3.5
0–70mph	7.6	6.8	4.5
0–80mph	9.8	8.4	5.5
0–90mph	13.1	10.4	6.9
0–100mph	18.9	13.3	8.3
Standing ¼-mile	13.1	13.6	11.9
Top gear acceleration (sec)			
20–40mph	–	6.6	–
30–50mph	–	5.7	–
40–60mph	–	5.7	3.7
50–70mph	–	5.6	6.0
60–80mph	–	6.0	6.8
70–90mph	–	6.7	7.6
80–100mph	–	7.5	7.0
Overall fuel consumption (mpg)	26.7	20.8	17.0
Kerb weight	1,207lb	1,366lb	1,168lb
Price	£14,553 (1990)	£18,492 (1990)	£34,950 (1992)
Test source/date	*Classic Cars*	*Autocar & Motor 1992*	*Performance Car 1992*

	K-series	K-series Supersport 6-speed	K-series 1.6 Supersport 6-speed
Engine	Rover 1.4 (non-Cat)	Rover 1.4 (modified)	Rover 1.6 (modified)
Power	110bhp	128bhp	138bhp
Maximum speed	103mph	114mph	112mph
Acceleration (sec)			
0–30mph	2.3	1.9	2.3
0–40mph	3.5	2.7	3.4
0–50mph	5.0	4.2	4.5
0–60mph	6.8	6.0	6.0
0–70mph	9.4	7.7	8.0
0–80mph	13.1	10.4	10.1
0–90mph	20.5	13.6	13.4
0–100mph	–	20.8	18.3
Standing ¼-mile	15.6	14.6	14.7
4th gear acceleration (sec)			
20–40mph	6.4	4.7	4.6
30–50mph	6.3	4.4	4.4
40–60mph	6.6	4.6	4.7
50–70mph	7.9	4.8	4.7
60–80mph	9.6	5.1	4.9
70–90mph	13.3	6.0	5.8
80–100mph	–	–	8.0
Overall fuel consumption (mpg)	29.2	25.7	27.6
Kerb weight	1,190lb	1,269lb	1,221lb
Price	£13,883 (1991)	£14,950 (1994)	£17,039 (1995)
Test source/date	Autocar & Motor 1992	Autocar 1993	Autocar 1995

APPENDIX E

40 THINGS YOU NEVER KNEW ABOUT THE SEVEN

The first 100mph Seven arrived in 1958 with the 1,100cc Climax-engined version.

Racing drivers who cut their teeth on Sevens include Graham Hill, Derek Bell, Patrick Depailler, Emerson Fittipaldi, Henri Pescarolo and Francois Cevert.

The original Caterham Seven was one of the few cars to have a perfect 50/50 weight distribution. All de Dion cars have a slight rear weight bias.

Should it be 'Seven' or 'Super Seven'? The original Lotus was a Seven and the term Super Seven was reserved for the quickest member of the family. All Caterhams are correctly Super Sevens, although they are commonly referred to under either designation.

Patrick McGoohan took delivery of Chassis Number 6 of the Prisoner special edition (he played Number 6 in the famous TV series). Graham Nearn retained Chassis Number 2.

British Formula 1 driver John Watson shakes hands with Caterham's Andy Noble: "Caterham provides motoring as it should be, not as it has become".

Graham Nearn was filmed in the last episode of *The Prisoner* TV series, *Fall Out*. He can be seen cleaning the car upon delivery to Patrick McGoohan.

To date some 41 official Prisoner cars have been delivered.

The rarest production Caterham Seven was the S3 fitted with a Ford 1300 engine: just four were supplied by the factory.

Celebrity owners of Sevens include Chris Rea, Rowan Atkinson, Jonathan Palmer, Jools Holland, Aerosmith rock band members Steve Tyler and Joe Perry and footballer Paul Gascoigne.

TV presenter Jools Holland was just one of many famous celebrities who have owned a Caterham Seven.

Racing celebrities in the Caterham series have included Chris Rea, David Brabham, Dario Franchiti, Justin Bell, Lisa Thackwell, Gareth Rees, Steve Parrish, Clive Chapman and Tim Sugden.

The Silver Jubilee special edition offered from 1981 was taken up by only eight customers. Seven had the show car's silver paint scheme and one was ordered in British Racing Green.

Britain has remained Caterham's best market since the Seventies, but Japan buys around half as many as are sold in the UK.

Chris Rea featured a Seven on the cover of his best-selling album, *Auberge*. The front end of a Seven was used on stage during the *Auberge* tour as the mounting point for some of the stage lighting.

Rock singer Chris Rea's best-selling album, *Auberge*, featured a Seven on the cover.

Two Bugatti Blue Sevens were built as prizes to be given away with Chris Rea's album *Auberge*.

Caterhams formed the first-ever one-make series for non-domestic cars in Japan.

Starter kits were introduced in 1984 and within three years were outselling the component-form cars.

Richard Galloway, 6ft 5in, with his Long Cockpit Seven.

One of the first customers for the Long Cockpit Seven was Richard Galloway – all 6ft 5in of him. He has been an owner ever since, proving that lofty dimensions are no bar to enjoyment of the Seven.

Despite being offered as an option from launch, the catalytic converter for the K-series engine was taken up by just one customer in its first year on sale.

The most popular colour for a Caterham is red, closely followed by green. The other standard colours are white, black and yellow.

70% of starter kits and CKD kits are supplied by Caterham with an approved new engine.

Four Sevens were Caterham/Dartford cross-over cars whose builds started at Caterham and finished at Dartford in 1987. The relevant chassis numbers are 4733, 4736, 4738 and 4739.

More than 200 specialist suppliers contribute parts and services used in the manufacture of a Caterham.

The Seven is often described as having brick-like aerodynamics. Indeed, with the roof down, the Seven's drag coefficient (Cd) is 0.76.

Caterham Cars' biggest export market is easily Japan, followed by Germany.

Caterham's policy of buying in 100% of components and not manufacturing a single item itself is virtually unique among car makers worldwide.

The Seven is a true British car with 95% of its parts sourced from the UK.

In 1991 journalist Eoin Young, writing in *Autocar & Motor,* chose the Seven as his greatest car of all time.

Under new copyright laws, Caterham became one of the first car manufacturers to apply to copyright the silhouette of its product.

In a 1995 *Daily Telegraph* competition to discover the classic car readers would most like to own, the Seven emerged as the third most popular choice.

Caterham's technical director Jez Coates named his son James Patrick Edward (JPE!).

A Caterham was represented at the British embassy in Paris as one of four exhibits forming part of a presentation on the best of British cars.

Strictly a one-off special: Harry Barke's stupendous twin-turbo Rover V8-powered Seven.

Individuals have fitted many strange engines in their Sevens, including Jim Brooks' installation of Mazda rotary power, Arno Huberts' use of Sierra Cosworth four-wheel drive and Harry Barke's incredible twin-turbo Rover V8!

Graham Nearn was approached by one owner at a show who presented his son, whom he said had been conceived in the back of a Seven on the way home from Caterham!

Classic & Sportscar magazine in April 1996 rated the Seven among the Top Ten in its list of 100 all-time great cars.

In 1994, racer John McLean asked Caterham to fit a turbocharger to his HPC. The result? More torque than a JPE, a top speed of 135mph and 0–60mph in 4.6 seconds.

The vice-president of the Seven Owners' Club of Japan is also the official photographer of the Japanese emperor.

Caterham is an original equipment supplier to Reliant, which uses Caterham's bellhousings on its Rover-powered Scimitar.

The secretary of an MP visited the Caterham stand at the 1995 Motor Show. The subject matter of his discussion led to a question being tabled at the House of Commons.

The 1996 Caterham was the first to have no common mechanical parts with the original Lotus Seven. Before then, only the handbrake lever had remained completely unchanged.

In September 1995, four Seven owners each drove 2,700 miles in five days in a Land's End to John o' Groats charity run. Another Seven owner took his car to Moscow and back.

APPENDIX F

USEFUL NAMES AND ADDRESSES

Caterham Cars

Caterham Cars Ltd (Sales)
Station Garage
Station Avenue
Caterham
Surrey CR3 6LB
Tel: 01883 346666

Caterham Cars Ltd (Factory)
2 Kennet Road
Dartford
Kent DA1 4QN
Tel: 01322 559124
01322 559122 (spares)
01322 559125 (service)

A network of service agents and race centres is available in the UK (contact Caterham Cars for details).

Clubs

Lotus Seven Club of Great Britain
PO Box 7
Cranleigh
Surrey GU6 8YP
Tel/fax: 01483 277172

UK's only club dedicated to Lotus and Caterham Sevens. 1,700 members. Monthly magazine *(Low Flying)*, reduced insurance, track days including tuition, hillclimb and sprint series, regional groups, regalia, technical help service, international meeting at Harewood. Free membership with purchase of new Caterham.

Seven owners' clubs and importers exist in many countries across the world and information can be supplied on request.

CATERHAM SEVENS AND ME
by Chris Rea

Sevens have always been in the part of my world that is motor racing and driving. In fact, I can vaguely remember when Sevens were Sixes!

In my teens they were awesome, dark red things, and to a young boy in North Yorkshire a fleeting glimpse of one of these was a rare vision, almost like a fantasy…they were *so fast!*

When, as a struggling writer of music, I finally became financially solvent, my first call was to the small town of Caterham, so often through the years seen in my imagination whenever the Caterham adverts appeared in magazines (the wonder of it; a small old English village with a garage full of these little thoroughbreds).

My first Caterham came with four forward gears. I owned it for only six hours and immediately changed it for my present one, with five gears. Clearly, from the start, I was going to be a classic 'Seven' person: constantly evolving, talking, thinking about it. Many years have now passed, and E954 KYE has changed and developed considerably from being a 'home-made' Ford pushrod to what it is now. That's got a lot to do with the magic of Sevens; the basic engineering design is so wonderfully on the button that so many things are possible.

It became French Blue, changed its wishbones, suspension, steering (to fast racing rack), and its gearbox is now a straight-cut, close-ratio. It grew a bigger engine and developed a bigger-breathing tuned manifold and now it develops nearly 250bhp! It's amazing to think that the 135bhp I originally had used to blow me (and most other cars) away. That's Sevens, though, that's all part of it.

Magnus Laird of Hyperion has always balanced the car's handling for me. Over the years he has always looked after me when I've raced Sevens and is about the most experienced there is in Caterham Seven motor racing. He taught me how to drive racing cars, and some of my victories and podiums in other types have come directly from what he taught me.

More importantly, there is a psychological sub-culture in Caterham Sevens and it is one that makes these gorgeous cars unique in every way. It's difficult to explain, but definitely felt. It's a psychology of the ultimate best performance without the pretension of the so-called supercars it so often outclasses.